Cover design by Darius Teymour Yussof
Typeset by Wong Yew Onn

Extra Precaution for Mommies: The cover of this book has been sealed with a layer of non-toxic oil, like that used in the printing of children's books, so a Mommy's or Daddy's skin doesn't absorb the toxic chemical contained in the ink used for the printing cover. The colors aren't as pretty but I was more concerned about reducing the chemical exposure to anyone reading this book.

Post-pregnancy Wellness Company website: www.post-pregnancywellness.com

First printing, 2012.

This edition ISBN: 978-1-4675-2115-4

Printed by Percetakan Lenang Istimewa Sdn Bhd
29, Jalan Lengkongan Brunei, Off Jalan Pudu,
55100, Kuala Lumpur,
Malaysia.

Printed in Malaysia.

RESTORING YOUR POST-PREGNANCY BODY, NATURALLY

Using Women's Traditional Wisdom

the
M🌼mmy
Plan

by
Valerie Lynn

Dedication

This book is dedicated to all the women who experience the hardship of transitioning to motherhood, and to all the men who, while embracing fatherhood, face challenges of their own. May you find strength and support in one another.

Contents

POST-PREGNANCY PRECAUTIONS

REMEMBERING THE DADDY • 132
Fathers At Birth

This last section of this book has been written for Dads. Most of the time, Dads don't know to ask for guidance on how they could best support the Mommy and baby in the first few weeks after childbirth. This chapter provides Dads direction with simple to follow guidelines and suggestions on his important role. Also included is highlighted information on what to expect regarding the emotions a mommy may be feeling due to the re-balancing of her hormones in the weeks to following childbirth and how he may best help her.

Acknowledgements

What is life without family? I would like to thank my mother and father, Donna and Edward Szkodny, who have been there for me my entire life and have given me enormous support, especially so when my son was born. And mom, you were right, all we can do is to be the best parents we know how. I love you both. To my brother, Matthew, whom I didn't get to see develop into a man, as I've been away so long, but turned out to be a down-to-earth, well-grounded, good guy whom I love dearly.

To Scott, my husband, whose love has never faded and belief in me seems never ending – thank you for your support, patience and most of all, giving me the space to pursue all of my endeavours, whatever they may be. I love you. To my Jordan, who will always be my baby boy and the reason I was able to explore and get to know a completely new, and cherished, side of myself – the mommy-side. I love you more than life; please don't grow up too fast. To Heather and John McDonough, my in-laws, and Sherrin, my sister-in-law, you have been wonderful since the first day I came into your lives and remain so. I love you all.

I have cherished the people I've met along the way during my research, as well as the people who I haven't yet met personally, but have inspired me to be a part of the wonderful community of child birth professionals. Each person is passionate about helping women in their own way, with the epicenter being the journey women choose to go on through pregnancy, labor, childbirth, and recovery with the precious end result of the family that comes into being. Birth is not just a one day event; the entire process is recognized, respected and treasured. The world is lucky to have you all as a part of it and now I'm lucky to have you all as a part of my life. Thank you for taking the time to share your thoughts and wisdom with me.

Foreword, Ibu Robin Lim
CNN Hero of the Year,
December 11, 2011

One week ago, we Birth~Keepers, mothers, fathers, midwives, doulas, doctors, teachers, farmers, artists, citizens of Earth, and children… voted to choose me, for the CNN Hero of 2011. I am still astonished, as together we rocked the world with Oxytocin, the most valuable yet, free resource on Earth… it is the hormone of LOVE.

Now, having landed back on Earth, I sit here attending the labor of a first-time mom in Bali, and I am overcome with gratitude for Oxytocin as it drives conception, birth, breastfeeding and LOVE in general. As I bathe in this gratitude today I wish to introduce to you and share this amazing book; *The Mommy Plan* by Valerie Lynn McDonough. I am endorsing *The Mommy Plan* because postpartum is so important, and yet there is so little information available to enlighten us about this most precious time of bonding, breastfeeding and healing. My own book: *After the Baby's Birth… a Woman's Way to Wellness*, was the first published guide to postpartum. Bookstores had a hard time figuring out where to put it on the shelves, all by itself, as there were just no other books at that time, to help new mothers cope. The advent of *The Mommy Plan* makes me so happy to share the shelf for this book is so essential. I have read it carefully and I love it.

Mother Valerie advises us on the modern practical application of ancient wisdom about postpartum recovery. Wise women's wisdom reminds us how important it is to listen to our bodies' need for warmth in the time of healing.

In our modern world, obstetrical science has forgotten this ancient wisdom, and is craving the memory. Sadly, many OBGYNs are forced by insurance companies (who drive the steamroller of modern medical culture), to treat mothers like suitcases that "carry" babies. Babies are viewed as a product to be delivered. And, postpartum is a time in which the new mother's needs are nearly completely ignored. After all, the baby has now been born, so there is no longer a medical focus on the mother! Shocking? Yes. In fact, I feel that the medical habit of ignoring the postpartum mom, unless she becomes so ill that intervention becomes an emergency, is abusive. It is time to care for ALL new mothers, and this book is an important key to having the knowledge "toolbox" prepared to help.

A new mother in many traditional cultures is honored, protected and nourished with special care. I believe that this special care is clearly and eagerly outlined in Valerie's book. I would urge all families to have this book, as a timeless resource to be treasured by new mothers for generations to come.

However, do not expect the new mother to go out and buy this book for herself. Remember, she is busy nourishing and nurturing her new baby, she is doing the most important work in the world. Get this book for her, and follow the steps for helping her recover from childbirth fully.

Postpartum is a time when each new mother is reinvented by her heroic efforts in bringing her baby Earth-side. It is a precious opportunity to rebuild her health from the foundation up. I am fond of saying: "You are pregnant for nine months, you are blessed to be postpartum for the rest of your life. Make the rest of each new mother's life better, healthier, happier, easier, follow THE MOMMY PLAN."

Love, OM Shanti, from Bali, Ibu Robin Lim

*A portion of the proceeds of this book will go to support Ibu Robin's free birthing clinic, Yayasan Bumi Sehat, (Free Mother Earth), located in Bali, Indonesia.

Preface

My "AHA" moment came in April 2007, during my pregnancy with my son, Jordan. My husband Scott, who is Australian, and I decided to spend a year in my home state of New Jersey so he could experience living in the United States. I had lived overseas for the most part since 1994, with the last ten years spent in Malaysia, Southeast Asia. Over the years I've learned about a range of post-pregnancy beliefs and traditions and have observed how all women in traditional cultures followed some type of after-birth recovery program according to their ethnicity and customs. Women from traditional cultures seem to make a full recovery in a just a few months time, which is a stark contrast to what is happening in Western countries.

I also noticed post-pregnancy support care came in the form of family and modern-day confinement women, or traditional post-pregnancy (or postpartum) practitioners. These women knew exactly what to do to help a new mother's body begin its healing process from the inside out during the first six weeks post-pregnancy, whether a mother's birth experience was natural or by cesarean birth. Women seem to be free from lingering unstable post-pregnancy emotions, and I never met anyone that suffered from maternity blues, postpartum depression, or otherwise. Meanwhile, mothers in the United States, or other Western countries, did not seem to be able to cope with their emotions after childbirth as well.

Back to my "AHA" moment. I had assumed that the same products and services would be available after I gave birth. I mean, we have everything in the United States, don't we? Boy, was I wrong! One sunny spring day during my eighth month of pregnancy, I went out to buy recovery products, and much to my surprise, I could not find anything similar to the ones I saw overseas. What I did find was ample nipple and bum creams, stretch-mark lotion/oil, a few pregnancy teas, and prenatal vitamins. My search widened to other departments and then several stores. After two weeks of searching, making telephone calls and researching, I came to the realization that I wouldn't have the benefit of any such products or treatments –bummer! I had my son in May and went through my recovery with no massages, treatments, or abdominal wrapping services, but life went on. We returned to Malaysia in August and resumed our lives there once again.

It was Mother's Day 2008 when I came across an article about the exceedingly high rates of post-pregnancy-related mood disorders in the United States. It was very disturbing as it dawned upon me the sheer numbers that the percentages in the article equated to. The figures were referring to well over one million mothers annually. I understood that every woman who goes through pregnancy experiences temporary emotional instability (as I also experienced such emotions during the first week), as her hormone levels rebalance, whether a birth is carried to full-term or not. However, the statistics coming out of the United States concerned me and seemed much higher than compared to other Western and eastern countries. This got me wondering, "Was the experience of maternity blues, even though temporary, felt more severely by women in Western countries than in traditional cultures? Were such emotions felt for a longer time? And why weren't Western women coping with the post-pregnancy period like in the past?" I didn't know the answers, but I wanted to find out.

That's when I started to do in-depth research and found out that the country I was living in, Malaysia, happened to have a very low rate of postpartum depression of just 3.9%, and the specific social group I studied, the Malays, was 3%.[1] Once I made this surprising discovery I wanted to know more: 1. Why was this rate so low? 2. What were the contributing factors? 3. Why were Malay women having what clearly seemed like a better and more balanced recovery from childbirth? 4. What are they doing differently?

Postpartum depression and other related illnesses do exist in Malaysia, but after asking around it far less common than in Western countries or countries that do not have a supportive after birth culture. The women that did suffer from postpartum depression, natural alternatives were the remedies first sought as a solution.

I also examined the typical diet in Malaysia, and like many Asian countries, it adopted the Western diet of fast food and junk food, and the sugar content of the local food is normally high, so that wasn't a primary factor. Eventually, I identified two major differences: (1) better family support, not perfect but better, and (2) post-pregnancy recovery wisdom passed down from generation to generation in the form of specific guidelines regarding diet, activity, and personal care during the first six to eight weeks after childbirth.

What struck me was that nearly all women had what I like to call a "post-pregnancy plan" in place, normally by the end of the second trimester. An expectant mother and her family would have already decided upon the actions to be taken after birth and

5

identified the temporary responsibilities that people would willingly take on during those first six weeks after a child is born. By having a post-pregnancy plan in place, most of the hard work had been prearranged, allowing for a mother to devote this time to her own healing and bonding with her newborn.

After making this discovery, the *no-brainer* conclusion for me was that American, and Western, women need to be aware of such effective post-pregnancy guidelines so they too could develop their own plan to manage their recovery because statistics aren't in our favor, with high numbers experiencing some sort of extended emotional mood disorder after childbirth. This is not to say that planning and following through is a 100% guarantee, but it is certainly a preventative action that can be taken to decrease the chance of experiencing extended, or serious, postpartum emotions. In my opinion, the post-pregnancy recovery plan is one of the most important plans a woman could develop.

Throughout this book, I may be repetitive at times, but please bear with me as I believe any new concept must be repeated several times before the mind absorbs the information and then processes it, which renders the information to be easily recalled and utilized. This will ensure that there will be *no doubt* in your mind why you need to have a post-pregnancy plan in place *before* you give birth and exactly what needs to be included in the plan.

Introduction

Women's status has been considered relatively *higher* in Western cultures than in non-Western cultures, yet paradoxically *less recognition* seems to be given to new mothers in the United States.

Post-pregnancy Beliefs & Practices
Among Non-Western Cultures,
The American Journal of Maternal/Child Nursing.
March/April 2003

In the United States, a mother's recovery from childbirth is not given much attention and often completely overlooked. The perception of the transition of a woman's body from pregnant to a non-pregnant state is one of a natural revision, with the process taking care of itself. Therefore, a non-pregnant body no longer needs special care. This is only half true. The transition *is* natural and will complete itself given time; however, the healing process can be better and stronger if a mother's post-pregnancy body is given "tender love and care" (TLC) in the immediate six weeks after childbirth, which can be easily done as normally most of the first six weeks or more are normally spent at home. In my opinion, a mother's body needs even more care in the post-pregnancy weeks than throughout pregnancy.

If you are questioning whether a little TLC for yourself is really necessary, ask the 1,240,000 mothers in the United States who are diagnosed annually with some sort of post-pregnancy or postpartum emotional mood disorder. Ask them how it disrupted their life, and I'm sure they will vividly share their heartbreaking experiences, which takes many women years to process. Go online and read the countless pregnancy, labor, and childbirth forums, and you will see topics such as maternity/baby blues, postpartum depression, postpartum anxiety, postpartum panic attacks, postpartum exhaustion, postpartum obsessive-compulsive disorder, and the worst of the worst, postpartum psychosis. The stories are very sad and frightening as they are written by women just like you and me who may not have had any prior experience with depression, so they didn't know what was happening to themselves or how to stop it. Worse yet, they don't know how to make themselves better, until the only course of treatment is antidepressants. I've been in tears many times reading such stories as these women write directly from the heart and many times without family or friends knowing as they are embarrassed or don't want to admit it to themselves.

So I ask you, gentle reader, with those odds, would you take the chance of ending up as another statistic? Or, would you do everything in your power to recover as healthy and strong as you can, to enable you to take care of the life growing inside you? Your newborn will need you to function at your best, so it's up to you to do everything in your power to ensure your body recovers to the best of its ability. The immediate six weeks post-birth is a short, but critical, window of opportunity to place yourself on the path to a healthy recovery, therefore make the most of this downtime.

When I came to the realization of the seriousness of post-pregnancy-related illnesses that had spread throughout the United States, I also came to find out that this topic was a "black hole in our healthcare system." There aren't many insurance policies that address this specific maternal health problem, leaving the only readily available recommended solution to be pharmaceutical antidepressants that are not safe for a breastfeeding baby, no matter what the claims may be.

What I would like to convey is that ample evidence-based proof exists in the form of millions of women who have, and still are, heeding post-pregnancy precautions and following proven after birth recovery programs. They don't dare throw caution to the wind and do nothing. This is something you can also follow, and have just as good a result, as long as you are committed to having a healthy recovery. Traditional beliefs and practices that have been discounted by Western medicine are making a tremendous comeback as people recognize their merit and effectiveness.

I haven't come across the particular post-pregnancy guidelines in this book in Western countries, presented in a comprehensive written form. American women who give birth, generally speaking, don't follow or engage in any type of post-pregnancy recovery program with specific guidelines. This is the "first item of business" that needs to be changed in order to start reducing the number of diagnosed cases of postpartum-related mood disorders.

I hope the knowledge in this book will start an awakening as more and more women seek natural alternatives to the existing healthcare system. If we have many messengers to carry this wisdom, it will spread from shore to shore. Women will have the information they need to heal and recover in a safe, strong, and most importantly *"balanced manner"* from childbirth. All evidence points to the fact that most new mothers in Western cultures are having an *"unbalanced recovery"* from childbirth.

Since I am American, it is easiest for me to refer to my home country of the United States. However, postpartum related conditions seem to occur in most Western countries as well as countries that do not have tried and true after birth traditions. Therefore, the information contained in this book can be followed by all women.

ONE

The Postpartum Epidemic in America

DEFINITION OF EPIDEMIC
Affecting or tending to affect a disproportionally large number of individuals within a population, community, or region at the same time.

Official rates of postpartum depression (PPD) based on 4.2 million live births in 2010.[1]
- 10%–15%[2] = 420,000–630,000 mothers

The national figure of *"clinically recognized births,"* which includes fetal losses, miscarriages, and stillbirths is 6.2 million.[3]
- 10%–15%[4] = 620,000–930,000 mothers

Unofficial rates of postpartum depression (PPD), 15%–20%[5] based on the figures above.
- 4.2 million = 630,000–840,000 mothers
- 6.2 million = 930,000–1,240,000 mothers

These figures are based on the number of *reported* cases, and therefore, realistically the numbers are even higher because many cases of PPD go unreported.

Let's compare these figures to the following incidences of other *major diseases* among women in America:
- 800,000 women will get diabetes.[6]
- Approximately 300,000 women will suffer a stroke.[7]
- Approximately 230,000 women are expected to be diagnosed with breast cancer.[8]

According to the definition of an epidemic, based on the official figures, it could be easily argued that there is a "postpartum epidemic" taking place annually in the United States.

US Natal and Postnatal Information

The pressures of modern-day life force women to recover as quickly as possible from childbirth, resulting in an "unbalanced" recovery that can be linked to several post-pregnancy-related illnesses:

- Maternity/baby blues
- Postpartum anxiety
- Postpartum exhaustion
- Postpartum OCD
- Postpartum panic attacks
- Postpartum depression
- Postpartum psychosis

These medical labels are common household phrases in the United States when in other countries post-pregnancy-related illnesses are far less common, if not rare. We need to ask ourselves, "Why is there a postpartum epidemic in America and other Western countries? More importantly, as the segment of the population that is susceptible to such illnesses (we women) - how are we going to protect ourselves from becoming a statistic?"

Facts about the United States:

- US population October 2011: 312 million.[9]
- Number of live births in the United States in 2010: 4.2 million.[10]
- The annual National Vital Statistics Report indicates that the total number of clinically recognized pregnancies is on average 2 million higher[11] than the number of live births as it includes fetal losses, including miscarriages and stillbirths. (2010: 6.2 million).
- 1 new birth occurs every 8 seconds.[12]
- 1 person is added to the US population every 14 seconds through birth or immigration.[13]
- The United States is the only industrialized nation that doesn't require employers to offer *paid* maternity, paternity, or adoption leave.[14] The US Family and Medical Leave Act allows for 12 weeks of job-protected leave, but only covers those who work for companies with 50 employees or more.[15]
- Average maternity leave taken: 6.6 weeks, because in many cases the typical family cannot afford to take 12 weeks of unpaid leave,[16] therefore generally maternity leave is taken two weeks before childbirth, leaving only four weeks to spend with a newborn.
- A Harvard study found that out of 168 nations, 163 countries had some form of paid maternity leave, leaving the United States in the company of Lesotho, Papua

New Guinea, and Swaziland.[17] This is still the case as of 2012.
- Up to 10% of American women (2010: 420,000) will experience depression or anxiety during pregnancy.[18]
- 80% or 1 in 8 American women (2010: 3.36 million) experience some sort of post-pregnancy mood disorder.[19]
- 15%–20% of American mothers (2010: 840,000) experience postpartum depression following the birth of a child,[20] but only 1 in 5 will seek professional help.[21]
- 1 to 2 in 1,000 women experience postpartum psychosis or 4,200–8,400 women per year.[22]
- 40% of all births are to unmarried women, an increase of 26% since 2002.[23]
- Among African Americans, the number of children born to single mothers is more than 70%.[24]
- The number of multiple births has increased due to infertility treatments:
  - Twin births doubled: 68,000 in 1980 to 132,000 in 2004.[25]
  - Triplet-plus births: increased more than fivefold from 1980 to 7,727 in 2004.[26]
- US population 2015(E): 315.5 million.[27]

Pharmaceutical Antidepressants
- The only readily available treatment for PPD and other emotion related illnesses is antidepressants.
- Antidepressants are now the third most prescribed type of drug in the United States, behind cholesterol-lowering medications and painkillers.[28]
- 11% of American women take antidepressants[29:] (17,160,000 women as of 2008)
- Sales from antidepressants are currently more than $13 billion annually in the United States.[30]

My Interpretation
What these figures represent to me are mothers, women, sisters, aunties, cousins, and friends of all races, creeds, and religions who do not know how to take care of their post-pregnant body in the immediate period following childbirth. These figures represent newborns that have inconsistent care as their mothers aren't able to fully care for their needs. It represents siblings who are neglected and aren't able to understand what is happening to their mommy. It also represents daddies, husbands, or partners who are frustrated and don't realize that postpartum-related mood disorders are real. In the United States, more divorces take place during the first year of a child's life than any other age (on average when a baby is eight months old). The first year of a child's

life is a time period when a mother and father need to help and support each other to take care of a young child. Then why do mothers and fathers feel they are better off separating? In my opinion, there may be some relation between a woman's unbalanced recovery from childbirth and this divorce statistic.

Statistics also indicate that most new mothers in the United States do not have the luxury of taking six solid weeks of downtime. For this reason, women feel pressured to recover from pregnancy and childbirth as quickly as possible to return to work or resume their previous life. Therefore it is essential that women maximize each and every day during their maternity leave and provide what their body needs for a strong recuperation. Time is of the essence. This is why there is a real need for post-pregnancy precautions and recovery techniques that are proven, well-defined and effective.

Don't Be a Statistic

For the record, I am *not* against antidepressants. This type of drug has gotten so popular and would not continue to be in demand if there wasn't a social need for it. Therefore, it serves an important purpose. However, what I am for is sharing knowledge and providing options to women, ideally while still during pregnancy, so that a post-pregnancy, or postpartum, plan can be developed and ready to be followed from the day a woman gives birth. A woman's body begins the transition back to its non-pregnant state as soon as she births the placenta in a vaginal birth, or when an obstetrician removes the placenta in the case of a caesarean birth. This is considered as Day One.

The Increase of Hormone Levels During Pregnancy

By the time a mother is in her third trimester, there is up to three times the normal level of hormones in her bloodstream. The hypothalamus, the part of the brain that helps regulate hormone levels, becomes dormant during pregnancy since the baby and the placenta have complete control over the endocrine system, which is the system in our body that is made up of glands that produce and secrete hormones. However, the vast majority of those hormones disappear within the first five days of giving birth, and it takes the hypothalamus up to three weeks to regulate the endocrine system again. This hormonal fluctuation is considered a main contributing factor in the onset of maternity blues.[31]

Traditional Postpartum Emotional Disorders

Maternity Blues or Baby Blues, is the most common type of emotions experienced by mothers; it is the passing state of heightened emotions. It occurs in approximately

80% of new mothers in the United States within two to four weeks after birth. Hormones are furiously rebalancing during this period. A woman suffering from the blues may cry more easily than usual and may have trouble sleeping. This state peaks three to five days after delivery and lasts from several days to two weeks.[21] The blues *do not* interfere with a woman's ability to care for her baby and is so common, and expected, that these feelings are not considered an illness. However, if such feelings persist, it is *not* normal, and a mother should recognize this and confide in someone.

There is a more gentle and traditional belief about the blues, that it is felt when a mother's milk fully comes in on the third day or so and will last for a few hours to a few days. I like Robin Lim's view on the blues in her book *After the Baby's Birth, A Complete Guide for Postpartum Women.* "The arrival of your milk and the blues at about the same time inspires the wise-woman saying, "Letting loose the tears help the milk flow."[32]

For most women, the symptoms are mild and go away on their own, but as highlighted earlier, anywhere between 10% and 20% of new mothers develop a more disabling form of mood disorder or postpartum depression.

Maternity/Baby Blues[33]

Affected: Up to 80%; 500-800 in 1,000 post-pregnant women.
Onset: Roughly 1-3 days postpartum; lasts from a few hours to several days.
Symptoms: Tearfulness and Exhaustion
Treatment: Review the story of your baby's birth with a beloved friend; Rest, eat well and cry if need be. Get the emotions out.

Postpartum Exhaustion[34]

Affected: *Nearly all mommies.*
Onset: *Can be from Day One, or birth.*
Symptoms: *The physical and emotional exhaustion from birth and taking care of a new baby that most women can expect in the weeks following delivery.*
Treatment: *Ask for help if you aren't getting enough of it, make sure you get sleep or rest.*

Postpartum Depression[35]

Affected: *10-20%, 100-200 in 1,000 post-pregnant women; Re-occurrence rate for women who previously had PPD is approximately 10-35%.*
Onset: *Can set in any time, however usually begins between 2 weeks and 18 months post-pregnancy and can last up to a year.*

Symptoms:
- Bizarre or strange thoughts
- Chest pains / Heart palpitations
- Despondency or feelings of despair
- Exaggerated guilt
- Fear of not bonding with baby
- Feel like you are "going crazy"
- Feeling of out of control
- Headaches
- Helplessness
- Hyperventilating
- Hopelessness
- Hostile behavior
- Impaired concentration or memory
- Inability to cope
- Intrusive thoughts
- Loss of normal interests
- New fears or phobias
- Nightmares
- No job
- Numbness
- Over-concern for baby
- Panic attacks
- Thoughts of suicide

Treatment:
- Get additional loving support from understanding friends and family; seek professional guidance.
- If your doctor prescribes medication and/or psychotherapy, make sure you get emotional support as well.
- Take a good look at your diet—you must eat well to be well.
- Take small steps toward feeling good: brush your hair, go for walks.
- PLEASE: The family must get professional guidance for the woman suffering from PPD.

Note: Symptoms' frequency and severity vary from woman to woman. A woman may experience some or all of the above.

<u>*Postpartum Psychosis*</u>[36]
Affected: *1-3%, 1-3 in 1,000 post-pregnant women.*
Onset: *Onset is severe and sudden; usually begins within the first month postpartum; 80% of the cases set in within 3–14 days postpartum; duration varies and recovery is gradual, but averages three months once treatment begins.*

Symptoms:
- Alteration in mood
- Agitation
- Bizarre hallucinations
- Delusions
- Distorted thinking
- Extreme confusion
- Failure to identify familiar people
- Fatigue
- Feelings of hopelessness and shame
- Frantic excessive energy

- Hearing voices
- Hyperactivity
- Inability to stop activity
- Incoherence
- Irrational statements

- Loss of memory
- Preoccupation with trivia
- Rapid speech
- Refusal to eat
- Suspiciousness

Treatment:
- Immediately the family must intervene and get the woman suffering from symptoms of PPS experienced professional help.
- The safety and well-being of both the mother and baby are at risk.
- This should be viewed as a medical emergency that requires immediate hospitalization and medication; psychotherapy and nonjudgmental love and support are essential.

Note: The above information regarding the traditional postpartum disorders is from the book, *After the Baby's Birth: A Complete Guide for Postpartum Women,* by Robin Lim, Celestial Arts (2001).

Modern Diagnosis of Postpartum Anxieties

In recent times, postpartum depression has been further broken down and categorized into three different anxieties. Postpartum anxiety disorders are characterized by the common symptoms of excessive anxiety and worry and can occur along with the other disorders, although it is not formally identified as a post-pregnancy disorder. According to Ann Dunnewold, past president of Postpartum Support International, "Postpartum depression is actually an inappropriate label. Postpartum anxiety is much more common than depression in new mothers, which makes sense in that mothers are adjusting to a whole new role and identity when they usually have had very little preparation and receive little support."[37]

Postpartum Post-Traumatic Stress Disorder (PTSD)[38]

Affected: *1-6%, 1-6 in 1,000 post-pregnant women*
Onset: *In the immediate days after birth or up to six months. PTSK is often misdiagnosed as PPD but it can also co-occur with PPD. A mother may have symptoms and not a full-blown occurrence but she is still disturbed and suffering. Most often, this illness is caused by a real or perceived trauma during delivery or partum. Such traumas include the following:*

- Baby going to NICU (neo-natal incubation unit)

- Prolapsed cord
- Feelings of powerlessness, poor communication, and/or lack of support and reassurance during delivery.
- Use of vacuum extractor or forceps to deliver the baby.
- Unplanned cesarean section.

Symptoms:
  (i) Intrusion: re-experiencing the event through intrusive memories, flashbacks, or nightmares.

  (ii) Arousal:
- Anger
- Difficulty concentrating
- Difficulty sleeping
- Easily startled
- Jumpy
- Hyper-vigilance
- Irritability

  (iii)Avoidance
- Detachment
- May avoid reminders – baby
- Numbing
- Sex
- Where birth occurred or another birth.

Postpartum Panic Disorder or Panic Attacks[39]
Affected: 2%, 2 in 1,000 post-pregnant women
Onset: In the immediate days after birth or up to six months.
Symptoms: A mother experiences panic attacks with:
- Health palpitations
- Shortness of breath
- Chest pain
- Shakiness
- Dizziness
- Fear of going crazy

Postpartum Obsessive Compulsive Disorder (POCD)[40]
Affected: 3-5%, 3-5 in 1,000 post-pregnant women
Onset: In the immediate days after birth or up to six months.
Symptoms:
- Postpartum OCD is the most misunderstood and misdiagnosed of the perinatal disorders.
- Obsessions or intrusive thoughts, these are persistent, repetitive thoughts or mental images relating to the baby. These thoughts are very upsetting and not something the woman has ever experienced before.
- Compulsions, where the mom may do certain things over and over again to reduce fears and obsessions. This may include things like needing to clean

constantly, checking things many times, counting or reordering things.
- A sense of horror about the obsessions.
- Fear of being left alone with the infant.
- Hyper-vigilance in protecting the infant.
- Moms with postpartum OCD know their thoughts are bizarre and are very unlikely to ever act on them.
- Risk factors for postpartum OCD include a personal or family history of anxiety or OCD. OCD is not the mother's fault and is temporary and treatable with professional help.[41]

Treatment for Modern Postpartum Emotional Disorders
Treatment varies for the modern postpartum emotional disorder however they closely follow the current treatments available for the traditional disorders.

AUTHOR'S NOTE
Even though anxiety is more prevalent, postpartum depression has been much more researched, and therefore, I will continue to use the term postpartum depression for simplicity.

What Causes Postpartum Emotional Disorders?
There are many schools of thought, opinions, and interpretations about the root cause of postpartum depression, such as chemical imbalance or genetic malfunction. However, no exact cause has been decided upon. Hormone imbalance is thought to play a role. Levels of the hormones estrogen, progesterone, and cortisol fall dramatically within forty-eight hours after delivery, and it is thought that women who go on to develop postpartum depression may be more sensitive to such hormonal changes.[42]

A new mother should not ignore or brush off persistent negative or depressive feelings. If you find yourself feeling this way, I would encourage you to conduct online research, speak with a friend, or a mothers group. You can call a state Helpline, Hotline, or even Warmline, so a mommy can ask experienced people anonymously to determine whether something serious may be developing in her state of mind *before* anxiety, OCD, depression or otherwise sets in.

It's Part of the Healing Process
I would like to emphasize that a mommy should not be embarrassed or ashamed if she feels emotional or unstable within the first few weeks post-pregnancy; or even at

a much later date (within the first year). Such emotions are part of the body's healing process. Any attempt to communicate your worries and concerns should be viewed in a positive light. In some cases, just speaking about such feelings with a person who is familiar with the subject is therapeutic in its own right. Don't count solely on your husband, partner, or family to understand how you are feeling; or for them to know the best way to support or console you the way that you need. Speaking with someone who has experienced what you are going through may be a better source of support, and she may be able to provide you with activities you can do to work through your feelings and emotions.

Internal Exercise

Women should be made aware that their body is doing its own *"internal exercise"* at a very high intensity during the first three weeks after childbirth. A woman's body is healing in high gear as it's naturally designed to do so. If you think about it, a six-to-eight week recovery, or even a three-month recovery, after a ten-month state of consistent pregnancy, active labor and then birth is not a very long time. For that reason a new mommy needs to manage her recovery and continue to closely monitor her diet and eating habits, the activities she engages in as well as her personal care (how she takes care of her body) during the first few weeks, especially if she is not having a strong recovery. Post-baby recovery is something that cannot be passively ignored but must be actively managed on a daily basis.

POST-PREGNANCY ANALOGY
Drug Addiction Withdrawal vs. Pregnancy Hormone Withdrawal
We can liken post-pregnancy mood changes (due to the sudden drop in hormone levels) to the "cold turkey" effect when a drug addicted person stops taking drugs. A mother's body goes into shock and has, to some effect, withdrawal symptoms as it tries to "rebalance" itself at much lower hormone levels. While we cannot control the rebalancing of hormone levels, a woman can take action by providing her body with identified nourishing foods and avoid foods that are known to interfere with the body's natural healing ability.

Sharing After Birth Wisdom

By sharing after-birth wisdom and knowledge from around the globe that is lacking in most Western countries concerning the temporary changes in a mother's diet, activity, and personal care during the first six weeks postpartum, women will better understand the actions they can take to help themselves heal better and stronger. I did not create the post-pregnancy do's and don'ts in this book; they are based on extensive research of existing traditional guidelines developed over thousands of years. As I mentioned previously, the specific social group I studied, the Malays, have a PPD rate of just 3%. I'd take the rate of 3% over 20% any day. Wouldn't you?

THE MOMMY PLAN

The Mommy Plan is a mother's *Post-pregnancy Plan*. It is a plan that should be customized to her own physical and emotional needs to enable her to recover in a safe, strong, healthy, and above all <u>balanced</u> manner. It is my conclusion that women in America, and other Western countries, are recovering in an *unbalanced* manner, which is leading to an extended postpartum-related emotional illnesses or complications previously mentioned.

TWO

What Do American Women Do to Recover from Pregnancy?

POST-PREGNANCY WISDOM

The global population is 6.8 billion people. By my conservative estimate, more than half or roughly 3.5 billion people, live in countries that have well-developed post-pregnancy recovery traditions that guide a mother's recovery from pregnancy, labor and childbirth. It is a common traditional belief that taking care of a mother is an essential part of the post-birth process. Well managed postnatal care will greatly benefit a mommy and her newborn baby, in the immediate time period as well as later in life. Well developed recovery programs do not exist in most Western countries. Pregnancy recovery traditions, that were part our history, were lost when births were moved to a hospital setting and managed by medical doctors. Being that the most common complication from childbirth is post-pregnancy emotional illnesses, don't you think it's time such traditions are revived?

While conducting research on post-birth recovery traditions, I am asked time and again, "What do American women do to recover from pregnancy and childbirth?" And my response time and time again is, "For the most part, nothing. American mommies hardly do anything more than rely on their bodies to naturally revert to its non-pregnant state." The normal response I receive is a baffled stare because the thought is incomprehensible that women in America don't follow any sort of post-pregnancy program nor are they aware of any post-pregnancy precautions they should heed. A follow-up comment is normally something like, "But America has everything! And Americans normally know everything! It's so organized over there! They must do something? The most innovative ideas, products, and services come from America!" My response always is, "Not when it comes to information and knowledge about after-birth care. It isn't part of the culture."

There is a wealth of information about pre-pregnancy, pregnancy, labor and childbirth; however, in my opinion, as well as the opinion of many people in the childbirth industry, it stops there. The void of post-pregnancy recovery knowledge is the size of the Grand Canyon! Through my research I've realized that the wonderful post-birth traditions I became familiar with were not recorded in English for the most part but in the local language or not recorded at all and simply passed down verbally in certain families from female generation to generation through hands-on teaching and training. In fact in many instances, traditional midwives carefully guard their after birth practices and wisdom and often take recipes, techniques, and knowledge to their grave. Post-pregnancy beliefs and practices are treasured wisdom in traditional cultures and normally protected like national secrets.

As birth was medicalized and brought into a hospital setting in the 1930s–1940s in the United States, the role of the midwife was minimized and discouraged by the medical community.[1] It was the midwives who previously checked on women after childbirth and made recommendations to facilitate a healthy recovery. This was a serious mistake by the medical community. As it stands today, midwives and home births are making a comeback with scientific recognition of the important role they play in the high success rates in facilitating natural low-risk births. Remember, birth is something that women do, not something that happens to them.

American and Western Beliefs about Pregnancy

The cultural beliefs in America, and most Western countries today regarding pregnancy, childbirth, and the post-pregnancy period center around the baby. The mother becomes secondary. Well, even that is a stretch - probably not even secondary. In most cases, she is rarely asked how she is feeling or how her recovery is progressing. I can attest to this as I remember during my first weeks after I gave birth, no one asked how I was recovering or feeling. In American culture, recovery from childbirth has never been given much attention and thus largely viewed as something not to be concerned about. For someone like me that has spent the past fifteen years in Asia seeing firsthand the wonderful, caring traditions surrounding a woman from when she discovers she is pregnant up to her post-pregnancy recovery, it makes me very sad to learn and observe how women are viewed and treated in my own country during the same period in life. The United States is the leading industrialized Western country in the world and a role model to other countries in many ways. Therefore, the barbaric attitude toward women doesn't seem fitting for a nation where it is polite to hold a door open or pull out a seat for a woman. Another observation I've had is how well women recover in less developed, more traditional countries, and by and large how they don't experience extended post-pregnancy emotional feelings, resulting in a much better recuperation. It was definitely an eye-opener when I returned home to have my son in 2006.

Women's Liberation Movement Pros and Cons

The mind-set of American women needs to be touched upon as this has a direct impact on a new mother. The phrase "women's liberation" was first used in the United States in 1964 and first appeared in print in 1966.[2] Women's liberation gained momentum in America in the 1970s, and I know I speak for many women that we are all very grateful for those women that stood up for future female generations. The feminist movement effected change in Western society, including women's suffrage, the right to initiate divorce proceedings and 'no fault' divorce, the right of women to make individual decisions regarding pregnancy (including access to contraceptives and abortion), and the right to own property.[3] It has also led to broad employment for women at more equitable wages and access to university education.[4] These are rights that none of us modern moms would give up; however, the downside of this movement is that it instilled a mind-set that if we as women were to ask for help, it may be viewed as a sign of weakness. We as liberal, modern moms and women are supposed to be independent, self-sufficient, and therefore not need any help. Needing help is viewed as a sign of weakness in most women's minds.

This outlook of being able "to do it all" even after giving birth is hugely apparent as we fully believe we will bounce right back to our old selves, slip on our jeans, put on our Super Mom T-shirt, and pick up our life as it was. That wanting to be seen as "having it all together" in everyone's eyes puts undue emotional stress on being a new mother, leading to a longer recovery period. The mind-set of "I'm independent and can manage *everything* in my life on my own" is naturally applied in this situation, which is the beginning of what could be an emotional downward spiral when we don't live up to our own expectations of our former selves. Women need to give themselves a break, realize they are in a precarious health situation, and for a few weeks devote time to their own recovery, and of course bonding and taking care of their newborn. Taking care of a newborn will expend nearly all the energy a new mother has during the first few weeks after child birth.

Providing Knowledge and Guidelines

My intention was to research and translate post-pregnancy knowledge and wisdom about after-birth care into practical, easy-to-understand guidelines that all women can relate to. There is a wealth of traditional post-pregnancy wisdom out there that needs to be introduced, in the right way, so that a Western woman and her family can understand the need for such precautions and incorporate the guidelines into their recovery care. It's as simple as that. There are many things that a woman can do to help herself starting from Day One.

THREE

Taking Care of Mom = Taking Care of Baby

TRADITIONAL POST-PREGNANCY BELIEF
It is a common belief that taking care of a mother is an essential part of the post-birth process, and that well managed post-pregnancy care will greatly benefit both her, and her newborn, in the immediate time period, as well as later in life.

According to the study, "Postpartum (or Post-pregnancy) Beliefs and Practices Among Non-Western Cultures," *The American Journal of Maternal/Child Nursing,* March/April 2003,[1] the differences between Non-Western and Western post-pregnancy practices are as follows:

Post-Pregnancy Practices

Non-Western	*Western*
• Holistic, personal system	• Biomedical medical model
• Involving moral values	• Pregnancy managed by a physician
• Social relations	• Role of the woman less important
• Relation to the environment	• Gifts/celebrations centered around
• Birth ceremonies	the newborn baby (baby showers,
• Special foods prepared for the	christenings, visits from friends and
mother	relatives to see the baby)

As you can see from the list above there are stark differences between how Western and Non-Western cultures view and treat women throughout pregnancy, labor, childbirth, and the post-pregnancy recovery period. In Non-Western cultures, pregnant women are viewed as being special and treated with great care and kindness. Allowances are willingly made for her at the workplace and at home, without question.

Pregnant women are viewed as carrying precious life inside their body and thus taken care of or looked after in a fundamental way by society. Isn't this how it should be? It

23

isn't common for people to have the attitude that a woman will be a burden, and less productive, because she is pregnant, which is common in Western cultures.

First and foremost, there is an established mind-set that it takes a minimum of thirty to forty days of complete rest for a woman to have a healthy recovery from pregnancy and childbirth. Furthermore, every woman is entitled to a resting period that may be extended, depending on the progression and strength of her recovery. The entitlement of a resting period is not questioned or scrutinized for any ill intention by society at large. Mothers are considered important and a vital component of a family. It is understood if the mother is allowed full rest, she will recuperate better and faster and be able to resume normal activities, thus once again being a productive family member.

Immediately after giving birth, the new mother undergoes a carefully structured post-pregnancy recovery program that she arranges or is supervised by her family, lasting thirty to forty-four days. This supervised regimen of post-pregnancy care, is arranged well before a woman's expected delivery date normally before the end of the second trimester. Afterbirth treatments and services are a preventative measure against an unbalanced recovery from childbirth. Such services are not in any way a medical treatment or prescription.

> **WIDSOM FROM JUDITH GOLDSMITH**
> **PAST-PRESIDENT, NATIONAL ORGANIZATION FOR WOMEN (NOW)**
> It is time to take a fresh look at what ancient world traditional cultures may have to teach us. By ignoring traditional practices and denying them a place in the body of knowledge of mankind, we cut ourselves off from the independent experimentation of the rest of the world. And it would take a research grant inconceivably larger than any foundation or government could give to duplicate all the experiments that have been tried in the eons during which women have given birth on this planet.

Abdomen and Uterine Massage Techniques
Traditional post-birth treatments include circulatory and energizing shallow massages, hot stone uterine massage, body scrubs and rubs, and abdominal belly wrapping. The products used are all natural and specific for post-pregnancy recovery.

The treatments improve a new mother's overall vitality as well as:
• Minimizes swelling of the abdomen area.
• Reduces discomfort.
• Aids in decreasing bloating caused by water retention.

- Breaks down blood clots and helps expel excess lochia.
- Improves blood flow and rejuvenate the circulatory system.
- Complements the body's self-healing process, resulting in a better and stronger recuperation.
- Encourages the body to release water retention, pregnancy fat, and flatulence.
- Nourishes and revitalizes the skin and major organs by stimulating blood flow.

Below is a photo of a woman getting a gentle uterine massage. The uterus is always supported on the outside while being massaged with the other hand. The Malay style of uterine massage infuses heat with a heated stone or hand held metal press. From my own experience, the heat feels absolutely wonderful on this area as well as all over the body.

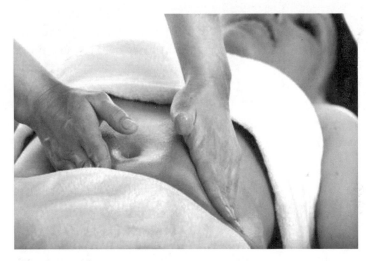

Anti-inflammatory properties of the ingredients in the herbal preparations assist the body in the reduction of overall swelling of the abdominal and torso areas, pelvic organs, uterus, and vagina. Daily usage of herbal products helps to minimize stretch marks by toning and firming the skin.

Many cultures around the world have wonderful traditions and ceremonies surrounding pregnancy, childbirth, and the post-pregnancy period. Women are honored in ways that recognize their rite of passage into motherhood for the first time or for successive children. It marks the most important experience and event of her life, and makes a woman feel truly special and have a sense of accomplishment after she births a child. For example in Malaysia, there is an ancient ceremonial practice to end the post-pregnancy recovery period on the 44th day. The mother is given a floral bath with seven varieties of scented flowers, seven citrus limes, and rose water. This special mixture is kept overnight and added together in a floral bath. After the bath, the mother will be given an exotic sweet scented floral herbal drink. This final treatment is to welcome the mother to a new healthy harmonious life.[2] Doesn't that sound like a lovely ceremony to honor a mother?

Traditional Post-pregnancy (or Postpartum) Practitioner

Traditional treatments related to women's health are very well-established, for both internal and external beauty, beginning from puberty through marriage, pre-pregnancy, pregnancy and post-pregnancy care.[3]

Women skilled in traditional post-pregnancy care are hired to take care of the mother during the first six to eight weeks after delivery and provide a regimen of specific body treatments akin to in-home spa therapies. There are still some practitioners that live with a family for the entire post-pregnancy period, but this type of practitioner is becoming difficult to find. Most practitioners are hired on an out-service basis where they come to the home to provide the treatments and often cook special post-pregnancy meals.

A traditional post-pregnancy practitioner brings the supplies needed to perform the treatments. The mother prepares her body before the appointment by taking an herbal sponge bath and feminine (vagina) sauna (the equipment is provided by the practitioner) prior to the appointment so her body is "preheated" causing the pores to open, which improves absorption of the products used during the various treatments. Typically, a lightweight portable mattress is brought so as not to get oil or herbal products on the mother's bed.

The standard number of treatments a mother receives is six, with the first three taking place in successive days between days five and ten after delivery, and the next three successive treatments taking place at the end of the recovery period. Each treatment lasts for about two hours. Needless to say, such treatments are very beneficial and expedite a mother's recovery.

Massage is an area that the Malay and Ayurvedic after-birth traditions have parallel beliefs.

AYURVEDIC POSTPARTUM WISDOM

Long time Ayurvedic Postnatal Doula (AyurDoula), Ysha Oakes, shares that warm oil massage and internal oleation are high priorities in Ayurvedic (Eastern Indian medicine) post-pregnancy traditions. *"The Ayurvedic tradition emphasizes extra dietary ghee (clarified butter, preferably from organic and pastured cows) consumption for the best contribution to structural and hormonal health. It serves as long burning, stabilizing fuel and contributes to a smooth functioning nervous system.*

This also supports a unique type of internal cleansing to take place, working in conjunction with maternal massage to gently and safely remove acidity and accumulated toxins from the tissues as a result of pregnancy and the work of birth. Internal oleation also helps move waste through the lower gastro-intestinal tract without strain. This particular type of internal lubrication is more slippery than water and naturally comforts strained tissues. It also provides special nutrition for deeper tissues when other dietary factors are properly supported.

External oleation takes place in the form of warm oil massages, using sesame seed oil most commonly as a base. These massages are recommended daily after birth or about ten days after a surgical delivery, for body, mind and spiritual balance. Massage helps a woman's ability to mother well in a number of ways after child birth. It helps with the re-balancing of hormones, restores a feeling of groundedness, connectivity, supports the immune strength, allows for good rest and rejuvenation, and helps circulation at a time when exercise is mostly contraindicated. And one of the Sanskrit words for oil means Love. I love it!"

Ysha Oakes, Author of Touching Heaven – Tonic Postpartum Care and Recipes with Ayurveda - founded The Sacred Window. This name stems from the belief that directly after child birth there is a sacred window of time, 42 days that should be devoted to a mother's recovery and her baby. Ysha has over twenty years' experience taking care of women and babies. For more information, visit: www.sacredwindow.com.

Asian Post-pregnancy Healthcare in a Global Lead Position

Asian healthcare traditions are in a lead position here. Not only does Asia have the raw materials, it has the knowledge as well. The world is increasingly reverting to natural forms of healthcare and demand for the same is high. The growing field of natural healthcare is now becoming well established in official government health policies in most countries of the world. To illustrate how Asian countries are far ahead of Western countries when it comes to post-pregnancy recovery care, I visited the post-pregnancy recovery unit in a Traditional Complementary Medicine (TCM) department of a hospital in Malaysia and interviewed the head doctor, nurses, and practitioners. Below is a story I wrote about my impression of the visit, imagining what it would be like if we had something like this available in Western countries.

A Heavenly Post-pregnancy Experience

Imagine walking into a hospital and then finding yourself in front of an entrance to a wonderful TCM spa-like wing. You walk inside and are met with beautiful herbal aromas and a relaxing spa ambiance. A spa nestled inside a hospital—herbal medicine, massages, acupuncture, and alternative treatments complementing modern medicine, supported by doctors, nurses and hospital staff. Not only postnatal treatments, but Alzheimer, cancer, injuries, surgical recovery, and so on are complemented and facilitated by alternative treatments.

Envisage this for your own post-pregnancy experience. On the day you check out of the hospital, your doctor prescribes six sessions of postnatal therapeutic massage and body treatments for you, to help your aching, sore body with its recovery. The treatments take place on the sixth, seventh, and eighth days after delivery and then again on the thirty-ninth, fortieth, and forty-first days.

Day 4 Post-pregnancy

You are sitting at home on the fourth day after delivery (since you gave birth naturally, you returned home in forty-eight hours) and the door bell rings. You answer it and are beyond surprised to find the nurse who tended to you at the hospital standing at your doorstep for the first of three home visits. During these visits, she makes sure the baby isn't jaundiced, checks your perennial area, helps with breastfeeding problems, and answers any questions you may have.

You learn that she will come by again on the fifth day and one more time after that within the first ten days. She reminds you that your post-pregnancy body treatments will begin on your sixth day post-pregnant.

Day 6 Post-pregnancy

On the sixth day, you return to the hospital to experience your first post-pregnancy treatment, not sure what to expect. You enter a noticeably different wing from the rest of the hospital. "Wait a minute," you say. "Am I in the right place?" A woman in a slightly different uniform calmly greets you with a warm cup of herbal tea and smiles as she says, "Yes, ma'am. You just sit right down here, and we will take good care of you." You sit down, sip the tea that warms you all over, and swear you've gone to heaven.

This wonderful spa facility allows you to bring your newborn with you as there is a soft bassinet for her to lie in. You made sure to have nursed her beforehand, and she is sleeping soundly next to the massage bed. You remove your clothes, all but your underwear as you are still bleeding. Your two-hour treatment begins with a heaty, warm oil massage that feels "Oh so good!" You drift in and out of sleep. Your body—the incredible vessel that has carried your child for nine months and then birthed her, and now feels like it has been battered, stretched, pushed, and pulled—is now being cared for in a way that you never imagined. During the massage, the traditional post-pregnancy practitioner asks you for feedback regarding various after-birth conditions as your body transitions to its non-pregnant state. She listens to you, letting you talk or choosing not to talk, and she answers any questions in a gentle caring manner. If there is anything that may be of concern, a nurse is informed, and it will be determined if you need to see your doctor.

After the oil massage, a heated stone, wrapped in a soft material, is softly but firmly pressed all over your body to infuse heat deep into your water-logged tissues and joints, focusing on areas that are particularly sore, bloated, or stressed; from birthing your baby and then slouching while breastfeeding such as your lower and middle back. Your uterus is pressed gently but firmly around its outer circumference encouraging it to shrink while blood clots in your lochia are being broken up through the heat and subtle pressure.

Finally, a torso wrap for your tummy, is placed on the bed. You are asked to lie down on your back, so the top of the wrap lines up just beneath your breasts when it is wrapped around your torso. Beforehand an herbal firming paste, that is warm to the touch and smells lovely, is applied to your abdomen. This paste helps firm the stomach muscles and sagging skin of the tummy area, as well as promotes the loss of water retention. A thin cotton cloth is placed over the firming paste so it doesn't get absorbed by the wrap. Then, the post-pregnancy angel, who has gently cared for your body for the past two hours, ties the belly wrap for you tightly but comfortably around your abdomen and helps you up.

You can't believe how much better your body feels. You actually feel like you have energy! The aches and pains have subsided for the time being, and you have a warm feeling all over. You swear you can feel the blood circulating inside your body, ridding it of built-up toxins and fats that it doesn't need any longer. Your bloated, floppy body is encased in a wrap that extends from under your breasts to just below your hip; and it feels like a warm hug, keeping everything together. You thank your post-pregnancy angel profusely and can't believe this is part of the hospital package for its maternity patients at no extra cost. You would certainly have paid for this treatment!

You leave the room and visit the nurse again. As the nurse hands you a second cup of aromatic herbal tea, she reminds you that you have two more treatments this week, the second one being tomorrow. You leave feeling calmer than you have in months, with a relaxed smile on your face, carrying your newborn with you.

Day 7 Post-pregnancy
Your appointment is at 10:30 a.m., but you arrive at 10:00 a.m., just in case you can get in early!

Care After Miscarriage
In traditional cultures, miscarriage is taken seriously. It is a must for women who have miscarried to heal themselves and follow the same dietary, activity, and personal care post-pregnancy guidelines for a two-week period. Even though the pregnancy was not full-term, a woman's body was still in a pregnant state, and therefore, the same hormonal and physical changes were set in motion. The massage treatments have the same effect of assisting the body to recover stronger in a shorter time period (the same way as if the pregnancy was full-term) by toning the uterus muscles, removing blood clots, and cleansing the uterus.[4]

A mental healing process occurs alongside a physical one. This allows a woman to have recognition that she was with child, but nature did not intend for the baby to be born. Honoring herself, and her body, by receiving treatments and knowing she is taking some action to strengthen her body allows her to work through and grieve her loss. The treatments heal, and prepare, the body for the next attempt to become pregnant.

Massage During Menstruation
The same hot stone, post-pregnancy uterine massage is given to women during

menstruation as the deep heat infusion into the tissues helps the blood flow, reduces cramps and the temporary water weight gain and bloatedness. In Indonesia, a component of the government's labor policy entitles women to have two days off per month during the heavy-flow days of their period. This is proof that traditional cultures better understand the importance of taking care of a woman's womb.

No Menopause Effects

Older generations of Asian women believe if a woman does not take the time to rest and recover after childbirth, paying particular attention to the healing and recovery of their womb, which they consider being the life force of a woman, then a woman will have poor health much later in life, normally referring to the menopause years.

I have spoken to several women in their menopause years or beyond (after sixty years old), where their menstruation cycle has stopped but have no signs of the effects of menopause that are experienced in the west. They all claim that it is because they followed post-pregnancy guidelines, and received treatments and massages to take care of their inner health, or more specifically their womb and body after childbirth. There is no scientific proof to support this claim, but there is ample evidence-based proof. Speaking to these women and seeing with my own eyes the good physical health they are in is proof enough for me!

There is no reason why all mothers can't have these same options of receiving non-medical, effective post-pregnancy treatments to help facilitate their recovery from childbirth. At the very least, all mothers should have the opportunity to hire a traditional practitioner to come to their home to provide such treatments. I've come across several online forums involving Western women who have flown in traditional post-pregnancy practitioners to live with them for one or two months to oversee and manage their recovery period.

Why Are New Mothers Having Post-pregnancy Treatments?

- They fill the gap of medical treatments for post-pregnancy care.
- They complement the emphasis of the medical community's focus on the mother's prenatal period.
- The treatments are nonintrusive and promote internal healing.
- A specified post-pregnancy program gives direction for new mothers to take the time and treatment needed for their bodies to heal.
- Post-pregnancy recovery programs and treatments are becoming more popular worldwide and available in various cultures.

Traditional Practices Gaining Global Popularity
Traditional post-pregnancy (or postpartum) practitioners are gaining popularity in Western cultures. New mothers, as well as women, want to train in the traditional ways, as the effects of such services and products are recognized. It has been documented in many reports from esteemed organizations such as the World Health Organization (WHO) that Western cultures could learn from traditional cultures when it comes to the benefits of post-pregnancy recovery traditions. Therefore, traditional post-pregnancy recovery practices are gaining interest from obstetricians, fertility doctors, midwives, doulas and massage therapists. You can read more on midwives and doulas in the postnatal section at the back of the book.

Natural Post-pregnancy Recovery Products
Sometimes using common sense and good nutrition isn't enough. There are natural products that are specific for a post-pregnant recovering body that assist with its healing and internal rebalancing.

POST-PREGNANCY TIP
The internal process of healing taking place during the first weeks after pregnancy, if well managed, is more essential than any physical exercise engaged in weeks later and can make a profound positive impact on a woman's long term health.

We assume our body has the innate ability to heal, and we are surprised when the healing that takes place isn't 100%. However, if we provide the necessary fuel the body needs, it would allow the body to recover, not only better and more holistically, but in a shorter time period, and in a more balanced manner.

What We Do Have Available in the United States: Doulas
A doula is someone, usually a woman, who provides nonmedical support to women and their families during birth, childbirth, and the immediate post-pregnancy or postpartum period. If you are unfamiliar with doulas, I'd recommend that you find out about the valuable services they provide to women and their families. Their services can be engaged from just prior to birth up to eight weeks or more after delivery. Hospitals are beginning to hire birth doulas as part of its maternity staff.[5] Therefore, if you can afford to hire a postpartum doula during the transition period of welcoming your baby into your family, do so.

There are several types of doulas: Perinatal or Antepartum, Labor or Birth, and Postpartum or Postnatal. The service that doulas off may include:

- Non-medical baby care
- Light household help
- Breastfeeding coaching
- Sibling care
- Child care tips
- Running errands
- Meal preparation

You have to find the right doula that will suit your needs. More and more doulas are becoming interested to be trained in traditional post-pregnancy recovery methods as this wellness trend spreads. The traditional treatments are a natural fit with the services offered by a postpartum doula because it's all about focusing on the recovery of the mom. There is a growing trend of insurance companies beginning to cover the cost of doula services, or a portion of the costs. However, the conditions insurance companies impose on doulas are normally not in the least favorable, resulting in serious under-valuing of the services they provide to families.

FOUR

The Womb is a Woman's Life Force

After-birth recovery beliefs and practices play a vital role in many traditional cultures. Such beliefs and practices are a vital preventative measure that provides a supportive environment for a new mother so she has a "holistic or balanced recovery" from childbirth. Balanced hormonally and physically, and mentally and spirituality. Post-pregnancy, or postpartum, recovery is overlooked in America and Western cultures in general, versus being an auspicious part of the pregnancy experience in other countries. I found stark differences in cultural beliefs between eastern and Western countries on this topic.

In eastern or more traditional cultures, there are deep-seated beliefs about post-pregnancy recovery that are ingrained and part of a shared-belief system. The emphasis of the importance of having a designated "recovery period" is recognized by all. Therefore, doctors are confident that a new mother will be well cared for by her family or by a traditional post-pregnancy (or postpartum) practitioner.

In the United States, doctors don't emphasize the importance of post-pregnancy recovery because it isn't their role. Most births take place in hospitals, and babies are delivered by obstetrician surgeons. Therefore, expectant mothers listen to the guidance their doctor provides them throughout their pregnancy, but the advice and care abruptly stops after the baby is born. Now, I'm not blaming the medical community. A doctor's job is to monitor a woman's pregnancy and to do everything in their power to deliver a healthy child; however, that is where their job ends. In other cultures, this is where traditional beliefs take over, and it is up to the mother and extended family to make the necessary arrangements to ensure a new mother has a healthy recovery. It's a family affair.

There is a deep-seated Asian belief that *"the womb is every woman's life force and affects the state of her overall health."* If a woman's reproductive organs or pelvic area is unhealthy, then it will affect every aspect of her health, inside and out. Therefore, to restore her physical health and energy levels, great emphasis is placed on the recovery of a woman's womb after childbirth. The belief also encompasses the notion that if a woman's womb doesn't heal properly, she may encounter years of bad health. I found this to be an interesting theory.

Traditional post-pregnancy recovery beliefs center around the notion that after childbirth, a woman's body is depleted of all its energy. Therefore the mother must have complete rest and follow recommended dietary, activity, and personal care guidelines for a minimum of six weeks to restore her vitality. After-birth services such as massages with specific techniques, body treatments, abdominal garments, and all-natural products are available to help a post-pregnant body heal from the inside out. Such services also assist the body to re-stimulate circulation and metabolism, encourages the loss of water retention, pregnancy fat, flatulence, and helps to break up and rid blot clots from the uterus via the lochia at a faster rate. The ingredients of the natural products have anti-inflammatory and antibacterial properties that help to reduce overall body and vaginal swelling. This allows shrinkage of the womb, cervix, vaginal, and perineum area to occur in a shorter time period.

The common theme throughout traditional post-pregnancy beliefs is that the mother needs special care, products, food, and services to help her recover from the significant life-altering experience of pregnancy and birth. Her body needs a lot of rest to be reenergized.

Post-pregnancy Analogy: Car Accident Victim

I'd like to use the example of someone who has been in a very bad accident resulting in hospitalization and complete bed rest. Unfortunately, we've all heard of or known someone who experienced this. In a few short weeks, this person who has had complete rest and was well cared for seemed to heal at an incredible rate and is up and walking around. Recovery from pregnancy and childbirth is a similar situation. Birth is a traumatic event for a woman's body. It is a natural event, but traumatic nonetheless, resulting in the body needing complete rest, nutritious food, and special care. You wouldn't expect someone in a serious car accident to get up and clean the house, go shopping, or cook during the first few weeks, would you? Don't expect that of yourself. Specialized care for a mother during the first six weeks after childbirth will provide her body with what it needs to heal, so she can mentally and physically manage the demands of her new baby.

Corporate America is Waking Up

The American government, as well as corporate America, is slowly beginning to recognize the connection between increasing social problems and the transition back to previous lifestyles by women after their maternity leave. Many women are not coping with the pressures of life, along with assimilating a new baby into their lifestyle, resulting in various post-pregnancy-related mental and emotional illnesses.

A Blue Cross and Blue Shield Insurance[1] branch in Anthem, Missouri, recognized this growing social problem and took action by introducing the Newborn and Parenting Resources policy in January 2010. This new service is designed to help new mothers adjust to their newborn baby and return to work after maternity leave. New mothers have eight weeks of counseling by licensed professional coaches who have advanced degrees in counseling and/or child development. The coaches provide support and help mothers set goals, address concerns and identify resolutions on topics including:

- Returning to work
- Adjusting to a new baby
- Work/life balance
- Issues with older siblings

- Health and nutrition
- Child development
- Parent well-being

The coaches are available via e-mail, instant message chat, online journal and telephone.[1]

As you can see, there is certainly a growing recognition that mothers aren't handling modern-day pressures due to the fact that they don't have the needed family support and thus aren't recovering soundly. These factors are directly contributing to the rising number of women experiencing extended maternity blues and/or unstable post-pregnancy emotions. Who do you think is ultimately suffering? Not only new mothers, but also, their newborn baby and other children if there are any. Normally the relationship with the husband or partner becomes extremely stressed, not to mention relationships with extended family members as well.

---

[1]Blue Cross Blue Shield provides 98 million Americans with health insurance.

Western cultures generally don't have the family support like years ago, so it is up to us mothers to take charge of our recovery after we deliver and actively and consciously manage it. We really don't have a choice as the odds are not in our favor that we won't be affected by some sort of post-pregnancy-related condition. We do need to be aware of what is going on within our body and why we need to recover cautiously and carefully, not rushing it. Make sure you pay attention to your emotions and feelings.

Traditional Post-pregnancy Recovery Practices
This period has many names:
- Confinement period
- Recovery period
- Resting period
- Lying-in period
- Sitting period
- Doing the month

The intention of all the names is the same. This time period is devoted to the mother to regain her strength and energy, to bond with her new child, and adjust to having a new baby in the house.

The general perception is that immediately after childbirth a woman's health is extremely vulnerable. She has gone through the natural, but traumatic, experience of birth where tremendous amounts of energy have been spent leaving her feeling weak. A woman may return to her mother's house or her mother (or another family member) may come to stay with her for one to two months to relieve her of all the domestic responsibilities including housework, cooking, cleaning, and looking after other children, if there are any.

From the wealthy to the poor, women around the globe engage in some type of post-pregnancy recovery practices. Caring for yourself from the day you deliver is *crucial* in order for you and your body to have a balanced recovery. The first week post-pregnancy is when the most intense healing takes place, but the subsequent five weeks are equally as important. After six weeks, your uterus and reproductive organs should nearly be back to their pre-pregnant size.[2] However keep-in-mind, that the post-pregnancy or postpartum period is not six weeks. It can last months or even years, with many women claiming it takes six to nine months before they feel somewhat back to their old selves, with many more women indicating they never feel normal again. So don't put pressure on yourself to think you'll have a full recovery in just six weeks. Odds are it won't happen. A six-week post-pregnancy recovery period is like an estimated due date (EDD). It's a *guesstimate* to give you a time frame.

Humoral Theory of Medicine: Relating to Pregnancy

Hot State vs. Cold State

Post-birth recovery precautions and traditions have largely been derived from the ancient belief in the following:[3]

There are four conditions in the human body: hot, cold, moist, and dry, and they must remain in balance.[4]

Pregnancy is considered to be a "hot state" as a pregnant body retains excess blood and fluids to support a growing baby. The excess fluids and presence of a baby cause a rise in an expectant mothers normal temperature of 98.6°F (37°C), of about 1.0°–1.5°F on average.[5] A pregnant body serves as an incubator for a baby over the subsequent nine months, and its temperature will stay elevated for the duration of the pregnancy.

A woman who has just given birth loses the following:

- Her baby's body heat.
- A lot of blood.
- All the amniotic fluids.
- The placenta.
- Is exhausted from pain.

This causes her internal body temperature to drop immediately, thus shifting the now-non-pregnant body to a "cold state."

POST-PREGNANCY WISDOM
Traditional post-pregnancy recovery practices followed during 30-40 day recuperation period after birth center around a mommy's food and drink intake, activities, and personal care.

The length of a mother's recuperation period is adjusted according to the following:
• How easy or difficult her pregnancy and childbirth was.
• The mother's overall health.
• How well her body is healing.

Traditional recuperation periods normally averages between 30 and 44 days but can be up to 100 days or more.[6] The purpose of the recuperation period is to restore equilibrium within a mother's body.

VIETNAMESE POST-PREGNANCY TRADITION
One Vietnamese saying is "three months and ten days" is the duration for a mother's post-pregnancy recovery. The months are considered to be based on the lunar calendar of the cycle of the moon.[7]

This extended resting period is a wonderful time for a mother to focus on taking care of herself and bonding with her child. However, it is just as important for a woman to take necessary precautions and monitor herself on a daily basis to ensure that her own recovery keeps progressing and doesn't regress. A woman recuperating from childbirth should have a holistic outlook and approach to her recovery as there are all sorts of activities happening within her body that she may not even be aware of. A holistic approach will provide a mother with better protection from the onset of the blues or worse.

POST-PREGNANCY TIP
Remember that the following information is only a <u>temporary</u> lifestyle change to be followed as strictly as you can manage during your recovery. It isn't forever!

American Mindset
Having read many studies about the immediate twelve-week period after childbirth in the United States, I realized that the mind-set of having a designated downtime for a "post-pregnancy or postpartum recovery period" must be nurtured even during pregnancy so that there is enough time for a new mother, as well as those around her,

to understand and accept the idea. As it stands now, the typical maternity period in the US is not a period that is devoted to a mother's recuperation. And unfortunately, the idea of a *lying-in period* after childbirth period doesn't seem to be an option for American women. The pressures and activities of modern life, not to mention financial obligations, don't allow a new mother to indulge in complete rest for four weeks. Two weeks has been deemed as a realistic time period that Western mothers feel comfortable with; however, one can come to their own conclusion that this is certainly not enough time. Even three weeks of following post-pregnancy guidelines and devoting the time to resting will make a difference; however, a full four to six weeks would result in a much better recovery.

FIVE

Why You Need a Mommy Plan

> Women's bodies have their own wisdom that has been refined over 100,000 generations.
>
> **Dr. Sarah Buckley**

Pregnancy and childbirth have always been a magical time for mothers, be it the first time or with successive children. Nearly all expectant parents have two strategic plans a birth plan and a baby plan.

Birth Plan
A birth plan is a written document that details a woman's preferences leading up to labor and childbirth. It normally includes information about labor techniques, medications, medical and professional childbirth practitioners, and so on.

Baby Plan
A baby plan consists of the purchases and preparations, undertaken by expectant parents, to ready their home to welcome their long-awaited, new baby as a member into their family.

The most commonly overlooked plan is the plan for a mommy's *own* recuperation from pregnancy and childbirth, or the Mommy Plan. This plan places a woman on the path to a *holistic recovery* and keeps her there with easy-to-follow food, beverage, activity, and personal care guidelines. With a solid physical and hormonal recuperation taking place, a mental and spiritual recovery will follow. These are the components of what I consider a holistic recovery. We mentioned in the previous chapter that a post-pregnancy or postpartum plan begins from the day a woman gives birth, or Day One, and continues for a minimum of six weeks, which can be extended depending on how a mother's recovery is progressing. In many cultures mothers target a full one hundred days for their after-birth recovery period, (especially when birthing successive children) making adjustments to their plan along the way as they heal and regain their energy levels.

Last but Not Least, The Mommy Plan

The third plan all women should have is the Mommy Plan. This plan focuses on the recovery and well-being of a mother immediately after childbirth for a minimum of six weeks, which can be extended week by week according to how her recovery is progressing.

A Personal Journey

Each woman's recovery is a personal journey, as is her pregnancy. Nevertheless, women tend to base the progression of their recovery, whether it's physical or emotional, on someone else's experience. This will often make her own recovery all the more stressful if it is not as fast or sound. It should be made clear, that one woman's recovery will not be like another's, and that a woman needs to listen to what her own body is telling her and respond accordingly.

Early Intervention

It is apparent that most women do not realize, or understand, the internal chaos their body is thrown into as it goes through the natural healing process. Precaution and early intervention can make all the difference in a woman's recovery and hopefully lessen or avert any extended emotional feelings.

First, let's review what happens from conception to pregnancy and wrap up with what's in store for your post-pregnancy period. By the time you finish reading this chapter, you will have no uncertainty that you need a Mommy Plan.

Pregnancy: 280 Days

Pregnancy is a specific, *temporary* condition lasting for a period of approximately nine months. An average pregnancy lasts 280 days from the last menstrual period (LMP) which is roughly 266 days from conception to birth. The first two weeks of pregnancy includes the time of menstruation, ovulation and fertilization. Conception occurs approximately 14–16 days after the first day of menstruation. The date of conception is not always known and can vary between women. The date of the LMP is known by most women so doctors use this date as a starting point for pregnancy.[1] From the LMP a birth practitioner will add 280 days to give an estimate due date (EDD), of which 80% of babies are born within the 2 weeks before or after 40 weeks and only about 5% of babies are born on their due dates.[2]

40 weeks = 9 months + 1 week ¦ 4.4 weeks = 1 month

In general, all birth practitioners agree that pregnancies, when using the LMP dating technique, average approximately 280 days or 40 weeks."[3] However, pregnancy is considered "full-term" anywhere between 37–42 weeks, with known cases of pregnancy safely lasting up to 44 weeks.[4]

In contrast to the general mathematical approximation of the EDD, there is no way of estimating how long the post-pregnancy period will last. This period could last longer than the pregnancy if a woman doesn't take precautions to place herself on the path to a healthy recovery. Both pregnancy and the immediate period after birth are times when a woman has to closely manage her health. In spite of this, high rates of postpartum depression indicate most women fail to plan for their own recovery or don't even think about it until after the six-week medical examination.

Pregnancy Health

A woman's body is inherently designed to provide the perfect environment for the growth and development of a baby. However, many aspects of our modern lifestyle may affect a baby's development. Such factors include stress, worry, poor dietary habits, sedentary lifestyle, and a polluted environment. As mother and baby are a single unit during pregnancy, whatever the mother does to herself will directly affect her baby. One of the most important aspects during pregnancy is adequate nutrition; therefore, a pregnant mother must incorporate nutritious food into her diet for both herself and her growing child. The worst advice I ever got in my life was not to worry about what I ate during pregnancy, to just enjoy and worry about it afterward. I would never pass on this advice. So please *do* worry about what you eat because if you don't, you will be worrying about it for a long, long time afterward.

In addition to taking care of her health, a pregnant mother should also take care of her emotions. It is a common belief in many cultures that a pregnant mother who is always unhappy, has low spirits, stressed, has a negative outlook, or worries a lot is susceptible to postnatal blues.[5] Make every effort to be positive; enjoy being pregnant. This is a very special time in your life. Even if you are having a difficult pregnancy, identify three good things about being pregnant and focus on them. Keep the list on the refrigerator or somewhere you can see or read it when feeling down. In most cases, women say afterward that they missed being pregnant. So savor this experience as it is a *temporary condition* and will be over before you know it.

There may be a link between chronic negative emotions and pregnancy depression. Uncertainty causes fear. If you are experiencing negative emotions during pregnancy, your first instinct may be to hide or suppress those feelings, which isn't the best thing to do. Accept the emotions or your fear about the unknown, whether it is the birth process or something else, and write a few descriptive sentences or even paragraphs so you can understand why you are feeling this way.

For example, "I am feeling a lot of stress and anxiety because I am afraid of actually going through the process of childbirth. I have heard, and read, many scary stories that I don't know if I can do it. I don't know how to do it."

These types of feelings are caused by the uncertainty of the future. Now that the above has been expressed, I would begin researching what happens to a woman's body during childbirth, or find out about popular birth strategies such as hypnobirthing. There is so much information on the Internet you can access that can direct you to your next action such as attending a talk on childbirth, or talking to a childbirth professional, such as a midwife, birth (or labor) doula, or antenatal (or perinatal) doula.

PREGNANCY TIP
Write down why you are feeling negative and work through them, then do your best to enjoy the rest of your pregnancy.[6]

How Does a Woman's Pregnant Body Change? [7]
During pregnancy, a woman's body goes through a profound transformation whereby virtually every part is affected:
- Cardiovascular: the amount of blood the heart pumps increases along with the heart rate.
- Breathing: more oxygen is inhaled and extra carbon dioxide is exhaled as a result of breathing for two.
- Blood: the amount of blood increases to regulate the body's core temperature to keep the baby's environment at a comfortable temperature.
- Hormones: estrogen and progesterone hormones increase.
- Thyroid gland: enlarges and the metabolism speeds up.

How Does a Pregnant Woman's Anatomy Change? [8]
As a baby grows, a woman's anatomy changes along with it:

- Ligaments and cartilage loosen (Ligament Laxity) because the hormone relaxin is released.
- Ribs, pelvis, and other joints expand to accommodate a growing waist.
- Back pain may occur due to postural distortions.
- Feet, ankle, and knee alignment may shift to adapt to postural changes.

Persistence of Hormonal Imbalance for Months

The hormonal changes that occur during pregnancy may persist for months afterward. The time period from delivery to the point when the reproductive organs return to their original shape and size is known as the postpartum period (a medical term).[9] A new mother is more vulnerable during this time than she thinks, and her body has special needs during this brief, but critical, phase.

Asking for Help Is a Sign of Strength and a Protective Mechanism

We've established that the mind-set of American women is normally fiercely independent, and that it may work against us in this situation. Being independent is a good thing; however, have you heard the saying "It takes a village to raise a child"? This is one of those times when it is OK to ask for help. It is a point in life when not only is a mother recovering from nine months of pregnancy and then childbirth, but she is also taking full-time care of a new little person. A little person that is unable to do anything for himself, and therefore, his needs are largely met by the mother. So during this transitional time period, every aspect of a new mother's life will be affected by change. This change will, without a doubt, enhance your life but have no illusion that it will also be a challenging process. You will never have loved someone so much, who places more demands on you at the same time. Getting to know your newborn will take patience as every child is different. The crying cues and behavior can only be learned over time. This is why to focus on your child and yourself for the first few weeks will make things easier in the long run.

> **POST-PREGNANCY REASSURANCE**
> If there is a right time to ask for help in your life, it is during the first six to eight weeks post-pregnancy. You will not seem weak or incapable. In fact, taking charge of this period and ensuring you receive proper nutrition and sleep will make all the difference in the world for your ability to function properly and take care of your newborn.

All mothers need time for themselves

When a mother doesn't get any time free time for herself, she may begin to feel overwhelmed. Caring for a baby day after day, or week after week, without a break causes stress. Not having any down time, to unwind, can lead to depression and render a mother unable to take care of her baby; as well as herself and her family. Therefore a necessary action is to ask for a break, or *temporary* help. Remember, the transition to a non-pregnant state means that a woman doesn't have 100% control over her own body, and sometimes emotions. Being the strong, independent, stoic, American woman is certainly not to a mother's benefit in this situation. You will know when you need assistance, and in what manner; and you will be surprised what the benefit of two hours, or more, to yourself will do to your state of mind.

> **PROTECTIVE MATERNAL INSTICTS KICKS IN**
> Asking for help is indicative of a mother's inner strength, as it is a protective mechanism toward her newborn.

I'm sure there are many people in your life that would gladly help you out during this time. I strive to believe that the innate nature of people is good. Surround yourself with good people. I will predict that you will be surprised by how many people are willing to lend a hand if all you do is ask. Then when the time comes later in life to repay the kindness, help out someone that needs it whatever their situation may be. Keep the good karma going. What goes around comes around!

It Takes a Village to Raise a Child

Find out who is part of your village or community, people you can rely on. Members of your community can be nonfamily, as well as family members, as it is common that many people move away from their immediate family for employment or personal reasons. Make a list not only of those people who are close to you, but of mother groups and similar support organizations near you. The trend of creating community support groups led by mothers is gaining popularity as there is a need for it. Create your own mother group if there aren't any in your area.

When I had my son, my parents lived just down the street. Two months after he was born, my husband returned to Southeast Asia to prepare for our move back. During this one-month period, I was a single mom, and boy, was it difficult! My son did not sleep well at night, I was getting up nearly every hour or two to nurse him. Most mornings my son and I were still sleeping at 10:00 a.m. My mother would come over every morning and watch him while I continued to sleep, took a long hot shower or had breakfast. For me these were the simple things that I needed most met. I was allowed time for myself. However my mother didn't come over at first; I had to ask her for her help. I had to admit to myself, and to her, that I needed help. Because my mother was retired, it worked out beautifully. That month would have been even more difficult if I didn't have someone dependable to rely on. My husband and I talked about it afterward, and we agreed that we would never do it again. But we, or I, didn't think it would be *that* difficult. I mean, I've lived and backpacked around the world for many years. Certainly, I could manage a little baby for a month on my own. Nope, definitely not the case! I'm very grateful to this day for all that my mother, father and brother did to help during this time. Here's to living and learning.

Who Is Benefiting from Your Silence?

Ask yourself who is it benefiting if you are suffering in silence? You? Certainly not your newborn, other children, or husband/partner. It is benefitting no one.

> **It is benefitting no one if you stoically suffer in silence.**

Do not suffer in silence as it almost always compounds any negative feelings you may be having. When a woman reaches out for help, she is reaching out for her newborn child and family in the same breath. Dr. Shoshana Bennett, past president of Postpartum Support International (PSI) and author of *Postpartum Depression for Dummies*, says, "Women with a past history of depression are at higher risk than others, however no woman is immune. Any woman even with a 'clean history', meaning with no history at all of mood disorder or depression or otherwise, doesn't mean they couldn't get PPD or otherwise."[10] Stress and a history of depression may influence whether the blues go on to become major depression. If such feelings are ignored, persistent negative emotions may worsen and could lead to postpartum depression.

The Mommy Plan, for a Balanced Recovery from Childbirth

Having a post-pregnancy plan in place for your recovery will prove to have many benefits. One of the most important benefits is that it may reduce the probability of being affected by pregnancy-related mood disorders that strike one in eight women in America today. This is a plan that is best developed and in place *before* a woman gives birth. It is not a guarantee that you won't experience some postpartum emotion. That is normal; however, to have a preventative recovery plan in place to help yourself heal from the inside out is certainly worth doing rather than doing nothing at all.

> **A POST-PREGNANCY PLAN...**
> is a proactive and preventative measure to ensure a mommy does everything she can to recover in a strong, healthy, and balanced manner.

Self-Care Must Continue Through the Post-pregnancy Period

A new mother doesn't have any control over the hormonal rebalancing that is taking place, but she can help her body by lessening some of the physical stress it's undergoing which helps hormonal levels rebalance at a more consistent rate. The mental and spiritual balance will follow after hormones stabilize and confidence becomes stronger as a mother gets to know her baby.

After a woman gives birth, the process of her body reverting back to its non-pregnant state begins immediately, and given time, this process will complete itself. However, it is important to optimize this recovery process by understanding the body is in a weakened state and has specific needs for the first few weeks post-pregnancy. Nine months of pregnancy and then childbirth is taxing on a woman's body, to say the least. During pregnancy, a woman takes care of her body by taking prenatal supplements and making adjustments in her diet because in essence she is already taking care of her unborn child. Therefore, pregnant women need to have a paradigm shift and realize that after her baby is born, she must continue to take proactive care of herself. It isn't over yet!

This is why a Mommy Plan that focuses on a woman's healing and recovery after childbirth is an essential precaution to provide the body with the *best internal environment* possible to heal itself. No one but a recovering mommy is going to know how she is feeling, physically and emotionally. A woman must pay close attention to her feelings during this period, and if she is feeling down for an extended time, a red flag should go up. It is a time to ask for understanding and help from the people in her life. Help in any way that relieves stress and allows her to recoup her energy. This is about what the mother needs, not what other people around her believes she needs—and she must communicate those needs very clearly.

American and Western Cultures Need a Paradigm Shift

American, and Western cultures in general, emphasize the preparation period up until the baby is born through the birth and baby plans. Then the focus shifts to the baby, and the mother becomes less important. Plainly put, this is wrong. A paradigm shift is needed among the psyche of Western cultures recognizing that:

> The well-being and healthy recovery of a woman after childbirth should carry the same importance and priority as taking care of the needs of a newborn child.

When a woman's body starts to revert to its non-pregnant state, an intense internal transformation is taking place as her body goes through the process of rebalancing itself from the shock of the significant drop in the levels of hormones as they are no longer needed. If a mother takes care of herself and is well looked after and supported by those close to her during the immediate post-pregnancy period, this will lay the groundwork for a healthy recovery.

It is vital for a woman to take special precautions to recover to the best of her ability. This will promote a healthy state of mind and physical condition, which will allow her to care for her baby and resume normal life activities, minimizing the risk of any major emotional complications. A woman is pregnant for nine months, but the human body has the capability to dramatically heal itself in a much shorter time. Yet most women don't even allow themselves a full week of complete downtime to recover and push themselves to function "normally", resuming previous responsibilities too early. This is when post-pregnancy complications may begin.

Other Traditional Cultures

In many Asian, Latin American, African, and Middle Eastern cultures, emphasis is placed on *both* the new baby, and the mother's recovery.[11] There are specific traditional herbal remedies and recipes that have been used for thousands of years to help a woman heal in a balanced manner, in a relatively short time period of three to four months, on average. Have this time frame in mind for your own recovery. Outside of America, post-pregnancy recovery products and services are widely used by women in many countries.

POST-PREGNANCY REVIEW

The Mommy Plan emphasizes the immediate six weeks after childbirth and can be extended week by week according to the progression of a mother's recovery. It should consist of post-pregnancy diet and drink in-take, activity, personal care and specific services and products for women after childbirth.

Post-pregnancy Precautions

The traditional information contained in the next four chapters:
1. Diet DON'TS
2. Diet DO'S
3. Activities
4. Personal Care

was accumulated through many lively discussions and interviews over bottomless cups of Malaysian *teh tarik** and *kopi***, with traditional and modern post-pregnancy practitioners as well as traditional and complimentary (TCM) doctors, friends, and people familiar with Malay post-pregnancy recovery traditions. Whether it was a scheduled interview or someone I met at a social gathering, I would always seek out opinions, knowledge, family recipes, and their experiences. I loved each and every discussion and thank everyone for sharing their time, stories, and wisdom.

*Teh tarik, or Malaysian "pulled tea," is a made from tea and condensed milk that is poured from a large cup or container, back and forth at least three feet apart. The tea is deemed to be "pulled" when a lovely froth develops on the top of the glass.

**Kopi is Malaysian coffee with a distinctive flavor derived from roasting the coffee beans with butter and sugar.

SIX

Post-pregnancy Precautions: Diet DON'TS

Caring for yourself immediately after childbirth is crucial to restoring your body in a strong, healthy, and "balanced" manner.

Background on the After Birth Traditions in This Book

The post-pregnancy recovery dietary guidelines that I'm introducing are commonly followed in Southeast Asia. The guidelines may differ from country to country as the region consists of ten nations, but there are definite underlying commonalities. The Southeast Asia region is home to over five hundred million people, is predominately tropical, and contains some of the oldest rain forests in the world originating over 130 million years ago, making them among the oldest on earth. The biological diversity has been recognized as one of the twelve global mega-diversity areas.

Influences on these Post-pregnancy Traditions

Globalization, a contemporary term for an ancient phenomenon, was very much a part of the way of life in Asia. Traders from the east and west came through Southeast Asia stopping in various trading ports, in countries like Malaysia and Singapore, as their vessels sailed from India en route to Indonesia, Vietnam, and ultimately China. Over centuries, crews of ships and their passengers made up of scholars, physicians and monks traveling the long sea journey in each direction would impart knowledge with the locals in the countries they came to port in. The Southeast Asian populace grew rich with cultural influences from China and India, and peoples from these countries settled in the region.[1] Therefore, Indian Ayurvedic and traditional Chinese medicine beliefs regarding post-pregnancy recovery have influenced the local beliefs in the region.

Back to Basics

We've established that traditional post-pregnancy practices center around the belief that a woman's body is *unbalanced* after childbirth, i.e., a cold state, and needs to be rebalanced and its energy replenished. With this in mind, the immediate after-birth period is accompanied by specific dietary, activity, and personal care guidelines. I've deciphered this particular post-pregnancy wisdom into a form that Western women could understand and accept. The practical reasoning behind these guidelines can then be easily incorporated into their Mommy Plan. I may have omitted some recommendations that are purely cultural, and therefore I cannot present a logical explanation.

Adaptation of Information for Western Diet and Lifestyle

Please note that the information in this book *had* to be adapted for women in countries where there isn't any (developed) post-pregnancy culture, in order to find value in traditional ways. I have made adaptations for a Western diet, and preferred healthy cooking styles, as some of the food recommendations may not be available around the world. I've also included recommendations based on recent scientific information that is relevant for post-pregnancy recovery due to the model of the global food supply and how it may interfere or affect the healing process the body will go through. This book is a blend of the best of the old and the new. Do keep in mind when reading the dietary guidelines that traditional cultures, still to this day, use food as part of their healthcare system.

You can also, gentle reader, make adaptations to suit your post-pregnancy temporary lifestyle. You may have had a healthy strong birth and don't need to follow all the recommendations but pick and choose which ones will work for you. Perhaps you don't need to have three weeks of downtime—it's really up to how healthy your body is after pregnancy and childbirth. Pregnancy is not an illness, but your body is in a weakened condition. What I've done is present the information in the most basic form, knowing full well that Western women will take what they feel works best for them and disregard what they feel won't work. Some of it may make you think, "Seriously? I'm not doing that!" and others, you'll say, "Hmmmm. That makes sense." But rest assured, I can attest to the effectiveness of traditional post-pregnancy practices because I've researched the science behind how they heal a woman's body.

If you start to feel unhealthy, have low energy levels, and feel like you aren't recovering well, review the guidelines again and adapt a few more into your post-pregnancy plan whether you are three weeks or twelve weeks after delivery. It can't hurt, and it can only help your body continue with the healing process.

As it stands, I haven't come across any comprehensive post-pregnancy recovery books, recommendations, or readily available programs that exist in Western countries. I have come across many articles by Western women who have written disapprovingly about post-pregnancy traditions because they view it as being too restrictive or not making any sense. I hope to change some mind-sets, fill the knowledge void, and provide each and every woman with the information she needs to create her own Mommy Plan, or post-pregnancy plan, for a healthy, strong, and above all balanced recovery from childbirth.

Bear-in-mind that each person is different, and what works for one person may not work for another. It's about monitoring yourself and your recovery, and making conscious adjustments in your food, activity, product usage, and so on as your recovery progresses. If you are having more than five consecutive days of feeling very stressed, having negative thoughts, are depressed, or the like, then do something about it. Do whatever you feel you have to do or what your mind responds to, to break this cycle before it gets entrenched in negative thoughts and you find it easier to just be sad or have anxiety than to break out of it. Shake it off before it envelops you.

> **POST-PREGNANCY REMINDER**
> Pregnancy is a temporary state and so is the intense healing process directly after childbirth, especially within the first three to six weeks. If you tell yourself that the change in your personal habits and diet is temporary, then the psychological acceptance, follow-through, and success rate goes up dramatically. People can accept the idea of a "temporary" state of change much better than a "permanent" state of change. This will allow you to create a plan with a beginning and an end in mind, so you can actively manage your own recovery.

The following dietary guidelines for the first six weeks after birth and beyond are based on the ancient belief of the Humoral Theory of hot and cold wellness. To understand traditional cultures is to comprehend that food is used as medicine; it always has been. Consuming and avoiding certain foods while having an illness, or imbalance, in the body is the basis for healing. Pregnancy is viewed not as an illness but as a temporary imbalance of a woman's body that can be easily healed, or rebalanced, according to specific guidelines. With the advent of modern medicine, most Western cultures have gotten away from this fundamental idea.

Since we've established that a woman's body after childbirth is in a "cold state," it makes sense to avoid foods that are cooling to the internal body temperature. Alternatively foods considered "hot" or those that bring warmth to the body, but not too heaty, should be consumed. The word 'heaty' refers to the capacity of a particular food, spice, or product to generate a "hot sensation" within the body. For example chilies are considered heaty as they contain capsaicins in the membrane. The hottest part of a chili is not the seeds, as many people think, but the white flesh that houses the seeds, known as the placenta. Interesting, no?

Someone may perspire after eating food containing chilies as this spice produces heat in the body. This is the heaty effect of eating chilies. Also, foods that are tough on the digestive system should be avoided as after childbirth, a mother's digestive system is weakened and sluggish and therefore not functioning normally.

POST-PREGNANCY TRADITIONS
Cambodia, Laos, Malaysia, Philippines and Thailand
Birth in these countries is considered to be an event that leaves a woman's body dangerously cold. A tradition called "mother roasting" or "smoking or roasting the mother" was a popular post-pregnancy tradition (and is still followed) that involved a mother lying on a thick wooden bed with a charcoal fire lit underneath and aromatic plants are laid out, thus enabling the essential oils to vaporize to provide warmth to the mother's body. The woman would lie on the bed from anywhere from one to seven days. The reasons for roasting was to strengthen things such as ligaments, tendons, nerves and blood vessels which were believed to be weak and in danger of becoming damaged after the stress of giving birth. This practice of an open fire has largely been replaced by modern heater for the most part due to the obvious dangers to the mother of accidently getting burned if the bed gets too hot, however it is still practiced in remote villages. Mothers also wear multiple layers of clothing to keep in her body heat and keep out any cold air.[2]

If You Are More Than Six to Eight Weeks Post-pregnant
The ideal time to plan for your recovery is while still pregnant; however, if you have obtained this book after the first six to eight weeks post-pregnancy, you certainly can follow the dietary guidelines, as your body is still healing. If you don't feel like you are having a healthy recovery, physically or mentally, I would recommend following the guidelines for a minimum of two to three weeks. That way the chemicals and disruptive foods will be cut out of your diet, which would give you better clarity to evaluate your physical and emotional state of mind.

Understanding Traditional Post-pregnancy Dietary Wisdom
Even *good* foods can be trouble for the digestive system during the immediate post-pregnancy period due to the unique state of a mommy's body after delivery. Some of the food avoidance recommendations in the book are foods normally found on health-conscious lists of nutritious and healthy foods. Therefore, please take note that it is *only* during the post-birth recovery period, when the body is in a weakened state, specific food is to be avoided; by no means are these permanent recommendations. You will have a complete understanding by the end of this chapter.

The Condition of a Woman's Body Immediately Giving Birth

- **In a cold state:** Due to the birth of the baby, placenta, loss of blood and amniotic fluids, and exhaustion from the birthing process.
- **Water logged, bloated, and swollen:** Due to retention of fluids needed to support the baby during pregnancy, commonly called edema. Areas normally affected are feet and legs, hands, arms, and abdominal cavity.
- **Carrying excess fat:** Due to the need to physically support the weight of a baby during pregnancy.
- **Sluggish circulatory and digestive systems:** These systems are temporarily sluggish due to the experience of birth. Constipation normally occurs.
- **Joint pains:** Joints are supple and soft, which is attributed to the body releasing the relaxin hormone. In most cases, this condition will persist for a few weeks as the hormone makes its way out of the body as it is no longer needed. Weight-bearing joints are normally affected, such as the neck, ankle, knee, pelvis, and lower back. Overall body aching and soreness from the birth experience will likely prevail.[3]
- **Sore breasts:** Breasts will be sore as the breast milk comes in; nipples may also be sore.[4]
- **Episiotomy:** If an episiotomy procedure (the cutting of the skin between the vagina and the anus) was performed by your doctor or if the area was torn during birth, the stitches may make it painful to sit or walk for a little while during healing. It can also be painful when coughing or sneezing.[5]
- **Hemorrhoids:** A common condition of swollen anal tissues as a result of pushing during childbirth although frequently unexpected by most mothers.[6]
- **Hot and cold flashes:** The body's adjustment to lower hormone and blood flow levels can wreak havoc on a woman's internal thermostat.[7]
- **Urinary or fecal incontinence:** The stretching of pelvic floor muscles during delivery can cause a woman to inadvertently pass urine when coughing, laughing, or straining, making it difficult to control bowel movements, especially if a lengthy labor preceded a vaginal delivery.[8]
- **Uterine after pains:** After giving birth, a woman's uterus will continue to have contractions for a few days as it shrinks and reverts to its normal size. These are most noticeable when a baby nurses or when medications are taken to reduce bleeding.[9] After-pains are not so profound after a first baby, however after second and subsequent babies, or after a miscarriage and/or pregnancy termination, after pains can be significantly strong. This is normal as the uterus contracts.
- **Vaginal discharge (lochia):** Initially heavier than a period and often containing blood clots. This vaginal discharge gradually fades to white or yellow and then

stops within two months.[10]

• **Inducement, epidural, and cesarean:** Such medications and medical procedures more often than not affect the body by slowing its circulatory and digestive systems; therefore, healing may take longer as the body normally has both side effects and after effects to process.

• **Breast engorgement:** Breasts feel swollen, tender, throbbing, lumpy and uncomfortably full, which sometimes extends to the armpit due to supply of breast milk coming in that needs to be release through feeding or pumping.

• **Hair Loss:** Hair may fall out or become thin due to drop in hormone level, this will not last and new hair will grow back.

• **Other conditions:** Varicose veins, sagging breasts, flabby tummy, stretch marks, darkened nipples, linea nigra, and possibly pregnancy melasma.

Post-Pregnancy Vocabulary
Linea nigra is a dark vertical line that appears on the abdomen of about 75% of all pregnancies. This brownish line about a centimeter in width runs vertically along the midline of the abdomen.[11]

Pregnancy melasma appears as irregular patches of brown skin on the forehead, cheeks, upper lip and nose. It is caused by hormonal fluctuations and in most cases tends to fade in a few months. However for some women it becomes permanent. It is not dangerous to one's health. An increase in estrogen causes Linea nigra, melasma and darkened nipples.[12]

Do you see why a mommy's post-pregnant body needs special care? Some of these effects could last up to two months as your body readjusts internally. Therefore, please be kind to yourself and treat your body gently and caringly as it is in a temporary weakened state. I'd recommend making a copy of the above list and giving it to your loved ones so they understand what you will be going through. Remember, this is a *temporary* state with the majority of the physical healing happening within three to six weeks.

Food Temperaments: How They Affect the Body
"Each food has a temperament that it is grown or raised with. This temperament is a food's identity, what it is, and has the potential to effect the human body with that identity. Food temperaments are comprised of four basic temperatures; hot, cold, cool, and warm. These four are then paired with one of two degrees of moisture: dry and moist damp.

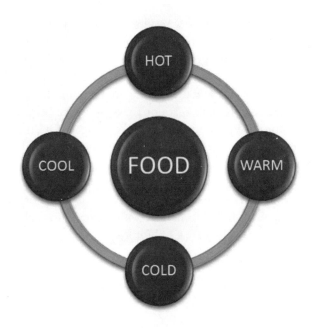

Generally, those foods that fall into the category of cold/cool are foods of plant origin that are high in water (juice), grown in water, high in vitamins and antioxidants, high in simple sugars, grow in tropical or semi-tropical climates, are fermented, and are lower in fat and protein.

Normally, those foods that fall into the category of hot/warm are foods of plant and animal origin that are lower in water content, grow in temperate climates, and are high in fat and protein or high in starches like some varieties of root vegetables, beans and some grains."[13]

POST-PREGNANCY EMPHASIS
These guidelines apply to <u>all</u> women after childbirth, whether they are breastfeeding or not. After birth a woman's body is in a super sensitive state, so foods that normally don't have any adverse effect on your body may have an effect during this period.

I. Limit Chemical Intake for the First Seven Days after Childbirth
This is going to be tough but is very important. Do your best from ingesting or exposing your body to any and all man-made chemicals for at least the first seven days

after giving birth for maximum recovery results. Chemicals interfere with the body's natural healing ability. If you could refrain from chemicals for thirty to forty days, your recovery would even be stronger.

In this day and age, organic or natural products are plentiful. Make sure you check product ingredients and buy products that don't contain chemicals. An extensive, free database from the nonprofit organization based in Washington DC, the Environmental Working Group (http://www.ewg.org/skindeep/) includes over 65,000 personal care products, ranging from toothpaste, cosmetics, lotions, shampoo, and so on. If you enter the brand name of the product you use, it will tell you the rating of the "health concerns of ingredients." You wouldn't believe how many products have formaldehyde as an ingredient! For those of you who are unfamiliar with the term, formaldehyde is used to preserve dead bodies, so it can't be very good for live ones!

Personal Care Products
- Shampoo, conditioner, spray, color, treatments, and products in general
- Toothpaste, soap, and deodorant
- Cosmetics, perfumes, and nail polish
- Lotions and sunscreens

Everyday household products as well as paint and plastic dishes can introduce harmful chemicals into your body and environment. We're also exposed to many potentially hazardous substances that you might not even think of, from dry-cleaning chemicals to the nonstick surface on frying pans. Even though most people equate clean with healthy, most commercial cleaning products take away dirt and grime but leave behind harmful chemicals.[14]

You may want to change your cleaning products to natural ones. The age-old cleaner of vinegar and water is fantastic and, for a more effective cleaning solution, add baking powder. Have you ever tried it? It's an excellent cleaner and all natural.

Household Products
- Dishwashing and dishwasher products
- Cleaners: bathroom, kitchen, floor, furniture polish, windows, oven, carpet, air fresheners
- Clothes detergent, fabric softeners, spot and stain removers, dyes
- Gardening products: fertilizer, insect repellant

Food Chemicals
Adjust your diet and refrain from eating artificial chemicals especially for the first seven days after childbirth and if possible cut most of them out for six weeks. Organic products are the best option to go in this case, although I know this is not an option for many people due to the expense. But remember, it is a temporary expenditure that can be budgeted into your household expenses. The second choice would be a combination of organic and commercial products. Whichever produce you eat, frequently buy organic. For example, in my house, my husband loves ketchup, so I buy organic ketchup. Research which produce or foods have a high absorbency rate of agricultural chemicals and make your own decisions. The fewer amounts of chemicals you take in, the more effectively your body will repair itself.

II. Food Preparation and Cooking Guidelines
Avoid excess oils and oily food.
Eliminate cooking with oils or even excessively brushing food or pots and pans with oil. Oily foods are heavy on the digestive system and may cause stomach upset and could be passed on to the baby. Avoiding margarine and shortening is also recommended.

Preferred cooking methods are as follows:

• Baked	• Grilled	• Healthy sautéing,
• Broiled	• Poached	frying or stir fry
• Crockpot	• Roasted	
• Dry fried	• Steamed	

These methods make food healthier and easier for your system to breakdown and digest. However, if you must use oils, this is the time to invest in a bottle of high-quality, nutrient-rich oil, such as olive oil or coconut oil. Use only a small amount when cooking.

Both olive and coconut oils are rich in antioxidants. Olive oil is the safest vegetable oil you can use. Choose oil that is cloudy, indicating it hasn't been filtered, and has a golden-yellow color, signifying it is made from fully ripened olives. This oil is best used for cooking at moderate temperatures.

Coconut oil is 92% saturated fats with over two thirds of it being medium-chain fatty acids. This is the good fat, like in avocados.[15] Coconut oil also has antifungal and antimicrobial properties. What is interesting is that this oil contains large amounts of lauric acid that is also found in breast milk, which is the why reason coconut oil is often used in baby formulas. This highly saturated tropical oil does not contribute to heart disease and has nourished healthy traditional populations for centuries.[16] You should acquaint yourself with the merits of cooking and baking with coconut oil as it is making a major comeback in the health-food industry.

> **POST-PREGNANCY TIP**
> Fill a spray bottle with 1/4 oil and 3/4 water and then spray the cooking surface. This way you'll drastically cut down on the amount oil used and your high-quality expensive oil will last much longer.

III. Post-pregnancy Diet DON'TS Guideline

1. No Cold Drinks and Foods

In America, we like our water cold, and with ice. In restaurants, most beverages are served at a cold temperature as well as with ice without a customer having to ask. There is the school of thought that ice water is good for us as it burns fat because it causes the body to heat it up and thus burn energy. That is true for a person that is dieting. In the post-pregnancy period, we don't want this to happen because we are already bloated.

Remember a post-pregnant body is in a cold state; therefore, it makes sense not to consume anything cold as the cool temperature will work against the body's effort to rebalance and raise its internal temperature. Cold foods normally cause the stomach to bloat, distending the stomach muscles at a time when you want them to tighten back up.

Foods classified as having a cold temperament by traditional explanation, as well as foods directly from the refrigerator that are cold in temperature, should be avoided. Consume nutrient-rich and dense food that is at room temperature, warm or hot. Cooling foods supposedly cause rheumatism, arthritis, and weak joints in a mother's body.

Cold dairy should also be avoided; therefore, if you like to eat cereal in the morning, please warm the milk, or if you eat salad, let the lettuce warm up to room temperature, including the raw vegetables. Also, drink juices that are fresh, not chilled or prepackaged.

2. Vine-Growing Vegetables and Fruit

This was a difficult guideline to understand. From my research, I think I've made sense of why it is a common after birth recommendation to avoid vine-grown vegetables such as pumpkin, squash, zucchini, cucumbers, watermelon, kiwifruit, and peanuts.

- Vine-growing vegetables and fruits have seeds and normally have higher water content. Eating produce that has high water content is traditionally viewed as working against body's natural process of releasing water retention. Since the body is releasing water, we don't want to interfere with the process.[17]
- Seeds of these particular vegetables may cause bloating in the stomach when eaten.[18]
- Peanuts are considered too starchy and often have traces of aflatoxin, a toxin found in a mold that grows on nuts.[19]

3. Nightshade Vegetables

Nightshade vegetables are actually fruit; however, we eat them as vegetables. What makes a fruit? It's all in the seeds and germination. Fruits have seeds that develop from the "ovaries" of flowers. Fruit gets snipped and leave the plant alive, while in the case of vegetables we're eating the entire plant so there's nothing left. Other popular vegetables that are really fruit include okra (lady fingers), cucumber, summer squash, and hard squash.[20] A common recommendation to people who have arthritis or joint pains is to avoid eating nightshades.

During pregnancy, a woman's body secretes and releases the relaxin hormone. Just as the name implies, the hormone allows a woman's normally inelastic joints, made of cartilage, to become supple and soft. This is necessary for the abdominal muscles to stretch and allow the uterus to grow out of the abdomen, and for the pelvic floor muscles to stretch for the birth of the baby. However, this adaptation severely reduces the support previously given by these muscles allowing increased movement, which in turn reduces joint stability.[21]

Nightshades are alkaloid and may cause further joint inflammation, causing pain and soreness in the immediate post-pregnancy period due to the level of relaxin within the body. Nightshades play a major role in bone and joint strength. Researcher Winifred Conkling states in *Natural Medicine for Arthritis*, "Eliminating vegetables from the nightshade family can promote cartilage repair."[22] I see a possible parallel effect for post-pregnant mommies.

Nightshades[23]
- Eggplant: all varieties
- Tomatoes: all varieties
- Peppers: green, red, yellow, pimentos, chilies, paprika, cayenne, hot and sweet, except for black and white pepper
- Potatoes: all white, except sweet potatoes and yams, which can be eaten in small amounts

  Products containing nightshades should also be avoided as in the case of tomatoes, which are used in many commercial products such as:

- Pasta sauce
- Pizza sauce
- Ketchup
- Salsa
- Juice
- Dips

4. Avoid Fruits That Are Acidic or Sour[24]

Acidic fruits are as follows:
- Lemons
- Limes
- Pineapples
- Grapefruits
- Sour versions of apples, plums, peaches, oranges and grapes.

An exception to this rule is oranges that are sweet not sour, such as mandarin oranges. It is acceptable to eat them in moderation as they contain vitamin C, which is needed for wounds to heal. For moms whose babies are jaundiced, it is a traditional recommendation for moms to drink pure, freshly squeezed orange juice so the vitamin C can be ingested by the baby through the breast milk. Don't confuse mandarins with the fruit tamarind, a different fruit altogether. Tamarinds have a sweet and sour taste and are a fruit traditionally eaten during the post-pregnancy period as it is believed to have properties that enhance the healing of wounds.

Choose red apples and red grapes over green ones. Refrain from drinking beverages that have lemon like ice water with lemon, ice tea with lemon, and foods such as lemon chicken. Again it is believed that the body is in an unbalanced state, and therefore, a post-pregnant mother needs to eat and drink neutral foods enhanced with herbs and spices to rebalance the body. What's more, the sourness of the fruit may be passed through the breast milk causing the baby to have bloating and/or diarrhea.

5. Foods That Cause Flatulence and Bloating

Certain beans, legumes, and vegetables such as artichokes, asparagus, broccoli, brussel sprouts, cabbage, lentils, sweet potatoes and onions have notorious reputations for causing gastric distress in the form of boating.[25] If you like to eat beans, cooking beans in soup can help with digestion of the large amount of fiber beans contain. The extra cooking time will start breaking the beans down even before you eat them.

Sodium may not cause gas, but it definitely makes you retain water. Cut back on salty foods and the salt you add to foods. Salt also comes in the form of food additives such as chemicals and preservatives. There are also fourteen thousand laboratory-made chemical additives to make our food appear fresher, more attractive, or last longer on the shelf.[26] Be a label reader to make sure you're not eating food with an excessive amount of salt or other chemicals.

Types of food normally containing sodium and chemical additives

- Fast food, drive-through, takeout, order-in
- Canned
- Processed
- Frozen
- Prepackaged
- Preservative-laden foods: hot dogs, sausages
- Caffeine drinks
- Soft drinks

6. Foods That Are Difficult to Digest

Pasta is not recommended, not even wheat pasta as it has a tendency to be difficult to digest, causing a post-pregnant body to retain water and bloat. According to the Glycemic Index group, "Pasta has a low GI because of the physical entrapment of ungelatinised starch granules in a sponge-like network of protein (gluten) molecules in the pasta dough. Pasta is unique in this regard."[27] Gluten free may be acceptable if you *have* to have a pasta fix but keep your portion small, as a side dish, instead of a main. If you can keep it out of your diet, then you'd be better off.

Fatty foods are definitely not good on your digestive system. Don't eat foods high in bad saturated fats, such as transfats, as it slows down digestion, and at this time, your system is already slow, which gives food more time to ferment in the stomach. Also avoid gravies or drippings from roasts as these are heavy on the digestive system as well.

7. Nothing Too Creamy

Don't eat anything that is too creamy, as this is not only heavy on the digestive system, but you don't want to eat too much dairy at one meal during this time. For example,

I've heard time and again that women who have given birth crave comfort food such as mashed potatoes, which are yummy but heavy on the system to digest, and they are from the nightshade family. The amount of dairy used in mashed potatoes is too much cow's diary to consume in one meal during this period. Also avoid foods like creamed soups, canned cream soups, or cream in casseroles. You can also substitute mashed sweet potatoes and carrots for regular mashed potatoes using a small amount of milk, butter or ghee, as well as sprinkle tamari soy sauce for minerals. It's a very satisfying and filling snack. Be careful not to eat sweet potatoes every day and keep portions small as they are known to cause flatulence for some women after child birth.

Cow's milk is hard on the digestive system. It digests best when boiled as boiling simplifies the protein molecules. Therefore, it is recommended to eat small quantities or have dairy every other day to give your digestive system a rest. Substitute cow dairy with soya or nut milk such as almond, hazelnut, or oat milk and make sure to eat protein-rich foods in order to have an adequate amount of protein in your body to produce breast milk.

Dairy products difficult on the digestive system:
- Fermented cheeses
- Sour cream
- Yogurt
- Homogenized, pasteurized, and/or nonorganic milk

Too much dairy in a woman's diet has also been known to cause excess and foul-smelling vaginal discharge.

8. Processed Sugars or Artificial Sweeteners
Products from white sugar or processed foods are not good for us at the best of times, least of all during post-pregnancy recovery. White sugar, raw sugar, or brown sugar (which in many instances is approximately 96% refined sugar) interferes with the body's ability to heal itself. Use alternatives, in moderation, such as the following:
- Date sugar
- Pure maple sugar
- Stevia
- Agave
- Blackstrap molasses
- Dehydrated cane sugar
- Raw, unfiltered honey, or honey directly from the honeycomb containing pollen.

> **IMPORTANT POST-PREGNANCY RECOMMENDATION**
> Do not use artificial sweeteners containing aspartame. This sugar substitute is sold commercially in two very popular sweeteners and was hailed as a savior for dieters unhappy with saccharin's unpleasant aftertaste. Unfortunately, one out of twenty thousand babies is born without the ability to metabolize phenylalanine, one of the two amino acids in aspartame. As a result, it's not recommended for pregnant women, infants, or during post-pregnancy recovery.[28]

Of course, all desserts should be avoided because of the high sugar content and the low sugar versions will have chemical additives. Even gum and hard candy shouldn't be chewed or consumed. In addition to high sugar content when you chew or suck on these, you end up swallowing, which means you're probably swallowing air that may cause further bloating.

9. Sauces and Condiments
Avoid commercially prepared sauces and condiments containing high amounts of sugar and fillers such as the following:

- Ketchup
- Mayo
- Mustard
- Salsas
- Hot sauces
- Salad dressings
- Spreads
- Dips
- Powdered mixes
- Marinades

10. Beverages
Fizzy, sparkling caffeine and alcoholic drinks should be avoided, including sparkling water. The fizz causes bloating and slows down the healing process, so pass up the sparkling water. Alcohol, specifically ethanol, is a central nervous system depressant with a range of side effects that can be felt more severely by a post-pregnant body.[29] Caffeine drinks such as coffee, black and green tea, and chocolate should be passed up consistent with the no-chemical guideline.

11. Prepackaged, Canned, Premade, or Leftover Food
Avoid the following:

- Packaged and processed foods
- Take-out food
- Fast food
- Junk food
- High-salt foods
- All food from a box, bottle, or can

Such food will contain preservatives and additive chemicals. Again, such foods are not good for us at the best of times, so it is imperative to avoid them during your post-pregnancy recuperation.

Leftover Food
Most leftover food has much less of its original nutritional value than when it was freshly made. If a microwave is used to reheat leftovers, you can be sure that the food will have hardly any or zero nutritional value. Your body needs all the vitamins and minerals it can get during this period, so try and eat only freshly made food. Leftover food is certainly convenient and fills a hole in your stomach when you are hungry; however, fresh food is what your body requires at this stage.

> **POST-PREGNANCY ADVICE**
> Eat every few hours and don't let yourself become too hungry.

12. Fish and Seafood
This recommendation is due to the fact that some fish and shellfish have high levels of bacteria that you don't want to put into your body. Also, some fish will cause the vagina to produce a "fishy" odor, and you don't want that either. Avoid eating the following fish and seafood.

- Tuna fish in a can, as well as any fish in a can
- Mollusks: clams, oysters, scallop, octopus, squid,
- Shellfish (crustaceans): shrimp, lobster, crab, crayfish
- Fish: Sardines
- Tuna fish in a can, as well as any fish in a can

Canned fish will contain laboratory chemicals and additives.

13. "Heaty" or Spicy Foods
In addition to foods containing chilies or that are very spicy, an overuse of spices, tonics, spirits, and medicine are also considered heaty, which will be passed on to the baby causing diarrhea.

14. Mushrooms
The variety of mushrooms is extensive with some varieties having medicinal properties (shiitake, maitake and the white button mushroom are being researched for all sorts of

health benefits). However, sometimes mushrooms are avoided as they are classified as fungi, and thus can have spores on them. Consequently, mushrooms are considered to have unpredictable health benefits during this time. If you like mushrooms consume them sparingly.

CHINESE AFTER BIRTH DISHES
Many Chinese recipes use sesame oil which adds a nutty flavor to a dish. Rich in Vitamin E, iron and calcium, sesame oil is used due to its "heaty" nature. Foods prepared with this oil are considered to take on heaty properties which internally warm a new mother. Sesame seeds are packed with antioxidants and can also be found in the oil. If you like sesame oil this ingredient could be part of the 20% of the 80/20 rule that you can use in small amounts for cooking.

I know the list of DON'TS seems extensive, so let's get to the DO'S!

SEVEN

Post-pregnancy Precautions: Diet DO'S

TRADITIONAL POST-PREGNANCY BELIEF

If a woman opts for a painless, speedy recovery, her outer shell may shine, but there could very well be inner damage. Prevention is far better than cure.[1]

REAL COMMENTS FROM REAL MOMS

"My weight isn't too bad as I'm still ten pounds over my pre-prego weight. I feel my digestive system is not well yet. I'm still constipated and don't have a bowel movement every day like I used to, and I have tons of stretch marks."[2] (3-months post-pregnant)

"I had my son via C-section. I have been breastfeeding and plan to continue until he is one years old. I currently weigh less than my pre-pregnancy weight, but I honestly look like I am about three to four months pregnant! I am looking for insight on what I can do. Will it just take longer because I had a C-section? Will it ever get better?"[3] (7-months post-pregnant)

Post-pregnancy Pep Talk

First of all, Mommy, please love your post-pregnant body! You've just given birth and should be proud of those stretch marks. Your deflated belly once held life inside of it. The remaining signs of pregnancy and childbirth that are part of your body's post-pregnant tapestry should be fully embraced and accepted, and then you can move on to your recovery with a clear mind. Don't compare yourself to Hollywood moms who have personal trainers, chefs, nutritionists, and a team of people to take care of them. Your journey through pregnancy has come to an end. So own it! Love your body! And be proud of yourself!

Post-pregnancy Dietary Adjustments

The post-pregnancy period is when a mother must adjust to caring for her baby while also caring for herself. This ensures she is not only strong but has enough energy to get through those first few months and beyond. The food a new mother chooses to eat will play an important role in her mood and energy levels. Eating the right foods your body needs can help you lose weight, and produce breast milk which is high in nutrients.

Nutritionally, rich breast milk will help your baby grow and develop. Nutritionally rich foods will lower your risk of experiencing post-pregnancy-related emotional illnesses as you are giving you body medicine in the form of food that it needs.

As far as eating and drinking is concerned, take into consideration your environment and constitution, as well as the season you have given birth plus the following six to eight weeks. In order to determine what your body needs, it is important to pay attention to your energy levels and identify which types of foods which cause you to feel tired or energized. There is a need to avoid contaminants in the form of processed food, food with high sugar content, coffee, alcohol, and cold food. Whatever a mother eats, the baby will also take in through breast milk, including residues of pesticides.

POST-PREGNANCY ADVICE
Continue taking your prenatal vitamins and iron supplements as recommended by your health care provider. A woman's post-pregnant body is in a weakened state. It has special and specific needs and, most of all, must be treated with kindness and given adequate time to heal.

Nourishing, nutrient-rich foods should be consumed. The basic post-pregnancy diet is a simple, wholesome and healthy one. It can best be summed up by the following guidelines:
- Eat foods that are either at room temperature, warm or hot.
- Eat foods that supply your body with essential fatty acids (EFAs) and Omega 3, 6, and 9 found in avocados, raw nuts and seeds and salmon.
- Eat whole, preferably organic, foods—whole grains, fresh vegetables and fruits, unprocessed meats, nuts, and seeds.
- Eat a source of nutrient-laden fiber, such as ground flaxseeds.
- Eat foods that supply your body with antioxidants; found it decaffeinated green tea, berries and herbs.
- Eat slowly and chew your food thoroughly.

Remember the preferred cooking methods are:
- Baked
- Broiled
- Crockpot
- Dry fried
- Grilled
- Poached
- Roasted
- Steamed
- Healthy sautéing, stir fry

For those of you not familiar with healthy sautéing or stir fry it is explained later in the chapter.

Eat High Quality Foods

During your post-pregnancy recovery, it is essential that you put high-quality foods in your body. Cheap foods normally equal low quality. Why do you think junk food is cheap and called just that? Prices are kept low because such foods are made of cheap ingredients and chemicals. What is happening inside your body is not predictable and therefore such chemicals may wreak havoc on your body during this intense transitioning and healing time. Therefore, it is very important that you do your homework and find out about the integrity of the products you purchase. There are many imposters out there that make claims only turn out to be bogus. For example, in a recent study, the Food Safety News reported that 75% of the honey found on grocery shelves contained no honey at all. In most cases, the pollen was filtered out to extend shelf life and replaced with thickened corn syrup.[4] Yuck!

POST-PREGNANCY MIND-SET

Adopt the mind-set of traditional cultures in that food is part of their healthcare system and is considered to be "medicine" in the way that it can help the body heal, not just fill the tummy. Therefore, eat foods that will help heal your body.

Post-pregnancy Dietary Guidelines: DIET DO'S

Eat Foods Considered "Warm or Hot"

Consume foods that are considered to have warm or hot properties that promote heat to be retained or brought into the body. Otherwise, make the food you eat to have a warming, or hot effect, on your body through the recommended cooking methods and by adding herbs and spices.

1. Fruits and Vegetables

Most fruit and vegetables are considered *cold*; however, there are exceptions based on traditional classification. Some produce can be made "warm or hot" by the cooking methods mentioned.[5]

Eat fruits and vegetables that:
1.   Doesn't remove the heat from your body.
2.   Are not too acidic or sour.
3.   Doesn't cause gas or bloating.
4.   Are easy on your digestive system.

Dried fruit from the approved list of fruit at the end of this chapter is acceptable; however, take note of the ingredients on the label and refrain from sugar or chemical preservatives.

Doctoryourself.com
I found a wonderful website called Doctor Yourself (www.doctoryourself.com), and below is the information from that website regarding chemicals used on produce.[6]

The average crop of fresh produce will be sprayed eight to twelve times with various agricultural fertilizers, pesticide, wax, and other chemicals before we purchase them. Such chemicals do not come off in water. If they did, farmers would have to apply them after each rain or even a heavy dew, which would be both labor intensive and expensive. Therefore, petrochemical companies make pesticides with chemical "stickers" that are insoluble in water to stay on the produce rain or shine. Wash your produce thoroughly.

Food Grade Wax
Many fruits and vegetables are not merely sprayed with chemicals, but are also waxed. So-called "food grade" waxes improve the shelf life and appearance of produce, but it also coats over, and locks in, any previously applied pesticides. This poses a problem, for waxes do not readily dissolve in detergent solutions. There are products that claim to be able to remove food grade waxes. The other alternative is to simply peel the produce. Frequently waxed fruits include apples, pears, eggplants, cucumbers, and squash. Even tomatoes are generally waxed. The lack of a high gloss is not proof positive that a fruit is unwaxed. Many waxes, like many types of floor polyurethane or spray varnishes, are not at all shiny. One way to tell if a fruit or vegetable is waxed is to run your fingernail over it and see if you can scrape anything off. Another way is to read the label and see if the produce is waxed.

Methylcyclopropene
This gas is pumped into crates of apples to stop them from producing ethylene, the

natural hormone that ripens fruit. Commonly known as SmartFresh, this chemical preserves apples for up to a year and bananas up to a month. Sulphur dioxide serves the same purpose when sprayed on grapes.

Please remember the information above when purchasing fruit and vegetables.

2. Meats and Poultry

High-quality lean meats such as beef, chicken, turkey, duck and rabbit are recommended in small portions of four to five ounces (115 to 140 grams) per serving. Liver is recommended as it a good source of iron. Avoid processed meats, cured cold cuts, and canned meats laden with preservatives.

Beef is known to be difficult on the digestive system, but it is also high in protein, so make sure you eat high-quality tender beef in small portions. Any type of hamburger patty made of beef, chicken, or turkey is not recommended as the meat used is normally not of high quality, unless you go to a butcher that will ground a high-quality beef for you.

If you are a vegetarian or vegan, then you will know which foods will give you the nourishment you need during this period. I find most vegetarians and vegans to have a good understanding of nutrition. In addition, follow the don'ts list for the vegetables and fruits you need to avoid.

3. Cold-Water Fish

Recommended fish to eat are as follows:

Anchovy	Grouper	Snakehead fish
Cod	Red sea bream	Spanish mackerel
Flounder	Orange roughy	Tilapia
Haddock	Red and golden snapper	Threadfin
Hake	Salmon	Tuna steak
Halibut	Shark	White pomfret
Herring		

If you are unfamiliar with some of these fish, look up their picture on the Internet or ask a fishmonger. Fish that are naturally oily and high in Omega 3, 6, and 9 are salmon, herring and anchovy.[7] It's very important for a recovering mother to replenish the omegas in her system, as they are normally siphoned off by the baby during the pregnancy mainly for brain development and growth. Dried fish is also acceptable, but please check the ingredients and make sure chemicals and preservatives are not added or used in the process.

> ## POST-PREGNANCY NOTE
> Keep-in-mind that pollution has sufficiently contaminated water resources with mercury and that some fish concentrate enough mercury in their bodies to pose a health hazard.[8] Tuna and salmon are the most commonly known fish to have high level of mercury. Before you purchase any fish, do your research and shop wisely. It may be easier to purchase chemical-free fish online and have it delivered directly to your house.

Astaxanthin

Almost 90 percent of salmon sold in supermarkets today come from farms. The diet of farmed salmon doesn't include crustaceans, which contains a natural astaxanthin that causes pink flesh in wild salmon. As a result, producers add astaxanthin to farm-salmon diets for that fresh-from-the-water appearance. Astaxanthin is manufactured from coal tar.[9]

4. In Addition to Plain Water, Consume Other Types of Fluids

A post-pregnant body retains water for a few weeks and therefore is basically "water logged." This has resulted in the traditional belief that large amounts of *plain water* should not be consumed. The idea is to try and "dry out" the body and give it time to release the retained water. Of course, you need to keep up your liquid intake especially when breastfeeding in order to produce an adequate supply of breast milk as well as not to let yourself become dehydrated, and to combat constipation. Reducing the amount of plain water and replacing it with liquids such as rich soups, broths, herbal teas, and non-dairy milks, (such as soy and nut) are recommended. Your body needs the extra protein to develop breast milk and rejuvenate the blood.

Drink Boiled Water

It is strongly recommended to drink boiled water that is room temperature, warm or hot. Bring water to a boil for a few seconds, and then turn off the heat and let it sit for half an hour. This should kill any bacteria (pathogens) that exists. Boiling water is a much better way of obtaining safe drinking water, even when compared to filtering devices or chemical treatments.[10] Other water sources such as tap water, spring, and even reverse osmosis may contain chemicals, or the container that holds the water may contain chemicals.

Lactation Teas

There are many lactation teas in the marketplace, and for a very good reason as lactating moms benefit from specific herbs that bring in a strong milk supply. Fenugreek and nettle teas are an example of highly recommended teas among lactation consultants.[11] Please choose herbal teas carefully and make sure they are safe while breastfeeding. I've added a chapter, "Herbs to Avoid While Breastfeeding," for this purpose.

5. Soups and Stews

Homemade broth, clear soups, blended soups (but not creamy), and stews are a nutritious replacement for of water and are very easy to make. Use any meat for the stock; meat supplies fat that is essential for extraction of fat-soluble nutrients. Drink as much soup as you can handle, consume soups that are full of protein-rich foods and devoid of hot spices. Drinking soup one hour before breastfeeding may help to increase milk flow. Soups warm the body from the inside out, which is what you want.

POST-PREGNNACY CAUTION
Many brands of stock cubes contain monosodium glutamate (MSG), a common chemical food additive to enhance flavor. There is a long-running debate on the health concerns of MSG. The Food and Drug Administration have labeled it as "generally regarded as safe (GRAS)." However, there have been studies that MSG causes headaches and other temporary but unpleasant reactions in people who are sensitive to it. There are also concerns that it may cause neurological damage, diabetes, or even be linked to the obesity epidemic.[12] Personally, I've suffered twenty-four-hour headaches after eating food that contains MSG, so I'd recommend avoiding anything containing this chemical as your system is extra sensitive during this period.

POST-PREGNANCY COOKING TIP
Healthy Sautéing or Stir Fry
Make a basic chicken and beef stock and freeze ice cubes out of the broth to use for cooking instead of oils. The broth gives food wonderfully added flavors and is an excellent way to eat healthy, not just during recovery but all the time as this style of cooking uses no heated oils.

I healthy sauté all the time. I start with about a quarter cup of broth and add diced onions and garlic (you may want to avoid garlic during your recovery) and let it simmer. I normally add a splash of soy sauce (low salt) or Worchester sauce and some spices for extra flavor and let them simmer for a minute or so on medium heat. Add veggies, cook for a few minutes and then add meat or protein last. You can let the broth simmer down until it browns the pan and then you could add a little more broth or water, to the pan, to get a nice yummy gravy. Again add diced onions, garlic or dried onion flakes (no salt used in drying process) if they were removed from the pan for even more flavor.

AYURVEDIC DIETARY GUIDELINE

Ayurvedic (Indian) dietary recovery guidelines recommend avoiding garlic as it can cause flatulence; therefore use this spice sparingly at first. If you find that you become gassy this will be passed onto your baby. In this case, refrain from using garlic when cooking.

Here's a recipe I put together from various recipes I've tried over the years. Both women and men should drink homemade broths, as they are nourishing for the body, which is why chicken soup always makes us feel better when we have a cold. You probably have your own, but this is a simple recipe:

Chicken Broth for the Post-pregnant Mommy's Soul
1 whole chicken (approximately 3 pounds)
2–3 tablespoons white vinegar
4 carrots
3–4 stalks of celery
2 large onions
2-3 bay leaves
2–3 tablespoons of black peppercorns
Fresh flat parsley and thyme

Take note that salt is not included in this recipe, or most broth recipes.

1. Chop up one whole chicken and roughly chop vegetables. Put in a stock pot or large pot.
2. Add 2–3 tablespoons white vinegar. Fill the rest of the pot with cold water, and soak for 1 hour. Soaking draws the marrow out of the cut bones, which is very good for us as it contains proteins, Vitamin B-complex, minerals (calcium, magnesium, zinc) as well as Lecithin and Methionine.
3. Add bay leaves and peppercorns.
4. Bring to a boil, remove any scum that rises to the top, and then simmer on very low heat for a minimum of 4–5 hours (I simmer for 10-12 hours). I start out uncovered but then put the cover on after about an hour when some of the water has evaporated. If you simmer too high, the water will evaporate too quickly.

5. Ten minutes before it finishes simmering, add the parsley and thyme as these herbs add mineral ions to a broth.
6. Scoop out chicken and veggies and strain the broth through a fine sieve into a large, clean bowl or stockpot. Discard the meat and vegetables as the flavor is normally boiled away and is therefore tasteless.
7. Place in the refrigerator until the fat rises to the top as a white topping. Skim off the fat. Do not drink or use broth until the fat has been removed.

Drink anytime you like. I have a cup in the morning, sometimes in the afternoon, and in the evening. Use for healthy sautéing and of course making any kind of soup! Freeze broth as ice cubes and keep in a freezer bag in the freezer so you have single servings for cooking.

HANNA KROEGER, *AGELESS REMEDEIES FROM MOTHER'S K ITCHEN*
Why chicken soup is superior and more relaxing to all things we have is because it has a natural ingredient which feeds, repairs and clams the mucous lining in the small intestine. This inner lining is the beginning or ending of the nervous system. It is easily pulled away from the intestine through too many laxatives, too many food additives... and parasites. Chicken soup...heals the nerves, improves digestion, reduces allergies, relaxes and gives strength.

Cream of Carrot and Ginger Soup
By Tan Kaw Ting, Culinary Arts Student, Berjaya University College of Hospitality, Kuala Lumpur, Malaysia
2 cups chicken or vegetable stock
4 carrots, cubed
1 inch fresh ginger root, sliced
1 stalk celery, cubed
¼ cup milk
1 stalk lemongrass
1 potato, finely sliced
½ onion, finely chopped
Add fresh or dried thyme, to taste

Sauté the carrot, celery, potato, ginger and lemon grass with the onion. Blend the sautéed ingredients until it is pureed. Add the stock stirring until it is the preferred consistency. Add the milk.

6. Nuts

Eating nuts and seeds are a great way to add vitamins, minerals, fiber, and essential fatty acids, like Omega 3, 6, and 9 to your diet. Nuts that support breast milk supply include almonds, cashews, and macadamia. Walnuts are also good for you. Like almonds, this nut contains leucine and isoleucine, which are amino acids that regulate growth, blood sugar, and wound healing.[13] Other nuts include pistachios, sunflower, flaxseeds, and sesame. Eat raw nuts, not roasted or salted. You can toast them yourself and sprinkle with a little sea salt or tamari soy sauce.

> **POST-PREGNANCY TIP**
> Make sure to chew nuts very well so they are not difficult on your digestive system. Soaking is a good option.

To Soak or Not to Soak

It may be beneficial to purchase your nuts and seeds raw and then soak them in clean water for a few hours before eating them. Soaking raw nuts and seeds stimulates the process of germination, which increases the vitamin C, B, and carotenes (provitamin A) content. It may also neutralize phytic acid, a substance present in the bran of all grains and seeds that can inhibit some absorption of calcium, magnesium, iron, copper, and zinc. Raw nuts and seeds also contain enzyme inhibitors that are neutralized by germination.[14]

7. Cereals and Oats

Choose cereals that are low in sugar. Before you purchase cereal, go online and read reviews by natural product websites that rate cereals as I've found them to be one of the most controversial products on the market with many bogus claims and genetically modified ingredients (GMO).

Oats or oatmeal (but not instant or prepackaged) is one of the most nutritious foods available containing proteins, vitamins, minerals, and trace elements that nourish nerves, and support the metabolism of fats.

8. Honey: High Quality, Organic, Unfiltered, with Pollen

Honey has many health benefits. However, it must be pure, *unfiltered*, high quality honey, containing bee pollen with no additives such as sugar or corn syrup. Do not buy inexpensive honey on the shelf of your grocery store as this honey is normally not the grade that will give you any health benefits. A newborn baby doesn't have a developed immune system. The benefit of honey is that it is a great immune system builder, and this benefit is gently passed on to the newborn through breast milk. Mothers in Southeast Asia usually eat honey twice a day for six weeks or until the baby has the first set of inoculations. However, if a baby is born weak, a mother will continue to take honey until she feels her baby is strong. There is no reason not to continue to take honey for the duration of the time that you breastfeed and beyond. It can only help you and your baby grow strong and healthy.

Dosage: Take two teaspoons per day, one in the morning after breakfast and one in the evening after dinner.

POST-PREGNANCY SNACK
Bread or toast with honey and cinnamon. Yum!

---

9. Dairy Products

In Asia, traditionally, people do not consume dairy products from cows, although consumption is slowly rising; therefore, there wasn't a traditional guideline on this topic but a modern one. Since the molecules from cow's dairy are quite large, it is difficult to digest, so avoid of consuming large amounts of dairy if you can. Also, cow's milk is a common cause of iron deficiency. It contains less iron than many other foods and also makes it more difficult for the body to absorb iron from other foods.

POST-PREGNANCY NOTE
Humans are the only mammal that drinks the milk of another animal, and yet other milk-producing mammals only produce milk for their offspring.[15]

If you consume dairy products, it is recommended to eat and drink full-fat dairy products versus low-fat or no-fat dairy products. In order to make up for the lack of taste, due to the removal of the natural fat content, additives in the form of sugar and preservatives are added. Consuming full-fat products will meet some of the nutritional requirements your body is searching for. Therefore, you will feel satisfied or full after consuming a moderate amount.

As previously mentioned, there are limitations as only *moderate* amounts of cow's dairy should be consumed, not more than sixteen ounces or two glasses every other day. Soy and nut milk, such as almond or hazelnut, are good substitutes for cow's milk. Avoid the light and flavor red versions as they normally contain a high amount of sugar and additives. Of course, don't drink them cold but warmed or room temperature.

If you do not consume dairy products, there are various types of vegetables and mineral sources which can enrich your diet with calcium as mentioned in previous guidelines.

- Sesame seeds, which can be eaten whole, in the form of tahini (sesame butter) and gomasio (a salt substitute that contains sesame seeds and salt) or can be added to many foods. They should be well chewed in order to increase the ability of the body to utilize the calcium they contain.
- Tortillas that are made using lime-processed corn are a good source of
- calcium. Be sure to check the label for additives.
- Some types of sea vegetables which are traditionally part of the Japanese diet, such as wakame, miso, soy sauce and tamari, can enrich a diet with calcium along with many other minerals.

CHINESE & AYURVEDIC POST-PREGNANCY DIET

Chinese and Ayurvedic (Indian) post-pregnancy dietary traditions are probably the best documented. Chinese postpartum dishes contain rice wine and sweet soup, pig's trotters (or feet) and papaya soup, sesame oil chicken dishes, black vinegar, old ginger root and drinks made with ginger. Hot drinks replace most of the water consumption contains red dates, ginger and longan fruit, which is known to warm the body. Such dishes are to dispel the flatulence in a mommy's body and warm it. However the Chinese normally wait ten days after child birth before consuming ginger.

Indian postnatal meals are rich with ghee, or clarified butter, and contain many warming spices such as cumin, black pepper, turmeric, fenugreek, fennel, saffron, cinnamon, nutmeg and cardamom. Within the Ayurvedic traditions, it is important to eat meals on time. Not letting a mother get hungry is believed to strengthen her digestive system. Lunch is eaten every day between noon and 1 pm, and never missed, as this is when the digestive system is at its strongest.

For both traditions, a variety of dishes must be eaten on specific days and weeks after birth to heal the uterus, restore the blood and to enhance milk production.

10. Egg Yolks

An egg is a chicken's unfertilized ovum (or egg). Egg yolks are considered "unsafe" food during recovery due to the possibility of bacteria entering the yolk while it's forming. This is like the dietary precaution during pregnancy, of not eating soft cheese or sushi. An egg yolk is the part of the egg which feeds a chicken's developing embryo, and is considered unsanitary for women who have recently given birth to consume another animal's ovum during this time period. If you want to eat eggs, stick to the egg whites. The primary purpose of egg whites are to protect the egg yolk, and to provide additional nutrition for the growth of the embryo, as it is rich in protein, and contains almost no fat.[16] This guideline can be relaxed after ten days, when the breast milk fully comes in, or twenty-one days depending on the progression of the recovery.

11. Grains and Breads
Whole grain breads are recommended over white breads and the following grains are more nutritious than plain white rice.
- Amaranth
- Barley
- Bulgar wheat
- Couscous
- Millet
- Quinoa
- Rice: brown, red, basmati or wild

12. Herbs and Spices
Consuming and cooking with all kinds of fresh herbs is recommended as they contain many health benefits. There are so many wonderful herbs and spices that it is impossible for me to list them, here is a sampling:

Fresh herbs: basil, lemon basil, chervil, chives, coriander, curry plant, dill, lavender, ginger, parsley, lemon verbena, lemon grass, mint, peppermint, spearmint, oregano, rosemary, sage, thyme, tarragon, and so many more.

Storage of Fresh Herbs
- Herbs that are sold in plastic boxes or cellophane bags keep well in them.
- Put loose herbs into plastic bags and store in the vegetable crisper of the fridge; herbs with more robust leaves will keep longer than fragile ones.
- Big bunches of mint, parsley and coriander will keep in a jug of water for a few days.
- Preserve fresh herbs by cutting and freezing in ice cubes.

Spices
Allspice, anise, bay leaves, black and white pepper, cayenne pepper, cardamom, cinnamon, celery, cloves, cumin, curry powder, fennel, graham marsala, garlic, ginger,

mace, marjoram, nutmeg, onion powder, pepper, peppermint, saffron, turmeric, vanilla and so many more.

POST-PREGNANCY TIPS

- You can use, young or old ginger, depending on your preference.
- If you add a bit of peeled, chopped fresh ginger to any food, IT automatically makes the dish "warmer." Drinking ginger tea is also beneficial.
- If you purchase a spice mix or blend, check the ingredients because sometimes sugar, flour, chemicals, or preservatives are added.
- Turmeric is a wonderful spice. It functions as an antibiotic and promotes a healthy circulatory system.

---

13. Jam Not Jelly

Jams made from the list of approved fruits, such as strawberry, are OK. Buy jams that are naturally sweetened. Jelly is to be avoided as it usually has high sugar content.

Recent Post-pregnancy Research

In addition to the above dietary guidelines, make sure your diet is rich in the good fats, of EFAs and DHA (docosahexaenoic acid) that can be found in a variety of fish, nuts, seeds, and oils. It is very important to keep both acids plentiful in your recovering body. EFAs: Omega 3, 6, and 9 are vital for a balanced recovery.

EFAs were drawn off during pregnancy by your baby through the placental cord as they are significant in fetal brain development.[17] When a baby is born, its brain is almost 25% of its adult size.[18] This is huge compared to anything else in the body. If a pregnant woman does not have enough Omega-3s in her diet, a growing baby will siphon the fatty acids from her tissues. If a woman has additional children and does not replace the missing EFAs, she will have lower levels of DHA with each subsequent child. Women need to replace what has been lost because if the levels aren't replaced, they will continue to decline throughout the breastfeeding period, which may have repercussions to herself and subsequent children. EFA deficiency has been shown to play a key role in many growth and developmental difficulties such as learning, behavioral, nervous, and immune-related disorders.[19]

It seems plausible that the widespread prevalence of postpartum depression could be due, at least in part, to EFA and DHA deficiencies. It is well established that EFAs play a substantial role in the prevention and treatment of depression. Chronic deficiencies originating during this critical time period may also explain why women tend to experience far more effects such as depression, fibromyalgia, chronic fatigue, and autoimmune diseases than compared to men.[20] In this day and age, a variety of high-quality EFA-rich oils are available in health-food stores. You should consider taking it on a daily basis to supplement your vitamin and dietary intake, especially during the post-pregnancy period and then making it a permanent addition to your diet. Please do your research.

If You Are More Than Six to Eight Weeks Post-pregnant
As I mentioned in the previous chapter, if you have obtained this book after the first six to eight weeks post-pregnancy, you certainly can still follow the dietary guidelines, as your body is still very much healing. If you feel you aren't having a healthy recovery, physically or mentally, the recommended food guidelines will cut out disruptive foods, and chemicals, from your diet. This will allow you to have better clarity to evaluate your physical and emotional well-being.

If your body still feels bloated, water logged, or weak, follow the guidelines as if it were your first week post-pregnant because your body is recovering at a slow pace and there still is much healing to be had. If you have lost most of the water retention and bloatedness, but still have body aches and a general lack of energy, then you should follow the dietary guidelines. Make sure you get an adequate amount of EFAs. It's very important to replenish them.

I would recommend following the guidelines for a minimum of three weeks, and then re-evaluate your physical and mental health, to determine whether you need to continue. I can't stress enough that this is a time when you need to pay close attention to how you feel, and the cues your body is communicating to you.

POST-PREGNANCY MINDSET
During your recuperation period, mentally prepare yourself that you will eat all, if not most, of your meals at home for the first three weeks. Then make the necessary arrangements to ensure you follow through and your food is made with as many whole and fresh ingredients as possible.

Portion Control Is Important
It is better to have small frequent meals of five to seven per day instead of the normal

three big meals a day. This allows for easier digestion. Do not have huge portions, and do not eat so little that your body isn't getting enough nutrients to fuel the healing process and produce breast milk. This is not a time for a severe restriction of the quantity of food but an adjustment of the foods that you consume.

Below is a review of the guidelines and a list of the recommended foods so that you may alter or develop your own recipes accordingly. Due to the countless types of food that exist, it's impossible for me to list them all. Therefore, if it isn't listed, consider adding it back to your diet after a minimum of three weeks, although if you can target the sixth week even better.

SUGGESTION

Buy two new cookbooks, one macrobiotic and one a natural, wholesome cooking type cookbook. Amazon.com has a baby registry feature and you could easily add the titles of two cookbooks, in addition to baby products, to your list, if you are using this website. There is always a birthday present, so let family members and friends know which books you would like. This way you will be familiar with the types of recipes that will benefit your body during your recovery and you could even try a few out before you give birth and teach the daddy as well!

Be Realistic

If you know that you won't follow through with a substantial change in your eating habits for at least thirty days, then follow the 80-20 rule. Customize your post-pregnancy daily life by adopting 80% of the traditional beliefs and practices and resume 20% of your normal lifestyle. Nowadays we live in a world where we can select the best of all cultural practices to promote and maintain good health after childbirth. Adopt what works best for you!

The most important thing to remember is that you *must* be comfortable with your own post-pregnancy plan. Do not force yourself to eat something that you don't like or it will cause problems later. Although you will be in a recuperation period, you are not a prisoner of your plan!

Sample Meals

Below are very simple sample meals to choose from to give you an idea that you should not starve yourself. Or take the recipes you normally make and adjust them to the guidelines. It will take some creativity on your part, but it shouldn't be too difficult, especially with the Internet at your fingertips. Most recipes can allow a healthful transformation without adversely affecting the taste or texture of the food. After three weeks, you could add more dairy and moderate amounts of *whole foods—* not processed, canned, junk, fast, or take-out food. If you are breast feeding you will have a hearty appetite as you will need approximately 500 more calories on top of your dietary intake to produce an adequate supply of breast milk. Therefore adjust your food intake to your hunger.

> ### BREASTFEEDING
> Not all women are able to breastfeed for various medical reasons. This is how Wet Nurses came about long ago, which were women that breastfed another women's child. Don't put undue pressure on yourself if you are unable to or if you feel strongly that you do not want to. There is an option of *Milk Banks* which provides screened and pasteurized donor mothers' milk, to families where the mother's own milk is not available for their baby. However do note that breastfeeding is the best option for a baby and reduces postpartum bleeding by inducing the release of oxytocin which helps the uterus return back to normal size faster.

The time between dinner and breakfast is too many hours to go without any caloric intake. Therefore you will need a before-bedtime snack to get you through the night. You may be eating wisely, but do not let your production of breast milk become dangerously low from not consuming enough calories.

Breakfast
- Oatmeal with honey, raisins, cinnamon, ground flaxseeds, chopped almonds with a dash of milk.
- Scrambled egg whites with fresh herbs such as basil, chives, or grated ginger.
- Low sugar, organic bowl of cereal, ground nut, with warm milk.

1 teaspoon of honey

Snack
Cup of chicken stock, baked sweet potato, fruit, nuts, warm smoothie.

Lunch
- A bowl of hearty homemade soup with whole meal bread.
- Couscous with vegetables and fish.
- Lightly stir-fried or healthy sautéed tempeh, vegetables and choice of meat over rice.

Snack
Avocado and cheese sandwich or crackers, warm smoothie.

Dinner
• Roasted chicken with rosemary, basmati rice with tofu and vegetables.
• Baked salmon with coriander, leafy green vegetable and carrots.
• Grilled beef, kale and Swiss chard with brown or red rice.
• Chicken with lemongrass and ginger, quonica, vegetables.

1 teaspoon of honey.

Before Bed Snack
• Toast with cinnamon and bananas
• Bowl of hearty soup.
• Leftovers from dinner that day.

Warm Smoothie Anyone?
Smoothies are popular but remember that you don't want to drink a cold one. Therefore make sure the water, milk or whatever base you use is either at room temperature, warm or hot. Try your usual smoothie this way as it may be good for you if it conforms with the recommended guidelines. Or come up with a "warm smoothie" recipe of your own! Use a nut-milk as a base - such as soy or almond - or you can even make your own nut-milk by soaking hazelnuts in soymilk overnight. You can add vanilla, hazelnut or almond extract, carob, honey or another natural sweetener, with various spices such as chai, pumpkin, or mint. I've even heard of hot oatmeal smoothies, where you cook your oatmeal as you like, then add extra hot milk and transfer to a blender and blend until smooth.

Spice Up Your Kitchen
Below are a few recipes for new mommies that follow the recommended guidelines that you may like to try.

After Birth Rice with Spices[21]
This is a popular Malay post-pregnancy recipe with a very simple name as you can see. I found it in one of the only books on Malay postpartum traditions I could find, written the local language of Bahasa Melayu. It was translated by a dear friend named Azura.

2 cups of rice
3 cups of fresh coconut milk or fresh milk
1 tablespoon of sweetened condensed milk
1 teaspoon of ginger – finely chopped
1 tablespoon of korma powder
2 pieces of cloves
2 pieces of cardamom seed
1 piece of star anise
1 cinnamon stick
1 piece of pandan leaf* (known as screw pin leaf)
2 tablespoons of (dried) fried onion
3 tablespoons of ghee (Indian clarified butter)
*Sometimes frozen pandan leaves can be purchased at an Asian grocer such as Thai, Filipino, and so on. Omit if you cannot find.

Wash and rinse the rice with running water three times to rinse out the starch. Heat the ghee in a pan on medium heat. Add the korma powder, fried onion and coconut milk/fresh milk. Then add a pinch of salt, keep stirring and bring to a boil. Once boiled add in the rice, pandan leaf, cloves, cardamom, star anise, and one cinnamon stick. Stir evenly. When rice is a little bit dry, turn down the heat. Put the lid on and let the rice cook fully until the rice is fluffy and dry. Fluff with a fork.

<u>Anchovies and Black Peppercorns</u>[22]
If you like anchovies, or would like to try them, below is a traditional Malay accompaniment sprinkled on meals during the recovery period as this fish is a good source of protein and calcium for new mommies. Black pepper aids in reducing stomach and intestinal gas and has been found to stimulate the heart and kidneys

2 pounds (1 kilo gram) medium-sized dried anchovy fillets
½ cup black peppercorns

Choose anchovies without heads and tails. Wash and clean the fillets, then drain the water and spread evenly on a baking tray. Bake at 180°C for 20 to 25 minutes stirring them half way through. Continue baking until they are golden brown. Blend in a food processor with the peppercorns until the mixture is fine granules or in powder form. Store in a glass container with an airtight lid.

Amount: ½–1 tablespoon per dish, mix with 1 tbsp black vinegar (optional).

Soothing Morning Oatmeal[23]
This is a recipe that I've tried that is wholesome, belly filling, and delicious! It is an Ayurvedic recipe from Robin Lim's book, *Eating for Two, Recipes for Pregnant and Breastfeeding Women*, who has kindly agreed to share her wonderful recipe.

So delicious, healthy, and above all, tender on a sensitive mother's stomach! New mothers need something warm, nourishing, and easy to digest to start their day. This is a very traditional Ayurvedic morning meal or midmorning snack. Almonds provide protein and can be ground in a blender.

1 cup brown, red or basmati rice, barley, couscous, millet, and quinoa.
4 cups water (may need more)
1 cinnamon stick
1 teaspoon cardamom
½ teaspoon dried ground ginger
2 cups milk or soy milk
½ cup of a natural sugar
½ cup blanched almonds, coarsely ground
½ cup raisins

Optional: ¼ teaspoon saffron threads *or* ¼ teaspoon sweet paprika

Grind the rice in a blender until it has the consistency of coarse sand. In a large pot, bring the water to a boil. Decrease the heat and add the cinnamon stick, cardamom and ginger. Add the ground rice while stirring with a whisk. Simmer, uncovered for about 30 minutes; enjoy the wonderful aroma. Stir often: don't' let the rice stick to the bottom of the pot. In a separate bowl, mix the milk, sugar, almonds, raisins, and saffron or paprika. Taste the rice to make sure it is well cooked; it should have the texture of a porridge or oatmeal. Add the milk mixture and continue to stir. Simmer for 10 more minutes. The rice should have the consistency of thin oatmeal. Serve warm.

Oatmeal Pancake with Date Compote
by Chef Sharifah Maria Syed, Instructor, BERJAYA University College of Hospitality (UCH), Kuala Lumpur, Malaysia

1 cup oatmeal
½ cup flour
3 tablespoons sugar or natural sugar substitute
Pinch of salt
2 egg whites
1 ½ cups milk, soy or nut milk
4 tablespoons olive oil

Date compote
10 thinly sliced pieces of fresh ginger root
20 dates
1.5 cups water, boiled and cooled
2 tablespoons honey
1 stick cinnamon
2 pieces star anise

Sift the flour and salt together. Then mix the oatmeal with the flour. Add the milk into the oatmeal and let sit for a few minutes until the oatmeal absorbs all of the liquid. Add a little milk or water if the batter seems too thick. Add in the olive oil into the mixture and mix well. Softly whisk the egg whites; just a few times to loosen up the whites. Then mix them into the oatmeal mixture. Pour the batter onto a greased preheated pan, allowing space for spreading. Fry the pancakes until the tops are full of bubbles and begin to look dry and the bottoms are a golden brown. Flip and brown the other side. Remove from the pan and serve with the warm date compote.

Date Compote
Place water, honey, sliced ginger, cinnamon stick and star anise in a small pot. Bring to the boil and reduce the heat. Add in dates to the syrup and simmer over a gentle heat for 2 – 4 minutes. Serve warm. Alternatively cool and chill in the refrigerator for up to one week. Just before serving, warm the compote in a pan, if desired.

POST-PREGNANCY WISDOM FROM IBU ROBIN LIM
In Bali there has been research that indicates porridge, or bubur, made with red rice stimulates a woman's milk supply to come in hours sooner, as well as increases the milk supply.

Traditional Fish Burbur
by Jerrine Teo, Culinary Arts Student, BERJAYA UCH, Kuala Lumpur, Malaysia

1 fish filet (your choice)
1 cup rice
2 cups water, boiled and cooled
1 inch piece ginger, sliced
2 tablespoon sesame oil
1 stalk spring onion
1 stalk Chinese parsley (which is celery leaves)
1 carrot diced
Dash soy sauce, to taste.
Garnish fresh cilantro.

Soak rice in water for one hour. Pour the rice and a little water into a blender and blend it coarsely. Sauté the ginger with sesame oil until fragrant in the pot. Pour the rice into the pot and add water. Add in the spring onion, carrot and Chinese parsley. After the porridge starts boiling, turn down the heat and put fish filet in. Simmer for five minutes. Pour the porridge in a bow and garnish with a few drops of soy sauce.

Steamed Chicken with White Vinegar
By Chef Azmin Amran, Lecturer, *BERJAYA UCH, Kuala Lumpur, Malaysia.*

Ingredients A
1 whole chicken cut into eight pieces
1 inch, fresh ginger root chopped
4 cloves garlic
Salt and pepper to taste

Ingredients B
3 tablespoons white vinegar
2 tablespoons coriander seed
1 teaspoon cumin powder
1 teaspoon fennel power

Garnish
Shredded ginger and spring onion

Marinade the chicken with Ingredients A and rest in the refrigerator for 30 minutes
– 1 hour. Steam chicken until cooked, then pour Ingredients B over the chicken pieces
and steam again for a few minutes and serve.

Ginger Yogurt Flavoured Chicken Curry
By Shankar Subramaniam, Lecturer, BERJAYA UCH, Kuala Lumpur, Malaysia.

1 pound of chicken cut into small pieces
1 cup full-fat plain yogurt
2 teaspoons salt
1 tablespoon ghee, (clarified butter) or butter
4 inch piece fresh ginger root, peeled
(2 inches of ginger for blending and the rest for sautéing)
3 cardamom pods
3 strips of curry leaves, fresh otherwise dried (1 strip for garnishing)
1 onion, sliced
1 teaspoon turmeric powder
2 cinnamon sticks
2 pieces of star anise
½ teaspoon cumin seed
8 garlic cloves
3 cups boiled water that has been cooled to room temperature

Pre-preparations
Marinate the chicken pieces with yogurt, and salt and keep it aside for 15 minutes
in a refrigerator. Blend onion slices, garlic and 2 inch fresh, peeled ginger root until
smooth paste.

Heat the ghee or butter in a thick bottom pan. First fry the cardamom, cinnamon sticks, star anise with the curry leaves, add in the rest of the ginger and sauté over a medium-low heat add in the turmeric powder. Add the cumin seeds and stir well. Cook until ginger is soft. Add enough ghee or butter to keep the spices from scorching or sticking to the pan. Add the blended onion garlic and ginger paste and stir well. While the onions are browning, add the marinade of yogurt mixed and then the water. Add the marinated chicken pieces, let it cook over a slow heat and cover for 15 minutes. Adjust the salt if required. Garnish with curry leaves and serve with plain rice.

Flourless Orange Ginger Cake
by Nigel A. Skelchy Just Heavenly (M) Sdn Bhd, Kuala Lumpur, Malaysia, www. justheavenly.biz/bakingbarn

2-3 oranges (total weight of roughly 450g), seedless is preferred.
6 eggs
1 oz (30g) of melted unsalted butter
1 ¼ cup of natural raw sugar
1 cup (100g) ground almonds
2 tsp of turmeric powder
¾ cup (100g) chopped crystallized ginger
1 ¼ tsp of baking powder, level
2 small teaspoons of white vinegar
Generous pinch of salt

Place whole oranges in a pot of cold water, enough to cover, and boil for two hours over a medium low heat. The oranges are boiled for a long time to soften the fruit and extract any bitterness or sourness. At the end of two hours, switch on your oven to 350F (180C) (320F or 160C for a fan forced). Prepare an 8" spring form tin. Line the bottom and butter the sides. Beat the eggs just to combine. Break the oranges up and de-seed (if not using seedless oranges). Chop the ginger to a size of a green pea. Not too finely, so there's texture when you eat the cake. Sieve the ground almonds, salt, turmeric powder and baking powder together. Put the deseeded oranges, soft rind and all, with the melted butter in a food processor. Slowly pour in the almond flour mix and white vinegar and blend. Pour into the prepared pan. Bake for an hour but perform a skewer test. The skewer should come out clean. Unmold after it has had a chance to cool for 10 minutes. This cake tastes better the next day as it allows for the flavors have a chance to develop. If you prefer to eat it warm, heat it in a microwave for 10 seconds. The result will be a dense cake full of flavor, not a light cake. Natural raw sugar isn't as processed as much white sugar, thus resulting in a heavier cake.

Ginger Tea

Ginger is one of those wonderful versatile spices, and for me, fresh is best! This is a typical tea made in households in Asia and drunk often, not only during post-pregnancy recovery. It has an invigorating spicy taste, and is also used as a home remedy against a sore throat, cold, flu, nausea, and indigestion. If you are new to ginger, I would recommend starting with fresh *young* ginger root as it has a softer taste than old ginger, which has a fuller and spicier taste. Below is another natural recipe for ginger tea from Ibu Robin Lim's book, *Eating for Two, Recipes for Pregnant and Breastfeeding Women.*

2 inch piece fresh ginger root, peeled and mashed
4 cups of water, boiled and cooled
Honey optional

*A squeeze of fresh lime, lemon or tangerine (optional)

Peel and slice the ginger root, then mash. Place in a teapot and pour in boiling waters. When the tea is lukewarm, and the add honey to your taste. When you have finished your recovery, you could also drink this cold.

Remember, there are Ayurvedic influences on the post-pregnancy beliefs found in Malaysia and Southeast Asia. Ayurvedic recipes are well documented and easily searched on the internet, the ones in Southeast Asia are not. Therefore Ayurvedic recipes can be easily researched and modified according to the guidelines in this book.

Yogurt with Honey and Cinnamon

This is a simple Ayurvedic snack recipe that Ysha Oakes recommends after birth. Make sure you use full-fat yogurt and add honey and cinnamon to your desired taste.

POST-PREGNANCY WISDOM

If you look beyond the typical Western diet, then you will realize there is an abundance of food you can eat during this time period. Take control over what is happening to your body. Precaution, planning, and preparation are the keys. If you take good care of yourself, you are taking good care of your newborn and your family.

BERJAYA University College of Hospitality is the premier niche lifestyle university college in Malaysia, specializing in Hospitality, Culinary Arts, Tourism and services management. The suite of programs includes Diplomas and Bachelor Degrees in culinary arts, hospitality management, tourism and travel, events management, and retail management and at post-graduate level a Master of Business Administration with specializations. The city campus is situated in prime real estate in Kuala Lumpur known as "the golden triangle." Located in BERJAYA Times Square, the campus is conceptually designed with a 5-star hotel ambience, equipped with the most comprehensive and advanced facilities to mirror the real world of industries for which BERJAYA prepares its students. For more information on BERJAYA UCH, visit www.berjaya.edu.my.

Recommended Guidelines and Food List

A recovering mother needs to eat healthily and make wise food choices for herself and her nursing baby, especially if the mother chooses to breastfeed.

Cold foods are prohibited for six weeks, especially during the first twenty-one days.[24] A nursing mother needs nutrient dense calories as her body requires more energy to produce milk.

Five to seven meals throughout the day is adequate. If you do not overindulge, then your body will start to burn the stored pregnancy fat that is no longer needed.

Body reaction to foods varies from person to person, so you need to observe if a food has a negative effect, such as bloatedness or flatulence, feeling cold, back ache, vaginal itchiness, or pain in the uterus. If this occurs, avoid eating that food, or eat it in small quantities.[25]

Post-pregnancy Cooking Methods
Grilled, broiled, steamed, baked, poached, roasted, healthy sautéing, crock pot, or dry fry.

Post-pregnancy Tips
1. If the first three ingredients listed is "sugar" or a chemical, then don't eat or drink it. The first three ingredients are always the primary ingredients of a product.
2. Drink boiled water, NO spring, tap, filtered, or reverse osmosis.
3. Soups are strongly recommended to be a part of your daily diet as they warm the body from the inside out.

Cooking Oils
High-quality coconut oil or olive oil.

Oils Rich in Omega 3, 6, and 9
Essential fatty acid-rich oils are available in health-food stores or online.
High-Quality Poultry and Lean Meats
- Beef, chicken, turkey, rabbit or duck, 3 ounces or 100 grams per portion.
- No processed meats, cured, cold cuts/deli meats, or canned meats.

Cold-Water Fish
- Anchovy, cod, flounder, haddock, hake, halibut, herring, grouper, red sea bream, orange roughy, red and golden snapper, salmon, shark, snakehead fish, Spanish mackerel, tilapia, threadfin, tuna steak, white pomfret.
- Salmon is high in Omega 3, 6 and 9 and is known to help with the production of breast milk. Dried fish is also acceptable, but please check the ingredients and make sure chemicals and preservatives are not added or used in the process.

Vegetables
- Avocadoes, beetroot, carrots, onions, celery, kale, Swiss chard, leafy green veggies, sweet potato, and yams.
- Veggies such as onions and celery are on the approved foods; however, for some people, they can cause gas. Monitor how the vegetables affect your system, and if you feel bloated after eating, refrain from eating for the first three weeks.
- Spinach is a considered "cold"; however, in the case of anemia, it is acceptable to eat.

Fruit
- Red apples, bananas (not too sweet or green), blackberries, blueberries, cherries, sweet oranges, tamarind, papaya, peaches, plums, seedless red grapes, strawberries.
- Dried fruits: take note of the ingredients on a food label and refrain from sugar or chemical preservatives.
- Make sure your fruit has been washed or peeled in case of wax.

Dairy
Full-fat dairy products are preferable.

Soy and Nut Products
- Avoid light or low-fat versions and be wary of flavored versions as they may contain sugar or chemical additives.
- Soymilk, soybean milk.
- Nut milk: almond, oat, hazelnut.
- Tofu and tempeh are excellent sources of protein. Soy products manufactured in Asian countries tends to be better quality as the fermentation period is longer, which has more health benefits. Do not consume genetically modified soy products.

Eggs
Avoid eating egg yolks for at least the first ten days.
Grains and Breads
- Whole grain breads are recommended over white breads.
- Grains such as amaranth, brown, red, basmati or wild rice, barley, bulgar wheat, cous cous, millet, quinoa.

Nuts, Seeds, Oils
- Raw, not roasted or salted.
- Almonds, cashews, flaxseeds, macadamia, sesame, sunflower, walnuts.

| **Natural Sweeteners** |
| Agave, black molasses, date sugar, raw, dehydrated cane sugar, high-quality organic honey, honey on the honeycomb, Stevia, pure maple sugar. |
| **Jams** |
| Berry jams, i.e., strawberry. Must be low sugar; make sure to examine the ingredients to ensure preservatives are not included. |
| **Spices and Herbs**
The addition of ginger to a dish make the dish or vegetable become warmer and is highly recommended in cooking as are most of the other herbs and spices. Begin cooking with ginger ten days after delivery.

Spices: allspice, anise, bay leaves, black and white pepper, cayenne pepper, cardamom, cinnamon, celery, cloves, cumin, curry powder, fennel, graham marsala, garlic, ginger, mace, marjoram, nutmeg, onion powder, pepper, peppermint, saffron, turmeric, vanilla and so on.

Fresh herbs: basil, lemon basil, chervil, chives, coriander, curry plant, dill, lavender, ginger, parsley, lemon verbena, lemon grass, mint, peppermint, spearmint, oregano, rosemary, sage, thyme, tarragon, and so on. |
| **Cereal and Oatmeal** |
| Low sugar, organic cereal or steel cut oatmeal. |

EIGHT

Post-pregnancy Precautions: Activities

In addition to dietary guidelines, there are recommendations regarding the activities a mother engages in within the first six weeks. This ensures a new mother doesn't try to do too much too soon, which often results in a setback of her recovery. In addition, simple strategies are offered to increase body temperature and to make sure the existing body heat is retained.

1. Resting and Bonding With Your Baby

I mentioned time and again that there are *only* two objectives for the first six weeks after childbirth: resting and bonding with your newborn baby. That's it, simple. Everything else is secondary, or isn't even remotely on the same level of importance, and ought to be overlooked during this time period. Again remember, this is only a *temporary* situation, so view this as a no-brainer and dedicate this time to your recuperation and baby. You won't ever get this time back, and many mommies that are able to take this time say it's precious.

Out of the three post-pregnancy guidelines, I find the activity recommendations the most difficult for Western women to follow as it requires slowing all the way down and being content to spend most of the six weeks at home. During the first one to two weeks, you may feel physically fine; however, you are definitely *not* fine and will tire easily. After two weeks, most women have more energy and attempt to resume normal household responsibilities. Then they come to find out that after completing a few chores, that they feel tired and need to rest. This is your body telling you that in no way are you ready to resume normal, domestic activities, so please stop! You may want to consider spending the first few weeks at a relative's home or split the time between your home and a relative's home, so that you have consistent help.

POST-PREGNANCY ANALOGY: AIRPLANE SAFETY DEMONSTRATIONS
When you are on a plane, before takeoff, the flight attendants will give the safety presentation and demonstration. When it comes to the part of how to put on the oxygen mask, the instructions are, "If you are traveling with children, please place the

oxygen mask over your face first, then place your child's mask on his or her face." This is because our first instinct is to sacrifice ourselves to take care of our children first. But, if we don't take care of ourselves, we won't be able to function properly to take the *best care* of our children that we can. Taking care of yourself means taking better care of your child in the long term.

We modern women think we are invincible, until we realize in three to six months time that, "Hey, wait a minute, I've lost that happy feeling. My body still has aches and pains, and I just don't feel right." Then we look back in hindsight, and realize we should have reserved the first six weeks for as much as non-activity possible. Do you remember the list of "Conditions of a woman's body immediately after giving birth" in Chapter 6?

Here's a brief review:
- In a cold state
- Uterine after-pains
- Hot and cold flashes
- Carrying excess fat
- Vaginal discharge (lochia)
- Varicose veins
- Joint pains
- Sagging breasts
- Sore breasts
- Flabby tummy
- Episiotomy
- Stretch marks
- Pregnancy melasma
- Hemorrhoids
- Urinary or fecal incontinence
- Sluggish circulatory and digestive systems
- Water logged, bloated, and swollen
- Effects of inducement, epidural, or cesarean effects

I believe, after taking in the above list, you will agree that you will need ample rest.

Baby Wellness: The Gift of Human Touch is Powerful Medicine

"Being touched and caressed, being massaged, is food for the infant, food as necessary as minerals, vitamins and proteins."
Dr Frederick Leboyer M.D.,
(created awareness of the functioning senses of newborns)

A well-documented way of bonding with your baby is through baby massage. It is very well accepted, and known for its calming effect for both the baby and the mommy and daddy.

Infant massage has long been practiced in Asia and has been shown to have general health and scientific benefits. Notable effects of massage on babies are calming, improved digestion, and reduction or elimination of colic fussiness and crying. My experience is of the Malay-style of baby massage, which is a common style found in Southeast Asia. In Malaysia, massages specifically for infants date back just as far as the specialized pregnancy and post-pregnancy massages – thousands of years. Most Malay mothers give their baby a massage every day for a minimum of three to four months, and in some cases up to six months.

There are two unique aspects to the Malay style of baby massage as it includes the use of a hand held, small herbal ball, called a *tunku,* and a little baby tummy wrap, called a *baby barut.* The tummy wrap is worn after the umbilical cord has fallen off and is wrapped snuggly, but gently, around a baby's torso (chest and belly).

Baby massage normally begins when a baby is two days old. A daily head to toe gentle massage is given after a bath, as this is when the skin is slightly moist and the pores are open. The most common oil I've seen used is high grade coconut oil, as it is the richest source of medium-chain triglycerides, has antifungal, antibacterial, antiviral and anti-parasitic properties and thus is very good for the skin. However, one can also use a high quality cold pressed virgin olive oil, as long as the oil is from a natural origin, and not processed or made from a petroleum base.

Baby Massage
A baby is given a nice warm bath to relax and be thoroughly cleaned. After bathing, lightly dry the baby and then place him back on a soft towel or cloth, one that you don't mind getting ruined, as excess oil will be absorbed by the material. It is also common for a baby to urinate or have a bowel movement while getting a massage. Most baby massages take place in the bathroom directly after a bath (with the door closed) as the room will be a warmer temperature than any other room in the house after a bath. This type of massage is given before the diaper and clothes are put on.

Baby Oil Massage
1. Put a small amount of natural massage oil on your palm and then rub your hands vigorously together to warm and stimulate the properties of the oil. Your baby will also appreciate the warmth of the oil rather than putting cold oil on his warm little body. *Your baby should not be too oily after the massage as you want the oil to be absorbed by the baby's skin and not by the diaper or clothes.*

2. Place the baby face up in front of you. Do not perform a baby massage with the baby being upside down, as in the baby's head pointed towards you instead of the feet. *If you massage with the baby upside down you will be massaging against the natural flow of the digestive system. The baby's tummy is the focus of this type of massage.*

3. Place your hand gently on the baby's tummy and softly massage the entire tummy area in a circular motion clockwise. Massage area around the belly button, as it follows the flow of digestion of the large intestine. Be careful not to get any oil on the umbilical cord if it is still attached.

4. In a wiping up motion massage your baby's waist area, towards the belly, using one hand after another. The tummy area is the focus, so make sure to spend a good amount of time on the tummy area which helps with a baby's digestion and any flatulence that may occur as the baby's organs are newly functioning.

5. Proceed to gently wipe down and softly pull the front and back of the legs in a downward motion working your way to the feet; gently caress the feet and toes.

6. Next, move up to the arms wiping down the arms in a soft pulling motion; stroking the back and front of the arms and hands, and then play with the fingers.

7. When you are finished with the front, place the baby on his belly on your forearm, supporting the head with the palm of your hand, and the body with your forearm. Then, gently stroke the baby's back and buttocks, like you are smoothing down a piece of cloth. Do not let any oil seep inside of the buttocks (or genital area) as it could cause irritation.

8. Turn the baby around to face you and place him on his back. You can then softly massage from the forehead down to the chin, in a downward motion.

9. Wipe the baby down with a towel before the diaper and clothes are put on. This may take only five to ten minutes, or, however long you and the daddy would like to bond with your baby. Babies usually like this sort of gentle touching, as long as the room is warm enough for their body temperature, not yours, so they don't feel cold. If your baby is crying check the room temperature.

Baby Sinus Massage

An additional focus of the face massage in the Malay culture is the mouth and sinus area. A mother or father places their pinky finger in the baby's mouth, with the underside of the finger touching the roof of the mouth. The nose and sides of the nose, where the sinus canals are located, are gently pinched and smoothed outwards to open sinus canals. Of course, be careful only to put a small part of your pinky in the mouth and that the airway of the baby is not blocked. This helps with sinus conditions and to keep the canals clear. If you choose to massage the sinus, it is important to use high quality or food grade oil as you will be sticking your pinky in your baby's mouth.

> **BABY WELLNESS NOTE**
> It is important to use "natural" or food grade oils as a baby will put his hands into his mouth or may rub his eyes. If you are using scented oils then do not massage the hands.

Malay mothers slightly warm the oil they use to enhance the effectiveness and absorption, but this must be carefully monitored as oil heats quickly, and if hot oil is applied to a baby's skin it could cause a burn.

Herbal Compress Massage
After the oil massage, a massage using an herbal compress in the form of a ball is given. An herbal compress may contain a combination of twenty or more of different types of traditional relaxing herbs. Some of the most commonly used herbs are lavender, ginger, lemon grass, kaffir lime, turmeric, camphor tree, and tamarind.

The herbal compress is warmed for five to ten seconds to a comfortable temperature for a baby's sensitive skin by the following methods:
  • steaming
  • heated, on a dry frying pan
  • warmed in a microwave oven

Below is normally how an herbal compress massage is performed on a baby:
1. Gently press the herbal compress vertically, on the baby's skin starting at the baby's tummy, and moving in the same circular, clockwise pattern around the belly-button, waist and hips.
2. Next move down to the legs, pressing the front of the legs, then lifting one leg and pressing the buttocks and up the back of the leg. Repeat with the other leg.
3. Press the top and bottom of the feet.
4. Press the back and front of the arms.
5. You can turn the baby around on his tummy, as previously done during the oil massage, and press the back. Do not press the genital area.

IMPORTANT BABY WELLNESS CAUTION
A baby's skin is very sensitive. A warm temperature to an adult may be too hot for a newborn. It is very important to test the warmth of the herbal compress on your own skin, at a sensitive area such as the inside of your forearm, and use your judgment to determine if the temperature is suitable for a newborn. If it is too hot let the compress cool down to a comfortable temperature. The temperature should only be warm, never hot.

Baby Tummy Wrap

I really like the baby tummy wrap. After the herbal compress massage a little baby tummy wrap is placed around the abdomen. A baby tummy wrap serves two purposes 1. It's meant to provide a baby with comfort, as he has just come out of the snug, secure peaceful environment of the womb. A tummy wrap is supposed to, to some degree, imitate the warm coziness of the womb – especially when a newborn cannot regulate his own body temperature. 2. It helps prevent a baby's stomach from becoming bloated, which may lead to colic, as well as tummy aches. It is secured

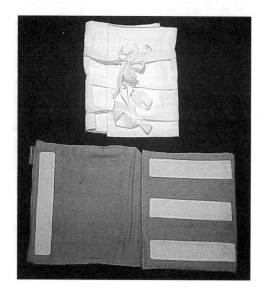

snug, but not too tight, giving the torso area gentle support while the digestive system and other organs begin functioning on their own for the first time outside the womb. Below is a photo of two types of baby wraps. One is with ties and the other is with Velcro.

The Malay women I've interviewed revealed that Malay babies have low rates of colic, or that colic passes in a shorter time period, due to the combination of daily massages and the baby tummy wrap, which functions as a supportive garment.

How to Put on a Baby Tummy Wrap
The baby wrap is placed open on a soft surface. The baby is placed face-up on top of the wrap; so his back is in contact with the wrap. The wrap is brought around the

baby's torso and is secured in the front. There are two types of wraps; one with a Velcro strip and one with ties in the front. There is also a version that ties in the back, and has a u-section cut out in the back for the diaper. A baby wrap comes in two lengths, a shorter size that is for just around the tummy area, and a longer one that covers both the chest and tummy area.

> **BABY WELLNESS TIP**
> A baby wrap is ideal on cool or cold nights to keep the core warm.

The Gift of Human Touch

There are many observed and proven benefits of baby massage: it calms difficult or colicky babies, alleviates gas, constipation and other digestion problems, relaxes, promotes better sleep, boosts the immune system, stimulates the senses, improves skin condition and blood circulation, and helps eliminates waste from the baby's body. However, there are also wonderful benefits for the parents, such as helping a parent learn about their baby's needs and desires. It also relaxes the parents, stimulates oxytocin production for mothers, and helps build parents' self-esteem about their ability to take of their baby.

The healing power of therapeutic touch has long been documented. A newborn baby instinctively responds to touch. A massage given by a mother or father to their baby is a wonderful way of enhancing the natural bonding.

To Swaddle or Not to Swaddle?

This is an important topic as there is a heated debate in the childbirth community over swaddling, with recent scientific information regarding Kangaroo Care being preferred to swaddling. Infant researchers claim it's in a baby's best interest to have the baby's hands accessible to the face, and claim that it helps calm a stressed baby. A baby wrap provides a baby's torso with comfort, without swaddling, leaving the arms free to move. Please research this topic and read more on this topic in the 'postnatal notes' section at the back of the book.

If you are interested in finding out more about this type of baby massage or the complementary products please contact me.

2. Minimize Domestic Household Chores

Make sure your home is well in order before you give birth--however you define "in order" to be. Activities you should refrain from doing include the following:

- Laundry
- Cooking
- Vacuuming
- Washing dishes
- Sweeping
- Cleaning windows
- Yard work
- Washing the car
- Loading the dishwasher
- Cleaning up after anyone

You should also include in this list anything else you can think of that is considered "work or "chores" including professional work. However, your home shouldn't get to a state of being too untidy or dirty as it is easier to fall into a depression in a messy house, than a relatively tidy one.

Meals

Meal planning and preparation is normally the most challenging to arrange if you are the primary cook in your household. Your body needs lots of rest and good nutrition to restore its energy level, which will be vitally important in the weeks to come. But *you* aren't supposed to be the one cooking the meals. Preplanning your meals isn't impossible, just challenging, so make sure you plan early and ask for help.

After three weeks of mostly rest, you can resume light housework, and I mean light. Nothing too taxing and don't do housework for hours at time. You are the best person to judge what is light for you, as each woman's recovery is exclusive to herself.

I realize that this guideline may not be entirely acceptable, or realistic, for American or other Western cultures. My hope is that mommies think twice before doing household chores that (may strain her body) that doesn't really need to be done and could be put off. Do your best to minimize the household work you engage in for six weeks.

AFTER-BIRTH WISDOM FROM BALI, INDONESIA

Ibu Robin Lim, founded a free birthing clinic in Bali 16 years ago and shared this Balinese post-pregnancy cultural tradition. In Bali, a woman is not allowed under any circumstances, to enter her own kitchen until the baby's cord stump has fallen off. This forces a mother to rest and keeps her away from house work. Of course, the family and extended family is intact and, in most cases, and they can take full care of the recovering mother.

3. Even Well-Informed Moms Need Help

American women are considered to be "strong." Strong-willed, strong-minded as well as strong physically. If we are so strong, then why do over a million of us experience some sort of postpartum mood disorder, every year? How did women that have never suffered from an emotional disorder and was able to adequately handle stress prior to giving birth, find herself experiencing unstable postpartum emotions? There are countless reasons why. But, I'm sure you'll agree, that's a lot of well-informed moms unable to understand or cope with what's happening in their own bodies.

I think with all of our control issues and in depth research, we assume that we are well-prepared *Super Moms* who are able to overcome any challenge motherhood throws at us! Hmmm, well, statistics clearly show we may not be as prepared as we thought. We read everything we can get out hands on before we give birth, but it doesn't sink in that we have *no real hands-on experience;* and the reality of bringing home our first or successive child normally sets in after a few weeks. Then, we realize we may have overestimated our ability to cope with the extra demands and changes in our life. That's OK. We are humans, and we are known for our ability to adapt to our environment. However, there are a few things we can do to help ourselves before we find ourselves at our wits end, exhausted and in tears while holding a crying baby in the middle of the night!

Family Support

Family support in the United States is not nearly what it used to be even just twenty years ago. Family members live separate lives, sometimes in different states and countries, and get together infrequently. That's OK too, as it's the world we live in and we make our own choices. However, with the celebration of a new baby, it is a time when families go out of their way to get together and make time to welcome a new addition to the family. So, why not piggy back on this happy occasion and ask for a little help with the new little bundle of joy? However, be very clear, in a nice way, that you won't be entertaining anyone but spending most of this time resting. You may only need help for a few hours a day, and even that would be something. It makes a big difference, believe me.

Deep Clean Your Home Before the Baby Arrives

In order for you to be able to devote more time to resting and the baby, I suggest that you do a deep clean of your home at least one month before your estimated due date. You will be at least eight months pregnant at this time so you need to enlist people to help you. This way anyone coming in to help you during your post-pregnancy period will know that they don't have to do any deep cleaning, only the daily or weekly tidying up.

Get the deep clean done well before your baby arrives. Make sure you use baby-friendly and natural cleaning products, such as vinegar, lemon and baking soda, as you don't want your home to have strong chemical smells. When you arrive home with your newborn to a deeply cleaned house, it will feel much better then coming home to an untidy or dirty home.

Below is a sample of a deep clean checklist:
- Dust intensively, as dust isn't good for a newborn. Dust ceiling fans, air vents and baseboard heaters.
- Wash floors, windows, cabinets and anything else dirty.
- Wash and clean carpets and furniture, if they haven't been cleaned for a long time. Again it's a dust issue.
- Deep clean electrical appliances throughout the house.
- Clean light fixtures.
- Clean window treatments – curtains, drapes; as dust and dirt easily collects in the fabric.
- Vacuum the inside, behind and underneath of furniture.
- Change air conditioning filters (in summer).
- De-clutter and/or reorganize any area that needs it.
- Check smoke alarms.

Stock your pantry with plenty of dried food items one to two weeks before your estimated due date. Restock anything that you are running low on – paper goods, pet food, laundry detergent and so on. Keep this list for the daddy or person that will be helping you after delivery.

POST-PREGNANCY TIP
Some supermarkets or smaller food stores have grocery delivery services available. Prepare a grocery list and have it ready to send to the store and they will deliver to your door step.

Don't expect the daddy to know he should change the bed sheets, put away the dishes, do the laundry, or tidy up. You may want to write up a "to do" list for him, or whomever will be helping you, and put it somewhere where it will be seen, like on the refrigerator. Or simply let him know what you would appreciate he do before you return home – from the hospital or birthing center.

Post-Baby Help Schedule

Expectant moms need to be aware that the transition is going to be more difficult than imagined, and that it's acceptable to ask for help from those around us. To develop this support network, we need to make a "help schedule" before we give birth. People have busy lives and making a plea for help at the time when we need it may not be conducive to other people's schedules.

Your help schedule should cover, at the very least, the first three weeks and hopefully up to six weeks post-pregnancy. Make a list of the activities you would like help with and prioritize that list. It could be cooking, cleaning, grocery shopping, picking up other children, coming over to watch the baby or anything else, so that you can have time to refresh yourself by taking a nap or just closing your eyes for a short time, take a shower, spend an hour to apply post-pregnancy recovery products, get a post-pregnancy massage and body treatments, take a walk to get fresh air, or just to have some time to yourself; whatever that would help to recharge your batteries.

Below is a sample chore list:

Kitchen
- Meals: plan/shop/prepare
- Set/Clear table
- Wash dishes/load
- dishwasher/put away

Kitchen clean
- Counter/Stove-top
- Drawers
- Floor: sweep/mop
- Appliances

Family areas
- General tidying up
- Dusting
- Vacuuming

Floors
- Sweep/mop/vacuum

Bathroom
- Sink, counter top
- Shower/Tub
- Toilet
- Floor
- Change towels

Bedrooms
- Make bed
- Change linens
- Pick up/put away clothes
- Vacuum floor

Laundry
- Sort clothes into loads
- Wash them
- Dryer items
- Fold/put away

Other
- Take out garbage
- Dust any other areas: hallway/foyer
- Pet care
- Vacuum stairs/other areas

Outside (only if needed)
- Pool care
- Lawn and plant care
- Car care
- Snow shovel

POST-PREGNANCY TIP
Do you have a friend or relative who is a clean freak? Those people may be good people to ask as they actually get satisfaction out of cleaning!

Don't be afraid to ask for help! You never know what people are willing to do unless you ask. People are always surprised by the kindness shown from those around them, and in my experience, I always get help from people I expect the least from! People are inherently good, remember that.

Make It Easy on Those Who Help You
When you are asking for help, you will want to make it easy on those that are willing to give their time. Let the person use your car for errands (picking up other children, shopping, and so on) and provide gas money. You won't need a car while you are resting. If your mother or relative can stay with you for a few weeks, keep the baby in your room and let the baby's room be a guest room; and borrow or rent a mattress for them to sleep on. There are many simple things that can be done to make the person, or people, who put their hand up to help you feel appreciated.

Show Your Appreciation
Give them a small gift when they leave, or have a gift waiting for them when they return home or send flowers. There are many inexpensive gift websites that have creative gift suggestions. A meaningful gesture, that costs nothing but your time and thoughts, is a handwritten note. Tell them how grateful you are for their help, and give real examples of how they've helped you over the past few weeks. These simple gestures go a long way. Sometime in the future, you can repay their kindness by helping them out when they need it. What comes around goes around!

4. After-Birth Journal

Every woman should keep a journal, file or record, comprising their experiences throughout pregnancy, labor and delivery. When childbirth is a satisfying experience, women seem to thrive afterwards. However, when there are unexpected outcomes, there can be anything from disappointment to extensive trauma.[3]

Examples of unexpected or adverse outcomes may be:
- If you had to be on complete bed rest for weeks or months during pregnancy.
- Labor was exceedingly difficult.
- A difficult vaginal birth.
- An unexpected cesarean birth.

- Unexpected episiotomy procedure.
- Medical interventions.
- Treatment by birth professionals or people who participated in your birth experience.
- Baby was handled roughly, or not brought to you as you instructed
- Cord was wrapped around baby's neck.
- Baby was breech.
- Baby became stuck in the birth canal.
- Baby had to go to a neonatal incubator.

and so on. The type of situations that could happen area many and what may not affect a friend, may affect very deeply affect you, therefore don't compare yourself to anyone else.

Research shows women who have negative experiences during labor and birth, normally need a great deal of support and comfort in order to work through what had occurred to heal and move forward. However, often women don't want to face or admit to themselves that their birth experience was far less than they had hoped for. This is when a birth doula can play an important role in protecting you and your birth experience, via your birth plan.

It is also important to record any medications, pharmaceuticals or herbal products and the respective dosage, taken during labor and be aware of the side effects, even if a product is deemed safe. If any post-birth conditions occur in the days, weeks and months that follow, then you have a detailed chronological history on hand to refer to in order to determine if there is a cause-and-effect relationship.

5. Avoid Exposure to Cold Temperatures

Your body temperature is slightly below normal, and therefore, it must be kept warm until it rises back to the normal 98.7°F (37°C). With this in mind, avoid the following:

- Drafts
- Direct fans
- Wind
- Cold air
- Excessive air conditioning

You don't want to get a "chill" or feel chilly. This includes exposing yourself to excessive cold temperatures in shopping malls, restaurants, movie theatres, and so on. Think about where you are going and take into consideration the temperature inside the venue or at the location. For example, taking a stroll on the beach in the evening may be chilly and windy—two combinations that are very bad for a woman recovering from childbirth.

If you give birth in autumn or winter when the temperature is cold, make sure to wear layers of extra clothes, although you are supposed to be staying home and keeping yourself indoors. Also, consider wearing a hat, wrapping your neck with a scarf and wearing undergarments such as leggings or thick tights. The temperature inside your home is also important as you don't want to feel cold. It may be a good idea to allocate a little more of your household budget, during the first six weeks of your recovery, as you may need to adjust the thermostat to a higher setting than usual. You can use hot water bottles to keep warm by placing it against your abdominal area, which will also help with uterine shrinkage and healing. I love hot water bottles! They are comforting and feel so nice, especially on the tummy.

6. Finished Basements

Many homes have finished basements that tend to be cold and damp due to the fact that it is underground. This may not be a good place for you to spend a lot of time unless you can raise the room temperature to consistently being warm; and take the moisture out of the air by using a dehumidifier.

Newborns and Varying Temperatures

Avoid exposing your newborn to varying hot/cold temperatures as they don't have the ability to easily adjust or regulate their body temperature. Keeping a skull cap on your baby's head, socks on his feet, and covering up the arms and legs will help regulate your baby's body temperature. What's more, a newborn's immune system is not developed, leaving him vulnerable to airborne or contact (skin) bacteria for the first few months.[1] Regularly cleaning your hands (and anyone else's who wants to hold your baby) with soap, hand wash, or sanitizer made with ethyl alcohol (like the kind that you drink in wine) that are nonchemical and natural, will reduce this risk to your baby.

7. No Swimming

Don't engage in any activity that may affect your body's internal temperature such as swimming, sitting in a hot or wet sauna, or even a cool shower. Swimming will reduce your body temperature, cooling it even further. Remember, you want to reheat your body. Even though you may be going through post-pregnancy heat flashes, which is a rebalancing mechanism, don't deliberately cool off your body too drastically. Think of your newborn - snuggling a cold mommy isn't as comforting as snuggling a warm one!

Of course, you should move around and take walks to get your circulatory and digestive systems functioning, but nothing too strenuous. If the bleeding of your lochia diminishes and then increases again, or turns bright red, you are doing too much activity. Stop whatever you are doing and rest. You may be inhibiting your body's ability to recover without realizing it.

8. Minimize Visitors

I know you don't want to be rude to the people who are close you, but it is strongly advised to minimize visitors. Friends and family normally want to rush over and see the baby the minute you bring him home. However, you shouldn't be engaging in activities like preparing the house for visitors, planning a menu, cooking, and cleaning up afterward. You don't want to expose your newborn child to the possibility of airborne bacteria, brought in by well-meaning visitors while his immune system is nonexistent. If you tell people you aren't feeling well and not up to visitors, the people you mean the most to will understand. The ideal time for people to visit is after one month.

Baby Happy Hour

If you have people that keep calling, wanting to come see your baby, and you are feeling pressured, why not hold a "baby happy hour". For one evening, plan a two-hour time period that *close* family and friends can drop in and see the baby. To make it simple on yourself, stipulate that it is only coffee and healthy snacks, and that everyone is required to bring a simple dish in a disposable container. Nothing too complicated or requiring elaborate set up. Assign someone like your postpartum doula, or a friend, the task of trying to subtly get people out the door by the end of two hours by starting to clean up, which is usually a polite, discreet signal.

Post-pregnancy Activity Review

Engage in *minimal* activity, not even housework for the first three weeks. After three weeks, light activities can be resumed. Grant yourself the time and space to recover by giving yourself permission to spend most of the next thirty to forty days at home with your new baby, other children, husband/partner, and close family members.

Explain to Other People

Explain to those people close to you that you will predominately be resting for the first six weeks after pregnancy. Be prepared for people to have their own opinions and expectations of the activities a new mother should be doing, as the idea of a "designated resting period" will most likely be a new concept. This will ensure everyone has a complete understanding of the activities you will, and won't, be engaging in. If anyone starts to give you a hard time, explain politely that the rates of post-pregnancy emotional disorders in the United States are at 80% of all new mothers, and that you'd rather not be part of those statistics. You want to be a part of the 20% that has a healthy recovery! There's enough information on the Internet for them to search and have this realization for themselves. This time is for you to recover, and to lovingly assimilate your new baby into your life and lifestyle. This adjustment period becomes even more difficult to manage if a mother's health is jeopardized by engaging in activities that can be put off for a few weeks. If you really cannot rest, then prioritize everything you feel you *must* do. Anything that is not important, delay it for at least three weeks, and everything else can be put off until after six weeks.

If You Are More Than Six to Eight Weeks Post-pregnant
You certainly can still follow the above guidelines because your body is telling you that something isn't right. You may not be able to have complete rest at this stage, but make it a point to slow things down if you've resumed normal activities too soon. Follow these recommendations for one week and see how you feel. Your energy levels should improve. You can relax some of the recommendations if you don't want to follow them strictly, just pay attention to your body. If something makes you feel noticeably better, or improves your energy levels, continue with it.

POST-PREGNANCY WISDOM
Don't engage in anything too taxing that will expend energy. You will need all of your energy to take care of your newborn, which is taxing enough. Designate the time to take care of yourself, and in turn you will be able to take care of your family even better. If you don't take the time, you run a real risk of extending the time needed for your recuperation beyond what you had envisioned.

NINE
Post-pregnancy Precautions: Personal Care

The post-pregnancy precautions in this chapter regarding personal care centers around keeping a mother's core temperature stable and not engaging in activities that may have a negative effect on the body's ability to increase the internal temperature back to the normal level of 98.6˚F (37˚C). Also included are insights from experts in the field of maternity recovery, who provide modern, alternative healing solutions for recovery that are becoming popular with moms the world over. All in all, a mommy must remember to continue to be gentle with her healing body, and to engage in recovery activities for the first few weeks not do too much too soon.

1. Showering and Bathing

I mentioned avoiding taking cool or cold showers. It is also advisable to blow-dry your hair after a shower or bath and not allow your hair to dry naturally. Think about it, the two primary areas our body heat is released is through the head and feet. Remember when you were a kid, and your mother told you not to go out with a wet head? Or, when you had a head cold and you were told not to get your head wet as this will expose the wet skin on your head to cool air and you could get sicker? This is the same principle, a wet head allows heat to be released from the body at a faster rate, thus cooling off the body and causing us to "feel a chill." This is a time when we are trying to keep the heat in and the cold at bay.

> **A TRADITIONAL POSTPARTUM PRACTICE**
> A well known postpartum practice in Asia is for a woman not to wash her hair until her baby's umbilical cord has fallen off, or not to wash her hair for the entire designated postpartum recovery period. It is thought that by not having a wet hair this prevents a chill from entering the mother's body.

There is a method of bathing or showering in traditional cultures recommended for women after delivery that will not shock their body. Starting on your right side, wet your foot, shin and thigh, continuing up to your torso, arm, shoulder, and head. Then, do the same for your left side, again working your way up to your head last. The notion behind starting on the right side is that our heart is on the left side of our body.

Therefore, we start with the right side so as not to shock the heart, and in turn chill the body. It's just another way of being gentle with yourself.

As you will be handling your newborn all the time, you have to make sure cleanliness and good personal care is a top priority, to reduce exposure of germs to your baby, as well as yourself especially if you have had an episiotomy or a caesarean procedure. Your wounds and the surrounding area need to be kept extremely clean.

2. Wearing Socks

This recommendation follows the notion that you have to keep as much of your body heat in as possible, and not let it escape or be lost. A common post-pregnancy recommendation is to wear socks or foot coverings at all times, so your feet don't come into contact with a cold floor, ground, or surface, thus causing a chill. Yes, this recommendation applies even in the summer time, so please wear something on your feet at all times.

POST-PREGNANCY WISDOM

Take care of how you walk, paying particular attention to the big toes so as not to bump or stub them. It is believed the body may become very weak and develop shivers.[1] This belief originates from the natural healing art of Reflexology, or Zone Therapy, that was introduced to the United States in 1913. Reflexology involves applying pressure to the feet, hands, or ears that have reflex points which or correspond to every part, gland, and organ of the body. Reflexologists claim the area of the big toe is said to be the point on the human body that is connected, or *reflex*, to the uterus.[2]

---

3. Engaging in Sex after Childbirth

The standard recommendation is to wait at least six weeks before engaging in sex. Many women in traditional cultures refrain for one hundred days if they do not feel up to it. There shouldn't be any rush or undue pressure by your husband or partner to engage in sex before you feel ready. The perineum area could become irritated or easily re-torn if not careful. Or, you just may not be into having sex for a few months and that's OK. Convey this to your significant other, because if you do engage in sex before you are ready, it may negatively affect your state of mind.

4. Wrapping Your Torso, Belly and Hips

A major concern for new moms is how to regain their pre-pregnancy body and flatten their tummy after delivery. This leads many women to seek out a modern version of the ancient practice of belly binding. The idea behind a post-pregnancy tummy wrap

114

is simple; to support the abdomen area by holding in the flabby tummy skin and fat so it doesn't hang, relieving the skin tissue from downward stress. Not only can further or new stretch marks be caused by hanging skin (depending on how much weight has been gained during pregnancy), but water retention and flatulence (or trapped air in cells) doesn't release as easily if there is tension caused by on the skin caused by hanging.

Do post-pregnancy belly wraps really work?
A common question still asked by most women is, "Do post-pregnancy belly wraps *really* work?" The short answer is, yes, without a doubt. Not only does a properly designed wrap help a woman reshape her stomach, it also provides needed support to the organs of the perineal area after birth by providing pressured support of the hips.

In addition to retained fat, water and air, are expanded organs in the womb area such as the cervix and vagina. The water retained by cells supported the amniotic fluid level surrounding the baby. The purpose of the air is to cushion the baby, internal organs and bones when a woman's center of gravity shifts as her baby grows larger and larger. This is why a woman gets more and more swollen during the last months of pregnancy. When the baby is born the excess water and air are no longer needed and the cells will naturally release and shrink back to their pre-pregnant size.   The purpose of a post-pregnancy wrap is to speed up this process with constant pressure on the abdomen and torso area.

BEWARE:
Shapeware vs. Post-Pregnancy Supportive Garment
Women need to be aware of the difference between a garment whose purpose is to be worn under clothes in order to compress the body to appear smaller, and a garment that is specifically designed to give support to a post-pregnant recovery body. They are two garments with very different purposes. Dr. Nor Mokhtar, a very well known obstetrician and gynecologist in Malaysia, makes an excellent comparison of the two types of garments, as well as gives a simple medical explanation of how, and why, a post-pregnancy garment helps a post-pregnant body in an article entitled, *A Belly Good Wrap*, (don't you love the title?) published by The Star newspaper. The following is an excerpt from the original article.[3]

"Mothers need to be aware that the shapeware market has been flooded with companies selling belly wraps, abdominal binders, body shapers, and girdles that are conveniently

labeled as "postpartum or post-pregnancy products". Many of these companies make unfounded claims that their post-pregnancy compression girdle or wrap will shrink your uterus, tighten your abdominal muscles, fade stretch marks, and return you to your pre-pregnancy figure in no time. We are all fans of shapewear and it's an excellent way to smooth and slim your body for a specific outfit, especially for a special event; however, shapewear is not appropriate support for a post-baby body."

During pregnancy, musculoskeletal changes are stimulated by hormone secretions and the continuous expansion of the uterus. Some of these changes include:

Abdominal wall expansion and abdominal wall separation (Diastasis recti)
The growing fetus and the increasing weight of the baby putting pressure on the muscles can stretch the abdomen as much as 50%. The abdominal muscles (rectus abdominis) on either side are joined by a narrow fibrous strip (linea alba), which thins as it stretches. Also, the hormonal changes which happen during pregnancy cause connective tissue to soften.

When the muscles separate, their strength is reduced and this can lead to back pain. The condition is more likely to occur where the abdominal muscles were weak prior to pregnancy. It is vital that the abdominal wall returns to its pre-pregnancy location to protect internal organs and properly support the torso. Using a post-pregnancy wrap may help with this problem.

Spine and Posture Realignment
Posture is greatly affected as a baby grows larger in the womb. The pelvis tips forward to counterbalance the baby's weight, which causes the pubic bones and tailbone to move backward, increasing the arch in the lower spine and creating a lordotic posture.

The upper spine simultaneously responds to this structural change by increasing its curvature, which rounds the shoulders forward, collapses the chest inward, and slides the head forward, creating a kyphotic posture. The combination of the kyphotic/lordotic posture results in the classic "S" shaped spine of a pregnant woman and is a direct result of a shifting centre of gravity.

This shifting of a woman's center of gravity and spine can affect the nervous system and cause aching, weakness, and numbness in the body.

Pelvic floor relaxation
The pelvic floor provides balance, body stabilization, and vital organ support. The pelvic

floor is the base of the core muscle system, attaching to the abdominal muscles and the sacroiliac joints. During pregnancy, hormones cause ligaments to stretch, which loosens the pelvic floor structure. This natural realignment allows the pelvic bones to open for the baby's birth and makes you feel a bit wobbly on your feet.

After the birth of your baby, the pelvic floor can remain loose and unstable for up to five months. Because the pelvic floor acts as the support system for the lower intestine, colon, and bladder, these vital organs may be less supported for a few months immediately postpartum. This lack of organ support is the primary reason why women suffer incontinence when coughing, sneezing, or laughing after giving birth.

Cesarean incision support
One of the major benefits of a post-pregnancy garment is that it can help to speed up recovery after a cesarean delivery. The girdle supports the muscles around the incision site and therefore helps to reduce pain. As this makes the wearer more mobile and active, it helps to promote recovery. Again, a number of women who used a girdle after a C-section have reported significant benefits from doing so.

Back Support
A post-pregnancy wrap helps to support your back and so relieves some of the back pain associated with the immediate post-natal period. This also helps to reduce the strain involved in lifting and carrying your baby as well as provides back support when breastfeeding as most mothers don't know they are slouching.

Properly designed and manufactured postpartum body garments will provide 360 degree support to assist in abdominal wall muscle retraction, improve posture, stabilize loosened ligaments, and provide support to the torso while vital organs returned to their pre-pregnancy position. For the best results, start wearing a post-pregnancy garment as soon as you can after giving birth and then continue to wear it each day for at least 40 days and even longer if you are not satisfied with the results.

When purchasing a post-baby body wrap please the following features in mind:
  i. Design
     Most modern post-pregnancy wraps only support the tummy area, which is just one area where the healing process is taking place. A longer design takes into account the other organs in the pelvic area that need temporary support as they shrink and become realigned. The design that provides the most comprehensive support should be long enough to wrap the area from under the breast to just mid-hip or just below the buttocks.

THE MOMMY WRAP

A longer design of a post-pregnancy wrap provides a holistic support to all of the abdominal and pelvic organs, including the muscles, in the pelvic area. Support to the pelvic area is <u>very important</u> in the immediate weeks after birth as a mommy's cervix dilates 10 cm when active labor is reached; this is equivalent to the size of an average bagel. Therefore the pressure of a longer Mommy Wrap on the hip area helps the cervix shrink and allows the pelvic muscles to heal without being further stretched. Such wraps are known to help heal diastasis recti with the constant supportive pressure on the abdomen area. Even if a longer wrap is worn for the first two weeks and then changed to a shorter wrap (that only supports the stomach area) for day time use it would be beneficial. Then the longer wrap can be worn overnight.

Below is a picture of a traditional longer Mommy Wrap. As you can see there is total support and no "muffin top" that can stick out on top or below. Western women who have worn such garments after giving birth have described them as, "a warm hug" holding their "floppy body" together, giving comfort.

ii. Material

The type of material is important so a skin rash doesn't develop. Unbleached cotton is recommended. The material should not be too elastic as post-pregnancy wraps are not meant to give or stretch too much, as this compromises the support of the organs.

iii. Tightness

A post-pregnancy wrap should be worn under loose clothes and tied as tightly as possible, but not too tightly until in causes major discomfort or cuts off circulation. The wrap should be worn for a minimum of twelve hours per day. For even better results wear it for twenty-four hours, removing it only when showering or bathing.

How to Make a Post-pregnancy Belly Wrap
You don't have to buy a pre-made post-pregnancy wrap, you can make one yourself. Go to a material store and buy 36-feet (12-yards) of unbleached, cotton material and wrap yourself. Tie one end of the material to a doorknob and start wrapping the cloth from mid-hip level making just one tie after the first wrap around the body to secure the materials; and then after each complete turn pulled the material tight and continue wrapping around your body to just under the breasts and then tie it off.

POST-PREGNNACY ADVICE

The day will come when you realize that your post-pregnancy wrap has done all it could to shrink your stomach area and the rest of the fat will be lost by exercise.

---

5. Strengthening of the Pelvic Floor

Two well known and experienced women provided insight into the very important topic of pelvic floor recovery after child birth. For advice on how a mother should begin her physical recovery, well-known international trainer Carolyne Anthony shares her views on the mentality mothers should adopt during their recovery, and expresses her support of wearing an abdominal wrap helps strengthen the pelvic floor. Biomechanical scientist, Katy Bowman, shared her view on Kegel exercise, the most widely known exercise for pelvic strengthening that is shaking up the childbirth community.

BEGIN YOUR RECOVERY GENTLY

Carolyne Anthony founded The Center for Women's Fitness, and designed her own unique Pilate's program for women throughout pregnancy and post-pregnancy. According to Carolyne, *"We need to give women permission to be 'postpartum.' Postpartum, not in the sense of an emotional illness, but to feel the normal heightened emotions as well as the condition a woman's body is indirectly after child birth. Nothing is wrong with recognizing this state. Women need to understand that it is a journey into another way of life that needs time to adjust to. Some women have a great transition and move forward naturally, but for others, it takes more time to adjust, especially if their new life, including a new baby, is totally different from the one they left behind.*

Most importantly, for new mothers, is to be acknowledged. Yes, they are very thankful for the healthy baby, but they are dealing with a huge change in life and sometimes they are frustrated and resentful. These are normal feelings that should not be brushed aside and dismissed. The issues they have with their bodies are also real and need to be dealt with.

However, when it comes to exercise, especially as a post-pregnancy exerciser, many programs do not take into consideration that a body after birth is different from the pre-

---

pregnancy one; and while it is different, it is by no means worse. If we all changed our mindset about how we should look as young girls, young women and then new mothers, older mothers and finally the grandest achievement of all-GRANDmothers, we would see that each stage of our lives is to be experienced in the present and to accept the body changes that come with it. So often I hear people trying to "get back into shape" after their babies. What shape would that be? You now have a body that has just done something amazing! Treat it with the respect and love it deserves and understand that recovering the body after birth is about restoring, strengthening and nurturing.

Exercise need not be intense and overwhelming to be beneficial. Just after birth, many women can begin a program of restoration using deep breathing and simple movements of their bodies. The exercises should be simple enough to perform anywhere and at any time. Rehabilitation of the pelvic floor, realignment of the pelvis to the spine and general stretching and releasing are all truly beneficial and will work wonders even though they are gentle.

I believe in the Asian tradition of binding (using a post-pregnancy wrap) the abdominals of the post-pregnant woman and even encourage them to perform their gentle exercises while using a tummy binder. The binder technically holds both the ribcage and pelvis stable, allowing the overstrained surrounding muscles to realign without undue stress. Nutrition and rest are equally important to help restore the body.

Beyond calming and relaxing the new mother, deep abdominal breathing will also act as a pump for the lymph system and will help remove excess hormones and fluid from the body. Deep abdominal breathing also activates the deepest abdominal muscle - the tranversus abdominus, as well as the pelvic floor, and helps to strengthen these muscles. All in all, the first few weeks post-pregnancy should be a period of quiet gentle nurturing of both the mother and child, filled with respect and awe for the miracle that has just occurred."

Carolyne Anthony has been in the fitness, Pilates and dance world for over thirty years, devoting herself to building movement programs that address the needs of the pregnant and post-pregnant woman. Carolyne is also a Birth Doula and Esoteric Healer. In 1994 founded The Center for Women's Fitness that includes 12 host sites worldwide and has certified over 500 instructors in her methods. For more information visit: www.thecenterforwomensfitness.com.

INCONTINENCE OR WEAK PELVIC FLOOR

According to Katy Bowman, a biomechanical scientist and Director of the Restorative Exercise Institute, eighty percent of all women, not just those that go through pregnancy and birth, end up with a weak pelvic floor. Below is advice that she presents in her pelvic floor programs:

"Problems with the pelvic floor are often misunderstood to mean that these muscles are too loose. In reality, most pelvic floor weakness and damage during delivery stems from excessive tension -- muscles that are too tight.

A normal pelvic floor, with the correct amount of tension, has the ability to support the weight of the pelvic organs as well as the fetus, but can also relax correctly at the appropriate times, i.e. bathrooming or birthing. Signs that the pelvic floor tone is compromised are small leaks from the bladder in everyday situations like laughing, sneezing, running and so on."

The most commonly recommended exercise, to recover and strengthen the pelvic floor, is the Kegel. The Kegel consists of squeezing (or tensing) and then relaxing the muscles that make up a portion of the pelvic floor. Bowman, however, makes a compelling argument that Kegels are a small part of what is needed to strengthen the pelvic floor and that too many Kegels can actually do more harm than good.

"Pelvic floor issues arise not from the one, two, or even five pregnancies a woman has, but from a failure to use the pelvic muscles, which include the piriformis, hamstrings, and gluteals, in a more-natural way," says Katy.

An advocate for the daily deep, bathrooming squats found in our ancestral behavior, Katy suggests that for optimal pelvic floor strength, we prepare or repair our pelvic muscles in a more holistic fashion. Bathrooming squats are much deeper than fitness squats and still remains a popular position to relieve one's self in Asia and traditional cultures. Bathrooming squats are referred to as the "natural position" to go to the bathroom. The first toilets were designed as squat toilets in out-houses; while the modern sit-down toilet became the preferred design in the west. Due to the preference of squat toilets, where women must get in a bathrooming squat position, pelvic floor dysfunction and uterine prolapse (a falling or sliding of the womb from its normal position into the vaginal area) is not as common in Asia like in many Western countries.

To prevent excessive internal pressure (called the Valsalva maneuver), relax the pelvic floor, don't suck the belly in, and hold onto something if need be. Once down, attempt to hold it for thirty to sixty seconds, as long as you aren't tensing your muscles. Two to three squat sessions throughout the day strengthens the buttocks, which help lengthen the pelvic floor back out to the correct length for optimal strength. Katy is depicted doing this deep squat at eight months pregnant (her tummy is blocked by her leg and arm). As you can see the heels are supported while doing this.

Crucial to the deep squat strengthener is the untucking of the tail bone. This untucking motion can be worked on even when not in a squat throughout the day by bending over holding onto a counter top, and lifting the tailbone until a stretch is felt down the back of the legs.

Katy also recommends for best results, spend more time lengthening the hamstrings and calves throughout the day. Squats take awhile to safely achieve, especially when the muscles are tight. She recommends doing bathrooming squats four to five times a day before, during, and after pregnancy. A strong, but supple, pelvic floor can improve both delivery and recovery.

Katy Bowman's work indicates that strong gluteal muscles are needed in order to have a perfect pelvic floor – not too strong, not too tight, but just right. This could be the missing link for many recovering postnatal moms!

Katy Bowman currently directs the Restorative Exercise Institute at-large. Analyzing human movement (biomechanics) was typically reserved for athletes and special populations, until biomechanical scientist Katy Bowman decided to apply these same engineering principles to the every-day use of the "human machine" for the purpose of reducing common disease. Katy provided the photo of the bathrooming squat above. For more information, visit: www.alignedandwell.com.

6. The Use of Aromatherapy for Anxiety and Emotions

Aromatherapy is the practice of using essential oils extracted from aromatic plants to restore or enhance health, beauty and well-being.

AROMATHERAPY FOR POSTPARTUM EMOTIONS

Master Aromatherapist Elizabeth Reynolds has been studying the human psyche, emotional and physical well-being, and their relationship to essential oils for over twenty years. Her most recent research included developing a line of essential oil blends specifically for prenatal and post-birth support that has had successful results in decreasing pre and post-pregnancy anxiety. *Elizabeth explained, "The use of essential oils in healing and spiritual practices dates back thousands of years. The National Center for Biotechnology Information (NCBI) has over 10,200 essential oil biomedical literature citations and abstracts. In my personal aromatherapy practice of over twenty years, I have witnessed both the physical and emotional benefits of essential oils hundreds of times; human emotions consistently respond to expertly blended essential oils. There is a direct connection between the olfactory bulb and the hypothalamus, providing a natural and effective connection to the glands in the brain that secrete neuro-chemicals affecting well-being.*

When my studies began to include essential oils to address symptoms of anxiety for women experiencing heightened post-pregnancy emotions, my expectations were reserved. I was skeptical that essential oils would in fact have an impact on the diverse, and sometimes hormonally driven, emotions after childbirth. I was pleased to discover that a clear pattern emerged from the test trials in which the blend of essential oils specifically selected for pre and post-pregnant women provided relief from anxiety and promoted deeper sleep. In a number of cases the essential oils were custom blended, according to a client's responses to the aromas of individual essential oils. Concerning the use of essential oils during or post pregnancy, I strongly recommend seeking a qualified aromatherapist experienced in custom blending."

Elizabeth Reynolds is the founder of Elizabeth Reynolds Lux Aromatics. She is a Co-Coordinator for Postpartum Support International, in Ventura County, California. Elizabeth is also the personality behind the well known, on-line aromatherapy, company Crown Chakra Café. For more information, visit: www.luxaromatics.com.

How the brain processes the aroma of essential oils

The methods by which essential oils are used therapeutically are inhalation, topical and in some rare cases, internally.[1] Inhalation has the quickest effect, because the molecules of the essential oils impinge on the olfactory bulb via the nasal cavity and thereby the limbic part of the brain. The limbic system controls your heart rate, blood pressure, breathing, memory, stress level and hormones, which is why essential oils can have a powerful effect on a person's mood and well-being. Effective methods of inhaling essential oils are from a tissue or palms of the hands, diffusing them in a vaporizer or diffuser, and by adding drops of essential oils to bathwater. Massage is also an excellent delivery system when essential oils are combined with a carrier oil such as grape seed or almond oil.

POST-PREGNANCY NOTE
Results of aromatherapy are specific, individualized and will vary from person to person. Each person can be impacted differently by an essential oil and results may be influenced by a person's surroundings, the time it is used, or the mood at the time of usage.

Documentary in the Making: After Birth Project

Elizabeth is directing and producing the After Birth Project, an eye-opening documentary, along with co-founder Joanna Whitlow of For Moms and Babies. The After Birth Project will expose the startling and largely unknown facts and conditions existing in the American culture for families after the birth of a child, which, for a mother, can be one of the most isolating times in her life. The film will also raise awareness and advance education around the needs of the postpartum woman and her family. More information visit: www.afterbirthproject.com.

---

[1]Consulting with a qualified aromatherapist is strongly recommended.

TEN

Herbs to Avoid While Breastfeeding

Breastfeeding mothers need to take extra care when consuming herbal products because even though herbs are natural, they are not always safe, as everything a mother consumes will be passed to her baby. Components in herbs may be passed through breast milk and ingested by a nursing baby just as easily as the foods we eat, and the medicines we take. Many herbal products contain ingredients that have effects similar to certain medications and could be potentially dangerous to a nursing infant. As the effect and concentration of herbs found in teas, liquids, pills, and food supplements may vary, breastfeeding mothers should be cautious and selective in their use of any herbal preparations. Please remember that breasts have no filter mechanism.

Herbs occur in natural form; therefore, the amount of an active ingredient may vary from leaf-to-leaf and plant-to-plant. New mothers should be aware of herbs that are safe, and even beneficial, while breastfeeding, as well as which herbs should be avoided. Below is a list of common and well-known herbs to avoid while breast feeding, as they contain constituents that may be harmful to the mother or baby, or, because they can decrease the supply of breast milk.

Herbs to Avoid

Common Name	Scientific Name
Alder Buckthorn	*Rhamnus frangula*
Alkanet	*Alkanna tinctoria*
Aloe	*Aloe barbadensis*
Basil	*Ocimum basilicum*
Bearberry	*Arctostaphylos uva ursi*
Black Cohosh	*Cimifugia racemosa*
Bladderwrack	*Fucus vesiculosus*
Blood Root	*Sanguinaria canadensis*
Blue Cohosh	*Caulophyllum thalictroides*

Bog Myrtle	*Myrica gale*
Borage	*Borago officinalis*
Buchu	*Barosma betulina*
Bugelweed	*Lycopus europaeus*
Butterbur	*Petasites hybridus*
Cascara sagrada	*Rhamnus purshiana*
Cat's Claw	*Uncaria tormentosa*
Chaparral	*Larrea tridentate*
Chinese Rhubarb, Da Huang	*Rheum palmatum*
Cinchona bark	*Cinchona spp.*
Coltsfoot leaf	*Tussilago farfara*
Comfrey	*Symphytum officinale*
Elecampane	*Imula helenium*
Ephedra/Ma Huang	*Ephedra sinica*
Goldenseal	*Hydrastis canadensis*
Greater Celandine	*Chelidonium majus*
Guarana	*Paullinia cupana*
Jasmine flowers	*Jasminum pubescens*
Joe-Pye Weed	*Eupatorium purpureum*
Kava Kava	*Piper methysticum*
Indian snakeroot	*Rauwolfia serpentine*
Licorice	*Glycyrrhiza glabra*
Madder	*Rubia tinctorum*
Male Fern	*Dryopteris filix-mas*
Mayweed, Stinking Mayweed	*Anthemis cotula*
Mate	*Ilex paraguayensis*
Parsley leaf	*Petroselinum crispum*
Peppermint leaves	*Mentha piperita*
Prickly Ash	*Zanthoxylum americanum*
Pulsatilla plant	*Anemone pulsatilla*
Rhubarb	*Rheum palmatum*

Sage	*Salvia officinalis*
Saw Palmetto	*Serenoa repens, Sabal serrulata*
Senna	*Cassia spp.*
Spearmint leaves	*Mentha spicata*
Tobacco	*Nicotine tabacum*
Wintergreen	*Gaultheria procumbens*
Wormwood	*Artemis absinthium*
White Willow	*Salix alba*
Yellow Dock	*Rumex crispus*

Post-pregnancy Recommendations[1]

- Avoid the pharmacologically active herbal teas.
- Drink herbal teas in moderation.
- Limit intake of any herbal preparation that combines several active ingredients.
- Always check labels. Even vitamins and common herbal products such as Echinacea, ginkgo, or ginseng may contain herbs that should not be used by breastfeeding mothers.
- Use only brands that have ingredients clearly marked on the label as well as the expiration date and the name of the manufacturer and distributor.
- Be sure to check with your physician before taking any natural remedy since it could interact with other medications you are taking or need to take.

Commons Questions by Moms

Common questions I get from Western moms are regarding the safety for a breastfeeding baby when taking such herbal remedies. The percentage of breastfeeding women is much higher in Asia than in the United States and other Western countries, and through centuries of evidence-based proof, the natural remedies have been proven safe. Normally the only adverse effect that women look out for is whether their baby gets diarrhea. If this occurs they stop taking the herbs until the diarrhea passes. After it passes, they being taking herbs again but at a lower dosage, all the while monitoring their baby for adverse reactions.

However, always seek advice from a certified professional specializing in herbal medications such as a naturopath doctor or herbalist before purchasing any herbal product. Your doctor, pediatrician, childbirth professional, or a certified lactation consultant can be approached, but they may not be intimately familiar with herbal medications. Herbs can be powerful medicines and should not be used frivolously or unnecessarily. However, with careful consideration of all options, you may find that taking an herbal supplement while breastfeeding is a perfectly safe and legitimate option.

Known herbs useful after birth include stinging nettle to rebuild the blood lost during birth, turmeric, to help prevent breast inflammation, and oat-straw to nurture the nerves and to help prevent nervous exhaustion. These herbs also increase milk supply, so keep an eye on your supply and reduce or increase your dosage of these herbs as necessary.[2]

POST-PREGNANCY PRECAUTION

If you do not have low milk supply and take an abundance of herbs and foods to increase your supply, you may create unnecessary difficulties for yourself such as over-supply, engorgement, plugged ducts, or mastitis. Your baby may develop colic from too much foremilk, or sucking difficulties due to an overly strong let-down reflex, both of which are common with over-supply. Use such herbs wisely, and reduce or stop their use if you notice such problems.[3]

ELEVEN

Turmeric, the Healing Spice

Long before modern medicine, Mother Nature gave us the gift of medicine in the form of natural herbs and spices in a variety of plants, leaves, stems, roots, and bark. In many instances all the parts of an herbal-healing plant has healing properties, and may be consumed. Such plants and spices were the primary component of nature's original healthcare system and utilized to treat most illnesses.

QUESTION: What do you think modern pharmaceutical medicine was founded on?
ANSWER: Herbal medicines.

Herbal products are used in many countries during post-pregnancy recovery to help with the body's internal healing. While breastfeeding, the amount ingested of a single herb is vital as a high dosage of a single herb should not be taken. However, herbs and spices used as a food additive, or in spice blends, are normally perfectly safe because the amounts are negligible.

A Commonly Used Spice after Child birth: Turmeric (Curcuma longa)
One particular spice that I'd like to highlight is turmeric. Turmeric has been used for four thousand years to treat a variety of ailments, such as: [1]

- Alzheimer's disease
- Bronchitis
- Cancer
- Colds
- Depression
- Diarrhea
- Fever
- Fibromyalgia
- Gallbladder disorders
- Heartburn
- Headaches
- Intestinal gas
- Jaundice
- Kidney problems
- Leprosy
- Liver problems
- Loss of appetite
- Lung infections
- Menstrual problems
- Stomach bloating
- Stomach pain
- Water retention
- Worms

Turmeric is one of the most commonly found ingredients used in post-pregnancy preparations around the world.

Medicinal Amounts vs. Safe Amounts

Taking turmeric supplements in medicinal amounts is unsafe during pregnancy. In this case, 300–400 mg per day, or more, is considered a medical amount.[2] Turmeric is known to be a uterine stimulant and could cause miscarriage as it could possibly promote a menstrual period, or stimulate the uterus, putting the pregnancy at risk.[3] Western scientists make the unfounded claim that there isn't enough information to rate the safety of turmeric during breast-feeding so it's best not to use it. This is a shame as women in Eastern countries have benefitted from turmeric for centuries. Let me explain how women in Eastern countries safely consume this wonderful healing spice while breastfeeding.

Why turmeric works

Turmeric contains curcumin, which has antitumor, antioxidant and anti-inflammatory properties. Curcumin is a remarkable substance that scientists have studied for its abilities to fight cancer.[4]

Healing Teas

There are many wonderful herbal tea blends consumed by new mothers in traditional cultures that contain turmeric as an ingredient as it greatly assists a mother's circulatory system, as well as has anti-inflammatory and antibacterial properties.[5] Below is an example of one tea blend I'm familiar with as being effective in helping a woman's body with its internal healing from childbirth.

This tea is drunk for two weeks twice a day after breakfast and dinner.

Postnatal Tea	
Total weight of tea sachet	3 grams
Total percentage of turmeric per sachet	19.0%
Total amount of turmeric per sachet	0.38 grams

As you can see the amount of turmeric in this particular tea formula per sachet is *less than 1 gram* or 0.38 grams = 0.0076 teaspoon per sachet; considerably less than 300–400 mg, which is considered the dosage amount to have a medical effect so it is absolutely safe to consume while breastfeeding.

Uses of turmeric

You may not know this, but there is a distinct possibility that you may already be consuming, or being exposed to, turmeric on a daily basis.

Turmeric is used as a coloring agent in the following:[6]

- Biscuits
- Gelatin
- Butter
- Ice cream
- Canned chicken broth
- Pickles
- Cereal
- Pharmaceuticals
- Cheese
- Popcorn
- Cosmetics
- Salad dressing
- Sweets
- Yellow mustards
- Yellow cakes
- Yogurt
- Dyes for hair and fur.

As mentioned, anyone taking herbal products must monitor the effects within their body. A common adverse reaction is a skin rash. If this occurs, stop using the product, and the irritation should go away in a few days. Because the effects of herbs may not be as fast as modern medicine, people have the tendency to "over medicate" themselves and take more than the instructions indicate, causing adverse effects. A person must be patient when using herbal products.

Below are examples of the use of turmeric during pregnancy and post-pregnancy care.[7]

Pregnancy

One teaspoon of turmeric with hot milk in the latter part of the ninth month of pregnancy is known to ease delivery.

Post-pregnancy Care

Ones teaspoon of roasted turmeric powder with natural cane sugar after delivery strengthens the body internally, and relieves uterus swelling.

The Use of Herbs for Recovery After Childbirth

In many Asian cultures, from the third week after pregnancy (for two weeks), women take specific herbal remedies, and tonics, to assist shrinking the perineum organs, and to strengthen the womb and body (Post-Pregnancy I) Then at five weeks, a different herbal remedy is taken for a further two weeks, which continues the internal strengthening (Post-Pregnancy II). Well known remedies, passed down from generation to generation, have been proven safe for breastfeeding by ample evidence-based proof. The women claim taking such herbal medicines at these particular weeks after childbirth is key in regaining uterine health. However, one should still take caution and consume only trusted homemade or commercial products.

After-Birth Herbal Products for Recovery

There are many all natural after birth recovery products, used in non-medical ways, in the form of oils for massages, baths, sprays, washes, scrubs, and rubs, where the ingredients permeate the skin and help a woman's body with the internal, physical recovery and healing process. Such products fall into the category of "natural cosmetics and personal care items or aesthetic products" specific to post-pregnancy recuperation. More natural products are becoming available in Western countries via the internet, not yet in mainstream retail stores. This means you need to do your homework before purchasing such products, including looking carefully at the ingredients. It is law, in most countries, that the ingredients must be printed on the label or outer box. Therefore it is an easy task to go on-line and research the individual ingredients and understand what the affect would be on a mommy's recovering body.

Remembering the Daddy

I used to build houses and one thing I learned is the importance of foundations. A well-planned, strong and stable foundation is what a house—and a family—needs, and the earlier the planning, the better the outcome.

Patrick M. Houser

Something I have discovered about the expectant fathers I have had the pleasure of working with is that they are fathers first and men second. They are keen to engage with and support their partner and child in every way possible. Yet they have few role models to draw on and virtually no social precedence or gender-specific community support. Our children and our families' futures are worth more than this, aren't they?

Today, nearly 90% of fathers are present at the birth of their children. Long gone are the days when a father paced back and forth in a smoky hospital waiting room while his wife gave birth elsewhere, in a room full of strangers. Fathers are now more in alliance with the creative process of pregnancy and birth and, therefore, mothers and babies. They have also taken up the mantle of being nurturers over the last several decades and have increased their participation in the family. This trend is producing astonishing results, ones that are also based in science.

Let's examine the father's experience during pregnancy and birth and how he supports the new family relationship. (Side note: I do not profess that all fathers should, or should be required to, be at birth; however, I do think it is a missed opportunity if not. Secondly, the role of primary support for a mother is not necessarily gender specific.) What if we actually included fathers in a meaningful way? Studies reveal that hormonal activity in a father increases during his partner's pregnancy, and more so if he is present at the birth and closely involved after. When a father is intimate with his child, especially through skin-to-skin contact, his oxytocin production increases. Elevated oxytocin in a father is recognized as a key component in jump-starting and maintaining his nurturing instincts and bonding with his baby.

Unfortunately in the world we live in, divorce/separation rates are at an all-time high. If fathers are made to feel welcome, included and safe while the foundations of the family are being laid, it will have long-term implications for the family. Fathers will stay if they feel like they belong. The alternative, leaving, can also look like emotional withdrawal, overwork, alcohol and drug use, infidelity, and being absent in general, with the almost inevitable outcome being divorce/separation.

Fathers are acquiring tenderness and a sense of belonging from engaging with mother and baby during pregnancy, birth and after. This then establishes a more durable foundation for a lifelong loving relationship between father and child. Our society as a whole is also benefiting as a result of this transformation in fathers. Fathers are beginning to discover, and put into action, additional facets of their instinctive nature, paternal love. Can it be a coincidence that this timing correlates perfectly with fathers entering the birthing room and becoming lovingly involved in their children's arrival?

Fathers at Birth

There is a monumental paradox surrounding birth that goes largely unrevealed. During birth, a woman is doing the most female, womanly thing any woman can, and yet she is using what is typically considered to be "masculine energy." Birth is often very energetic and physically demanding. Fortunately, if she is not interfered with, she has significant hormonal resources to assist her in carrying out this "work."

A father at the birth of his child is at his best when he enters into stillness, a quiet and reflective presence, more characteristically female. He is best at birth when supporting the birthing mother with his listening and calm. Yet how is a man to achieve this and be truly helpful to his loving partner, without proper preparation? How can he feel safe in this female world? Most fathers are not aware that they are going to have an emotional experience surrounding birth. The intensity of a woman's labor can weigh them down significantly if they are unprepared, under-informed or not feeling safe and welcome. The moment of the birth itself, or upon first holding their newborn, can open a floodgate for many fathers. Everyone does better if he has the opportunity to prepare.

For the majority of mothers, a significant key to her successful pregnancy, birth, breastfeeding, and recovery is the quality of care she receives from the father. When the father cares for the mother, he is most certainly caring for his child as well. So what is the potential for a father's contribution to his family, and what benefits might he derive during this intimate time between a mother and child? A father can carry out virtually any and all forms of caretaking for a new baby, except breastfeeding. Plus if a dad is regularly skin to skin with his baby (Kangaroo Care) they both benefit. There is a major movement in Western countries to make kangaroo care the standard method of care for all newborn babies, both premature and full term, as there are many benefits for both baby and parents. Please refer to the appendix for information on the magical benefits of kangaroo care for newborns.

Mothers and babies need to continue their close, intimate relationship that began in the womb. A child's security depends on it, and breastfeeding is a big part of this need for a baby. It is important dads understand this and differentiate their role in early parenting. Remember, dads are different to mothers and approach life, and especially parenting, differently. Mothers also need to remember that they are the gatekeepers to the baby, and it is important they support "dad's way" of being with his new baby.

Half the responsibility of taking care of your baby lies with you and half with the father. Some mothers exclude fathers without even realizing it. Be aware not to make that oversight as fathers can play an important role. They just need the educational, physical, and emotional support, as well as patience from you so they gain confidence in their ability to take care of their child. In the end, I'd bet he will exceed your expectations.

The above has been adapted from wonderful articles by Patrick M. Houser, author of the, Fathers-to-Be Handbook, *a roadmap for the transition to fatherhood. Patrick is a parent and childbirth professional, workshop leader, freelance writer, and speaker at conferences worldwide. For more information, visit: www.FathersToBe.org.*

Gentle reader, you may want to ask the Daddy to read this as it will serve as an introduction for the both of you to the important and irreplaceable role of the father and how wonderful and fulfilling it could be for him.

POST-PREGNANCY WISDOM FROM IBU ROBIN LIM
Robin's suggestion to many expecting parents she meets with is for the mother to take care of the input, such as breastfeeding, while the father takes care of the output, like diapering. Robin says that many parents appreciate and can understand this simple explanation.

PREGNANCY ADVICE
It is just as important for a daddy, as well as a mommy, to attend lactation classes so the importance of breastfeeding is understood by each parent. Successful breastfeeding occurs because of the support a mother receives by the daddy.

TWELVE

The Daddy Plan

Hi, expectant mommies! At this time, you should pass the book over to the Daddy, or significant other in your life, such as your husband, partner, paternal figure to your child, or post-pregnancy care provider, as I've written this chapter especially for them. This chapter explains how he/she can effectively support you during the critical first three to six weeks after childbirth.

POST-PREGNANCY WISDOM

The global population is 6.8 billion, by my conservative estimate more than half or roughly 3.5 billion people live in countries that have well-developed post-pregnancy recovery traditions, and social support system, that guide a mother's recovery from pregnancy, labor and childbirth. It is a common traditional belief that taking care of a mother is an essential part of the post-birth process. Well managed postnatal care will greatly benefit both her, and her newborn baby, in the immediate time period as well as later in life. Well developed recovery programs do not exist in most Western countries as they were lost when births were moved to a hospital setting. Being that the most common complication from childbirth is post-pregnancy emotional illnesses, don't you think it's time such traditions are available to our mommies?

Dear expectant Daddy, Father-to-be, or Post-pregnancy Care Provider,
Welcome! I'm glad to have you here, and I hope this book finds you well and looking forward to the impending birth of your child. Are you getting excited at the prospect of being a father for the first time, or again? I hope so, as it is truly a wonderful event, this miracle of life being born, wouldn't you agree? Bringing home a new baby will be one of the highs of your life, but it will also be one of the most stressful and challenging periods at the same time, and men and women handle stress differently. You, and this mommy, must be on the same wavelength to get through the first weeks post-pregnancy, which normally can be quite challenging. Keep-in-mind, when the going gets tough, you will need one another for strength and support in the weeks, months, and years to come.

It's my hope that by the end of this chapter, you will realize that the immediate three to six week post-pregnancy period is the most important time period throughout the cycle of pregnancy, labor, and childbirth. This is when support is most needed and valuable, even more so than during childbirth in my opinion. This is why you should develop your own Daddy Plan, which serves as a precautionary measure in order to ensure this mommy has a strong and healthy recovery from pregnancy and childbirth. You will have all your questions answered by the end of the chapter and if you don't, my email address is at the back of the book. Email me and I can point you in the right direction.

A DADDY'S PERSPECTIVE FROM THE INSIDE...

You have been waiting for nearly ten months, survived the birth, now what? There is much anticipation leading up to the birth of your new arrival, i.e. will it be a girl or a boy, where will they sleep, what baby accessories do we need to buy, how will we know how to look after a baby and how will this little one impact our own lives and social needs?

The day finally comes around and mamma is ready to give birth. Every birth experience is different. I was calm on the exterior, helping my wife with breathing exercises and patting her down with a cool cloth, only to be spread eagled on my back after an onset of low blood sugar, being seconds away from fainting and crashing to the floor. Then, there were several nurses at my side administering fruit juice and a muesli bar with my wife screaming, "Hello! Who is having the baby here?" Eager to redeem myself after gulping down half a glass of fruit juice and a bite of a muesli bar, I jumped up and resumed the breathing exercises and dashed over to hand my wife a glass of water, only to receive a static electricity shock, causing me to jerk forward with the glass spilling the cold water all over my wife. At this point she told me, not so calmly, to get away from her.

I can clearly remember thinking, (whilst my wife was enduring hour after hour of painful contractions, having difficulty squeezing the little fella out, his head coning and finally a decision was made to perform an emergency C-section) what have i done here? This could possibly turn out to be the worst day of my life.

Finally, our boy was born, and I was able to hold him, what a relief and what an amazing feeling holding my little boy all swaddled up in his blanket. Did I instantly bond and love our new addition to our family? Not really. I can remember other fathers talking about their experiences and how it was the best day of their lives and the immense feeling of love and pride of holding their new born baby for the first time. Strangely I felt a sense of guilt for not feeling this. It wasn't until he was around four months old that I can honestly say that I began to really discover a strong long lasting bond with my son. This may have correlated to the fact that my boy was starting to interact more with his dad.

After the birth of my son, it was a big adjustment for me. My wife was constantly tired and her moods were more erratic than usual. All her energy levels and affection was directed at our new born and little to none flowed to dad. I had to reach the stage where I didn't take this personally. My days slipping out the door to go sports training, or meet friends for a beer at any time of the day were somewhat curbed.

All in all, it was a difficult and frustrating time for all of us as a family. Fortunately, more and more is being written about the importance of post-birth care and well-being of the mother. I feel more needs to be written about helping fathers in their roles during this period. I can remember feeling a little resentment towards my wife, as I was really trying my best to help out with the changing of diapers, cleaning and general well-being of the house, but receiving what I perceived to be little appreciation in return.

In retrospect, having more of an education of what to expect and the specific things I could do to help out my wife, would have given me a greater range of skills to deal with the whole post birth transition. Guys are geared to want to solve things, and giving us more knowledge and skills to do so is empowering and gives us back a sense of control. The situation is hard on us dads, but it's harder on the family. You can better handle the situation if you are prepared.

I still feel that moms and your new son and/or daughter are the most precious family members that need caring and support during this stage, but dads need to put some time into themselves so they have plenty of deposits in their own emotional banks in order that they have plenty to give to their family and fulfilling what we all want: To be the best father and husband that we can be.

Written by Scott McDonough father of Jordan, husband of, yep – me, Valerie Lynn.

Now to give you background, that you may or may not be familiar with. Therefore, please bear with me if you are familiar. First, I'd strongly recommend that you understand the range of emotions this mommy may experience in the immediate post-pregnancy period and be able to differentiate between something called maternity blues, which is must less serious than other postpartum-related mood disorders and anxieties, which are in chapter five. Just familiarize yourself, don't wait until it may happen as you could miss vital warning signs.

AFTER-BIRTH REALITY CHECK
Unofficial rates of women experiencing postpartum depression are as high as 20% in the United States and the statistics in other Western countries are comparable.

Below is an indication of how serious the postpartum epidemic is in America. The president of the leading educational institution on maternity heath and care has finally recognized this social problem as it has devastating outcomes for families and far reaching social effects.

Gerald F. Joseph, Jr, MD, president of The American College of Obstetricians and Gynecologists, the foremost important institution on maternity care, stated, "As ob-gyns, if we can focus more of our attention on the emotional and psychological health of our patients during pregnancy and postpartum (period), I believe our specialty can have a positive and significant impact on the overall health and well-being of women everywhere. I'm so passionate about postpartum depression that I've made it the theme of my presidential initiative and a major focus of the ACM's scientific program this year."[1]

"Postpartum depression is a type of depression that affects women after they give birth. About 13% of women experience postpartum depression in the first year after childbirth, and it can develop any time up to a year after a baby is born. Postpartum depression has deleterious effects on a woman's relationships, her functional status, and her ability to care for her infant. The reduction of postpartum depression is a US priority healthcare need and a major public health concern."[2]

Drug Addiction Withdrawal vs. Pregnancy Hormone Withdrawal

A woman's hormones are a thousand times higher when pregnant. When the baby and placenta are birthed, there is a severe drop in the hormone level, which her body had gotten used to during pregnancy, and therefore, it goes into a type of shock as it tries to rebalance itself. I compare this to a drug addict that quits drugs "cold turkey" and the after effects the body experiences in the form of withdrawal symptoms. This is the same type of situation. A new mother cannot control the after effects of her hormones rebalancing, which can come in the form of unstable emotions, crying, hot and cold flashes, panic attacks and anxiety, and so on. Such emotions flare up a few days after she gives birth and may last two to five days up to a few weeks and even months if a woman begins to recover in an unbalanced manner.

Post-pregnancy-Related Emotions

The most common misconception men have is that unstable post-pregnancy-related emotions are *not real*. This, plainly put, is totally incorrect. The unstable emotions women experience after childbirth are very real. There is a simplified chart in Chapter 5, please take a look at it and become familiar with the signs as it could help you in the future.

What Is Normal and What Isn't?

It is normal for a woman to experience unstable emotions for a few days, but if you observe consistent instability or negative emotions happening for five days, a red flag should go up, and you need have a heart-to-heart conversation with her to try and gauge what is going on inside her head. A conversation may be all it takes for her to tell you what she is feeling and needs help with. If the unstable emotions continue for a few more days, have a conversation, and if that doesn't suffice, a realistic next step is to get her professional help before any sort of postpartum anxiety or depression really sets in.

US Postpartum Depression Statistics

The official rates of postpartum depression (PPD) in the United States are 10%–15%. Based on the national figure of "clinically recognized births," which includes fetal losses, miscarriages, and stillbirths of 6.2 million, this equals 620,000–930,000 mothers. Unofficial figures are between 15%–20%, which equates to well over 1 million women are diagnosed with postpartum depression each year.

To make a comparison, more women are diagnosed with PPD than men are diagnosed with new cases of erectile dysfunction, or impotence, annually. The average number of new impotence cases in the United States per year is over 600,000.[3] Yet you wouldn't know it, considering the overabundance of erectile dysfunction ads and people falling all over themselves to discuss impotence openly.[4]

You may be wondering why you haven't heard about the topic of postpartum depression or know about it in detail. Some of the reasons include the following:[5]

- Lack of information available to the general public.
- The general unwillingness of women to speak about it for fear of embarrassment.
- Underreporting.

The First Three to Six Weeks after Delivery

During the pregnancy period, you don't get to have many personal experiences like a woman does while carrying a child, but rest assured that you are a pillar of support nonetheless, and the most important and effective role you could play is yet to come if you determine you are up for it and take on the responsibility. Of course, it is the role of "Daddy" or parental figure or another significant role in this child's life; however, the role that is crucial at the beginning is of *"post-pregnancy care provider."* This is a temporary role only lasting three to six weeks post-pregnancy, but one of great significance as the care and nourishment a woman receives during those few weeks while her body is transitioning from a pregnant to a non-pregnant state can determine whether she has a balanced or unbalanced recovery from childbirth.

Your role in supporting this mommy during her labor and childbirth is also an important role, one that you will never forget. The moment your child is born into this world will be a memory forever. However, the role that has more practical impact for your family is one of post-pregnancy care provider.

In order to ensure this mommy is placed on the path to a healthy, strong, and most importantly, balanced recovery from pregnancy and childbirth, complete rest is needed for at least the first three weeks. After three weeks, light activities and household chores can be resumed if her recovery consistently progresses and she is getting stronger week by week. After six weeks, gradually more and more activities can be resumed as she gets back into the routine of her normal life. However, be very wary during the first six weeks after childbirth. If the mommy takes on too much, she may start bleeding again. If she gets tired or exhausted easily, then don't push her as her body is not ready.

Please understand and give this pregnant mommy permission, in your mind and heart, to have most of the precious first six weeks after childbirth devoted to herself and her newborn. You will not be forgotten about, but she and her baby's welfare has to be a priority at this time. If this mommy's recovery isn't sound, then there could be very real post-pregnancy-related emotional conditions that could last many, many months. Just imagine how this would impact your life as well as this mommy's ability to function, take care of her newborn, and resume her normal life. It would be significantly affected. In this case, an ounce of prevention is worth a pound of cure.

POST-PREGNANCY ANALOGY: SERIOUS CAR ACCIDENT VS. CHILDBIRTH

Have you ever known anyone that was in a serious car accident or underwent serious medical surgery? I'm sure the person spent their recovery period lying in a hospital bed for weeks on end, doing nothing but allowing their body to rest and heal itself. In a few short weeks, you were able to see a remarkable recovery, and the person was up and around and well on the road to a sound recovery. Childbirth leaves the body in the same type of condition. Even though childbirth is a natural event, it is nonetheless traumatic to a woman's body and warrants the same form of complete rest to have a healthy and strong recovery. Most women don't know this and resume their normal life engaging in too much activity and doing too much too soon, which sets back their recuperation.

The reason I'm including a chapter directed to expectant dads, father figures, or primary post-pregnancy care providers is that I was touched and inspired by the e-mails I received from mothers, in addition to the comments I've read in forums where women shared their post-pregnancy stories about the very dark days they went through and how they couldn't tell anyone for fear of being ridiculed or not being believed. A common theme time and again was about husbands or partners not believing that they just didn't feel right but they didn't know why. It seems that, in general, men normally think such feelings are made up or that women recovering from childbirth are being drama queens.

Below are real comments from blogs, forums, or articles by women who had experienced postpartum emotions or mood disorders; names have been changed or left out for confidentiality.

REAL COMMENTS FROM REAL MOMS

"I felt trapped in a disgusting body and felt 100% that my husband did not want me anymore. I felt that my entire essence had been stolen, like I no longer had a soul and it was replaced with negative nothingness. I stopped cleaning my home, too (which is NOT my normal behavior). There was this tiny little voice in my head telling me nothing but bad things, and I was convinced that it was true. I didn't feel suicidal, but I felt like: what was the point in living. For some reason, it was worse at night time. Then finally one morning, I woke up and I knew I was feeling better. In three days time, I was better. My depression started at three weeks post-pregnancy and lasted a week but felt like much longer."[6]

"It's horrible to say," said Christina, reflecting on her depression following the birth of her first child. *"but here I had this beautiful new baby, and I just didn't care about her. The feelings of love just weren't there. All I could think about was how meaningless everything seemed. I managed to feed her and change her, but that was about it."*[7]

"Hi, I am suffering from postpartum depression. It's very scary. I have no support from my husband. He keeps saying "What's wrong with you." I yell too much. I get so irritated with my five-month-old and lose it with my two-year-old. Then I cry 'cause I hate the way I'm acting and love my kids so much. HELP! I don't want to do meds!"[8]

"I began to cry a lot, beginning about two weeks after my baby was born. I could not make decisions or organize my thoughts—even something as simple as preparing a grocery list was too hard to do. I could not concentrate to read more than one or two pages, even though I had always been an avid reader. I was overwhelmed with feelings

of guilt and anxiety and felt that I was a terrible mother. All of the little issues in life that were manageable in the past became huge and overpowering. Sleep was difficult, and I felt continually exhausted. I sought professional medical help and with medication, therapy, and the help of a strong support system, made it through the lengthy process to recovery."[9]

"If you had known me during this time, you would not have realized that I was falling apart inside. After eight weeks, I had a breakdown: I could not stop crying. I told my mom I knew something wasn't right. I told my husband I felt inadequate. No one knew how horrible I really felt because I put on a façade. That was the day I called the PPD hotline and spoke to a counselor who recommended a therapist in my area; that was fifteen months ago."[10]

The State of a Mommy's Body after Childbirth

Below is a brief review of the condition this mommy's body will most likely be in after giving birth.

- In a cold state
- Water logged, bloated, and swollen
- Carrying excess fat
- Sluggish circulatory and digestive systems
- Vaginal discharge (lochia)
- Joint pains
- Varicose veins
- Sore breasts
- Sagging breasts
- Episiotomy

- Flabby tummy
- Hemorrhoids
- Stretch marks
- Hot and cold flashes
- Pregnancy melasma
- Urinary or fecal incontinence
- Engorgement of breasts
- Uterine after-pains
- Hair loss
- Inducement, epidural, and cesarean affects

If you breeze through chapter six, brief details are provided of each condition. Experiencing even half of the symptoms above would make anyone emotional, or irritable, as well lose self-esteem and confidence. After nine months of pregnancy and the trauma of childbirth, a woman's body has the innate ability to heal itself in a matter of three to six weeks *if rest is allowed.*

Dads or Post-pregnancy Care Provider

Maternity or baby blues, postpartum anxiety, obsessive-compulsive disorder (OCD), depression, and psychosis unfortunately are *real.* No woman wants to suffer from such illnesses that render her incapable of taking care of her child or unable to function productively. Do your homework online and find out about such illnesses. Follow men's forums on the topic. Many times, women try to hide or ignore what they are feeling only to suffer an emotional breakdown as its part of American culture for women to be independent and super moms at all times. It would be hard for an independent woman not to be able to "balance it all"—a new baby, home, work, and so on - and then having to admit that she needs help. It may be something she would struggle with.

When we don't live up to our own expectations and can't understand why we are not functioning as we used to, it can be very frustrating. This frustration may be taken out on you, so let's do everything we can to avoid that. Make your home a trusting, supportive environment for this mommy to feel safe. This will enable her to confide in you if she feels like something is not right and, please, make sure you take her seriously if she does. Also, a new mother might not recognize depression or anxiety because she is tired, overwhelmed, or simply adjusting to life with a baby.[11]

REAL COMMENTS FROM REAL DADS

"We did not have a perfect marriage, but it was pretty good. About mid-pregnancy she wanted to leave, then she came back. Our baby is six months old now, and she wants to leave again. She says she feels numb and disconnected from me . . . In every other way, she seems to be normal. Is it possible that she seems happy in everything else she is doing, but she has singled me out?"[12]

"I believe my wife is suffering from a post-pregnancy mood disorder, but refuses treatment. I have tried to convince her to see a psychiatrist because she may need medication, but she says her issues have nothing to do with any physiological issue. She has asked me for a separation. I am at a loss for where to turn."[13]

Things you can do:
- Whatever you do, do not be judgmental about her recovery, as she may not know herself what will help. Emotional care is vital in this situation; and certainly don't be judgmental if this mommy begins to experience unstable emotions. If you are negative and make condescending comments that may make matters worse. Not a very good environment for a newborn. A supportive daddy is much more helpful than a negative one.
- Don't expect this mommy to entertain people and carry on as she did before the baby was born. She will have fatigue, whether she tells you or not; it is important for a recovering mother to get more sleep and rest than usual.
- Do not base this mommy's recovery on another mommy's experience. Each

woman is different and will have her own unique experience of recovering from pregnancy and childbirth. Do not set unrealistic benchmarks for her.

- Think long term. Keep-in-mind that six weeks is a very short amount of time to put her on the road to a strong, healthy, balanced recovery from childbirth.
- Understand what is happening to a mommy's body internally from Day One, or the day she gives birth.
- Understand postpartum depression is real, not made up.
- Research the cost of antidepressant usage over a one year period, and the side effects that such drugs have on both mother and baby. Breasts do not have filters, therefore everything a mother eats, drinks or puts into her body in any way is passed onto a breastfeeding baby.
- Understand the long-term effects of an unbalanced recovery will have on your life over the next year or longer.
- Accept that you may not understand what is happening at times and ask for ways how you can help. Otherwise, fall back on things that would comfort anyone—a foot or shoulder rub, a hearty bowl of soup, an hour of quiet time for the mommy. Reassure by giving her a simple hug, tell her she's a fantastic mom and doing really well and that you are proud of her for all that she's accomplished being pregnant for nearly ten months and then birthing your child.
- Understand that this mommy may be scared of her own thoughts and feelings and may not be sharing them with you. She may feel ashamed or afraid and try to hide what she is feeling or going through. Most women don't want to be judged as weak, as mental health problems are normally viewed negatively. Reassure her that this isn't the case, that you love her and will support her through thick and thin. It is better to seek professional help sooner rather than later. For the sake of the family unit, first contact may have to be done by you.
- If you can afford it, plan to have a postpartum doula during the transition period of welcoming the baby into your family and house, and/or have a traditional post-pregnancy practitioner come to provide postnatal treatments for the mommy at home. If you aren't familiar with doulas, a doula is someone (normally a woman) who provides nonmedical support to women and their families during birth, childbirth, and the post-pregnancy period.[14] There are several types of doulas: perinatal or antepartum, labor or birth, and postpartum or postnatal.
- A postpartum or postnatal doula assists the new family at home after childbirth for one child or multiples. Services may include nonmedical baby care, breastfeeding coaching, child-care tips, meal preparation, light household help, sibling care, and running errands. Each doula is different and may provide more, or less, services. You can read more

about doulas in the postnatal notes section in the back of the book.

• Understand what The Mommy Plan is all about and how it helps a woman develop her *Post-Pregnancy Plan* for her recovery from childbirth. Read the whole book if you are up to it, as it will only benefit you in the long run.

• This is a time to dig down and be strong, mentally and spiritually. Your patience will certainly be tested.

POST-PREGNANCY ADVICE

It would be beneficial if you look into the types of post-pregnancy services available before your mommy gives birth, and see if they suit her needs. However, there is no reason why you can't hire a doula weeks, or even months, afterwards to provide needed extra help. Consider having a traditional practitioner come to your home, as your mommy shouldn't go out too often, and shouldn't leave your baby during the first few weeks. I learned this the hard way. When my son was four weeks old I thought it would be alright if I left him with my husband to go into New York for a half day of work, but my son cried nearly the entire time! Even though I had fully stocked bottles (with breast milk) in the refrigerator he wouldn't take the bottle, and only wanted mommy. The poor little thing was so distraught, not to mention my husband was extremely stressed out! So my advice is to have services come to you if when at all possible.

Schedule Vacation Time or Holiday Time Around the Birth

By now you've come to understand that the Daddy Plan is a post-pregnancy plan that men develop for themselves during the immediate six to eight weeks after the baby is born, detailing the strategies that will be followed and having assigned responsibilities for yourself and for those people who are able to help out (including hired services). It should also include the recommended diet, activity, and personal care guidelines detailed in this book.

I'm hoping that this book has been obtained early enough and you are reading it while the mommy is still pregnant. I know this is a big request and tall order but, I'm hoping there is some way that you could be home for the initial three weeks post-pregnancy period. This would help significantly. I also know this may not be realistic in America, where most people can take only one to two weeks' vacation per year. Nonetheless, it is a possibility *not* to take vacation during the pregnancy period. Assuming you have two weeks paid vacation each year, take an additional week without pay, during the first three weeks after delivery. If this is possible, perhaps you can speak to your company and arrange a portion of your pay to be held each week during the time of pregnancy. This way when you take paternity leave and vacation time, it can be paid out at that time so you still receive income. Please try to strategize and come up with a feasible plan. Most women feel very isolated in the first weeks after childbirth, which is when an unhealthy recovery could set in.

Spending Most of the First Six Weeks at Home
Plan to live simply and spend most of this time at home. Encourage this mommy to stay at home reminding her not to engage in too much activity. Make your primary focus be the recovering mommy's needs and willingly take on household tasks. However, the primary task that would greatly help would be preparing nutritious meals. This should be your priority as a woman's recovering body needs to have certain foods to help her heal and avoid other foods that interfere with her body's innate healing capability. Please read Chapter 6 "Post-pregnancy Diet Don'ts" and Chapter 7 "Post-pregnancy Diet Do's," and you will have a sound understanding.
Other household responsibilities should be viewed as secondary. This will ensure this new mommy will be able to take better care of herself and the baby and recover in a shorter time period. Get a good book, some movies, or a project that can keep you occupied during the time when you aren't needed by the mommy.

If Possible, Have a Family Member Live In
Arrange for a family member to come over and help out or live with you for at least one month. I know for some people this can be trying, however this is a time for "all hands on deck" so it's worth putting up with a little inconvenience and setting aside differences. Explain how they would be helping out and make it clear that it's not just about taking care of the baby, and that this isn't a situation where you would be entertaining them. This person could be there even if you are able to take a few weeks off from work. It is very common in other cultures for a third person to live in for one month to six weeks when a new baby comes home. That way the household responsibilities are shared and everyone can get some downtime. Remember, this only is a temporary situation.

You may have to step out of your comfort zone and take on responsibilities that normally are the recovering mommy's, but rest assured that your extra efforts will be very much appreciated. This is a time to come together as a functioning family unit, not fall apart or argue about who does what.

If Extended Postpartum Emotions or Depression Occurs
In all cases of extended postpartum emotions, depression or other related emotional

illnesses, including postpartum psychosis, there is an extra burden placed on the father of caring for the children as well as caring for the mother. Fathers who endure this stress should not be embarrassed to ask for help from other family members, friends or therapists. In most cases a father will have to continue working while taking on the extra stress of caring for a legitimately ill wife, a new baby and any other older children. Postpartum illness burdens any family excessively, and asking for help, whether personal or professional, should not be seen by fathers, as a weakness in any way.[15]

According to the Postpartum Dads website,[16] one of the very few websites dedicated to helping dads dealing with mommies suffering from postpartum depression, the following are very common mistakes dads make without realizing that it may contribute to the depression.

Comparing this Mommy to Other Women
Saying things like, "Why can't you be more like Linda? She has it harder than you, and she doesn't spend her whole day in bed crying."

Getting Angry
The frustration and disappointment that some men feel can change to anger that they take out on their wives or partner. Yelling, threatening, and humiliating are some of the ways that the anger can express itself.

Distancing Yourself
For some men, dealing with postpartum depression is just too much for them, and they find it easier not to deal with it at all. Ways that men distance themselves from their wives/partners include working longer hours, not coming home, or not talking.

Trying to Handle Everything on Your Own
We can't overemphasize the need to get quality professional help. We know that it is much harder to do than it should be, but she deserves the best treatment you can find.

Trying to Talk Her Out of the Depression
You may have a great philosophy toward life and feel like you know exactly what she needs to do to get out of the depression. However, comments like "All you need to do is . . ." or "Honey, of course, you feel bad, look at how you spend your day just lying around all the time. What you should do is . . ." aren't helpful.

Not Being Open About Your Feelings

Men don't like to talk about their feelings. Read any Venus-Mars book! There is more than just your feelings at stake here. The safety and well-being of your child could be a real concern. Get over any fear you may have about your feelings and take action. Call an anonymous postpartum hotline for starters.

Ignoring the Depression

Plainly put, don't ignore it and think it will go away. It may be more serious than you think.

Not Making Her Health and the Well-Being of Your Family Your #1 Priority

After reading this chapter, I don't think you will make this mistake.

Creating a Treatment Plan

If you find yourself in a situation where this mommy may have the signs of postpartum depression, you must act quickly. One of the biggest challenges many men face is getting their wives to recognize that they are suffering from depression. Often women reject their husbands, children, family, and friends, and still do not realize they have a serious problem. Some women refuse to talk to their husbands and blame them for all their problems resulting in separation or divorce in the first year of the child's life.[17]

You must act *quickly* and create a treatment plan. Depending on the severity of the depression, you may need to play a critical role in creating and implementing the treatment plan. While you will be relying on professional doctors and counselors for the specifics of the plan, you may be in the best position to observe the results and provide feedback to the professionals. This mommy may not be capable of making appointments, keeping appointments, understanding instructions, and following through. The doctors may not be able to get a good understanding of her condition without your input and evaluation. Your active participation can greatly help her recovery.[18]

Dads Can Get Depressed Too

Every day, over one thousand new dads, or one in ten, in the United States become depressed.[19] The term that describes the emotions dads face is "postpartum dads." The feeling of excitement of a new baby wears off after sleepless nights, a crying infant, and fights with the mommy leave you going to work exhausted. You may find yourself becoming irritable or withdrawn.[20] This is more common than you might think as dads must also make adjustments in their life. If you find yourself beginning to feel this way, there are websites and associations dedicated to helping dads through their transitional time. Know that you are not alone and remembered alongside the mommy.

Even talking to a good buddy who has children, may shed some light on what you may experience. If this is not your first child, know that all pregnancies and births are different and if this mommy had a good recovery or a bad recovery after her first or subsequent children it doesn't mean this time around she will be the same. You have to be astute and look for clues to what she may be feeling or going through.

Much of the information in childbirth education classes is directed towards the mom's experience, however you do need to understand what is going to take place after your baby is born and therefore have realistic expectations. There are very few childbirth classes directed at men and taught from a dad's perspective – but they do exist. Do your research and attend one. Such classes address the unique set of challenges that dads face while being integral in the birth process and beyond. When you are prepared for the birth process, then your anxiety will be reduced and your confidence increased. The benefit to you would be that you would know exactly what role you would play and effective bonding techniques that you could use with your newborn baby. Such classes benefit a first time dad or a dad of successive children.

ADVICE FOR DADS, FROM A DAD
Below is advice from Joe Valley, M.A., Therapist & Daddy Educator, the founder of Empowered Papa and coach to new dads. Joe equips dads with the knowledge they need to be valuable birth partners and post-pregnancy care givers.

Dear Dads,
I want to talk about the guy's perspective for a moment, and how you as a dad fit into this postpartum or post-pregnancy time. Unlike the pregnancy and birthing time, you actually get to directly experience your child in a way not possible before – you get to hold your child. I remember holding my boy, Sacha, for the first time and getting that good skin to skin contact on my chest known as Kangaroo Care (KC). He was exhausted from his birth and immediately fell asleep. I got a snooze in there, too. Pure bliss. I was bonding with my son, and it gave my wife, Andrea, a chance to see that her husband was a caring dad.

Our primary role as dads during the weeks immediately following birth is that of post-birth caregiver and organizer of physical support. Why? Because Western culture has sadly forgotten about postpartum care and we don't live in large family groups much anymore, which is where a woman would normally find her support. When my son was born, we lived away from both of our families. My wife suffered a really tough postpartum depression--largely because of a lack of support and awareness of how to care for a mom while she cared for a baby.

This time after the baby is born is rarely spoken about. However, it is just as important as in pregnancy and birth. If you make it your personal mission to see to the health and well-being of mama and baby during this time, then you are going to experience the kind of ongoing joy and satisfaction that you've been looking for in this landmark event of your life.

I am a practicing therapist and coach, and I specialize in helping fathers through this most transformative event of their lives. Postpartum issues of sadness and depression are more common than you may think, and fathers are often times at a loss of what to do. The reason why I say that is because the sadness and depression may not appear logical or rational, and your normal conflict resolution skills may be temporarily ineffective. In my experience as a therapist I have found that the best things you can do for your partner during the postpartum time are to listen with sincerity and take nothing personally. Be easy on yourself, too, and make sure you talk to your friends about what is going on in your life. Friends are really helpful for us to gauge how we are doing. It's important for you to have the support you need during this time.

If you are an expectant dad now, then I encourage you to start your involvement in the birth of your child by saying this sentence out loud, "I am a dad." Seriously, it's going to help. You may not feel like a dad right now, yet you are one. You matter and can positively influence the pregnancy, birth and postpartum time. I also encourage you to get involved with the childbirth education. When you are prepared for the birth process, then you are able to reduce your anxiety and increase your confidence, which means that you can effectively bond with your new baby when you meet face to face for the first time.

Dads matter, and you play a valuable role of emotional support at the birth of your child and afterwards in a physical support role as post-pregnancy care provider. When you are prepared, then your partner is more likely to have a balanced recovery from childbirth and you will be able to celebrate your new role as a father.

Joe Valley has identified the need for fathers to have access to paternal information and has developed childbirth education classes specifically geared towards fathers. For more information about how you can support a new mother effectively visit his website: www.empoweredpapa.com.

There is a lot of good information on the websites below including real life postings by dads about their experiences.

Postpartum Dads: www.postpartumdads.org.
Postpartum Support International: www.postpartum.net.
Postpartum Men: www.postpartummen.com.
D.A.D.S., Inc. www.dadsinc.com.
Bootcamp for Dads: www.bootcampfornewdads.org.

Thank you, Daddy, for taking the time to read this. I hope you were able to take in just one piece of information or knowledge that will assist you during the first weeks and months after your baby is born. I wish you all the best for a happy and healthy newborn and for extra strength during the immediate weeks and months afterward.

Post-pregnancy Parting Thoughts
"Be Your Own Hero"

Hi again Mommy! In closing, I'd like to stress that the journey back to a normal body after pregnancy is rarely an easy one, which is why a having a Mommy Plan is vital. Every woman needs to have a plan in place not only for your physical recuperation, but just as importantly, your mental recovery. Make a list of mommy groups you can take part in and do not isolate yourself at home after child birth. It only takes a few minutes of research on the internet to find out what is available to you within five miles of your home. Or, even host a mommy group in your home.

Don't put excessive pressure on yourself to recover too quickly. Make sure you enjoy this time with your newborn and be proud of yourself and this achievement of the miracle of birth. Feel your feelings whatever they are, whether it's one week after you've given birth or eight weeks. Don't be afraid of them - embrace them, write them down, talk about them. Only then will you begin a balanced healing process, which includes processing your own personal experience of pregnancy, labor and child birth. I'm advocating for you to make the most of those first few weeks, when a majority of the time is normally spent at home, and put yourself on the road to a healthy recovery, both mentally and physically.

Be Your Own Hero
Be your own hero means finding your inner strength, facing the things you don't want to face and coming through it stronger, better and more knowledgeable about yourself. No one but you knows what you've gone through and therefore only you can truly be your hero through this experience. For your post-pregnancy period – you are also the hero for your newborn baby as well as other children if you have any.

Fifteen or Fifty?
Whether a woman is fifteen or fifty years old, has given birth or has miscarried, she should take care of her body in the immediate post-pregnancy period and make every effort to adhere to a well-developed and planned-out post-pregnancy recovery plan. This type of plan is a *preventative* measure before any real postpartum emotion sets. It isn't a substitute for any professional or medical advice. However, keep in mind that this plan cannot be executed by a woman alone. She needs help and will have to rely

on her husband, partner, family members, or those close to her. It is certainly a plan worth seeing through, as a few weeks of healthy recovery will enable months and years of strong health.

I wish you a happy, healthy and most of all <u>balanced</u> post-pregnancy recovery!

Mommy Notes

Hot Topics Among Modern Moms

This section provides moms with short articles which highlight "hot topics" that moms are talking about. It is recommended that you continue conduct your own research on each topic of interest to get a full understanding.

What are the Differences between Midwives and Doulas?

Midwives oversee the medical parts of the birth, including the actual delivery, while doulas provide constant emotional and physical support and comfort to the mom-to-be.

Midwives and doulas work together and complement one another as they perform very different jobs. Midwives are clinically trained and have the responsibility for the safety of the mother and baby. Examples of the services they provide are:

- Prenatal care
- Vaginal exams
- Blood work
- Blood pressure
- Monitoring of the baby.
- Post-birth and newborn care.
- Delivery, or catching of, the baby.
- Charting the medical information.
- Checking the fetal heart for any distress.
- Monitoring the laboring mother's vitals.

Some midwives also provide family planning, annual exams, and other kinds of gynecological services. A midwife attends a birth when a woman is in full active labor, near full dilation of the cervix or has very intense contractions happening every few minutes.

Birth or Labor Doula
A birth or labor doula on the other hand doesn't perform any clinical responsibilities but provides emotional and physical support, comfort, advocacy on the part of the mother according to her wishes and birth plan. There is also prenatal consultation to discuss and review the birth plan. A birth doula will normally be with a mother from the very start of early labor (called lead-up labor) providing constant support as contractions start from light to intensifying which can be many hours till the cervix dilates.

A common description of the services doulas provide is, that they "mother the mother."

Doulas Do A Lot

A typical question is, "What does a doula do?" My response is, "Well, they do a lot." *Doula*, pronounced DOO-LAH, is a Greek word, and the translation of the meaning I prefer is "mothering the mother." Doulas, like midwives, believe that childbirth which is a natural event and should not be considered a medical procedure but rather a process controlled by a woman.

A doula provides emotional and physical comfort for mom while helping her partner support her as well. We now use the word to describe a trained antepartum, labor or postpartum professional who provides a mother and father with continuous emotional support, physical comfort, and assistance in obtaining information before, during, and just after birth.[1] Doulas are recognized as professional individuals (mostly women), who provide emotional, physical, and informational support during the antenatal, birthing, and post-pregnancy periods.[2] Doulas draw on knowledge and experience to provide reassurance and perspective, make suggestions for labor progress, helps the birthing mother relax through massage, acupressure, counter-pressure, positioning, and other techniques known to give comfort.[3]

The service provided by doulas has been known to:[4]
- Result in shorter labors with fewer complications.
- Reduce negative feelings about one's childbirth experience.
- Reduce the need for labor-inducing drugs such as pitocin.
- Reduce the mother's request for pain medication and/or epidurals.
- Reduce the need for medical intervention such as forceps or vacuum extraction and cesareans.

More specifically:[5]
- 50% reduction in cesarean rate.
- 25% shorter labor.
- 60% reduction in epidural requests.
- 40% reduction in oxytocin use, or pitocin to speed up labor.
- 30% reduction in analgesia use.
- 40% reduction in forceps deliveries.

Research shows that parents who receive support:[6]
• feel more secure and cared for,
• feel less pressure on a woman's partner to have all the answers,
• are more successful in adapting to new family dynamics,
• have greater success with breastfeeding,
• have greater self-confidence,
• have less post-pregnancy-related mood disorders or depression,
• have lower incidence of substance abuse.

Types of Doulas

The following definitions were provided by the Childbirth and Postpartum Professional Association (CAPPA) website, the largest childbirth professional association in the world (www.cappa.net).

Antepartum or Perinatal Doula

An antepartum doula is a person who has received specific training that relates to assisting pregnant women who are classified as high risk (who may or may not need to be on bed rest), or pregnant women with medical conditions necessitating for help. This assistance includes education and physical support such as bed rest assistance, sibling care, errands, meal preparation, home care, and emotional support. The antepartum doula does not perform any clinical care. This role is strictly non-medical. The antepartum doula has extensive knowledge and training in the area of high-risk pregnancy support.

Labor or Birth Doula

A labor or birth doula is a person who attends to the birthing family before, during, and just after the birth of the baby. A labor doula is trained to deliver emotional support from home to hospital, ease the transition into the hospital environment, and be there through changing hospital shifts and alternating provider schedules. The doula serves as a labor coach and information source and to give the mother and father the added comfort of additional support throughout the entire labor. They provide emotional support for a laboring woman with techniques such as massage, wiping her forehead with a cool cloth, leading relaxation exercises and suggesting positions that will make the stages of birthing easier. A birth doula will also advocate for a mother's wishes in her birth plan to be fulfilled or convey the mother's immediate wants and needs through clear communication to the care providers.

Other titles used by women offering these kinds of services are "birth assistant," or "labor support specialist."

LABOR/BIRTH DOULA WISDOM
Rena' Koerner, President of Doulas Association of Southern California (DASC)

The word has become more mainstream, it's not as Greek as it once was... well actually it is. Doula is the Greek word for woman servant or slave. We, as birth doulas, work to support a woman and her family through the prenatal period, the labor process, as well as her birth and the immediate postpartum transition.

Birth doulas are one of the primary constants during the birth of a new family. We aren't strangers, and are often hired to be the protectors of the safe space as a family grows. We have the pleasure of meeting with families prior to birth and learn what's most important to them for their big day and we help them create their birth plan.

On that day, or the day a woman gives birth, we are there to help them calmly navigate through the process of welcoming their child, hopefully without many unnecessary obstacles. We offer suggestions for comfort and for labor progress while also creating peacefulness; and just as important, we are there to help take the pressure off the dads or partners. We live in a time where the partners are expected to be the primary support for the birthing woman. With any hope at all, they have attended a childbirth class (and not just a one-day cram class at the hospital, or an online class) filled with other expectant parents, with an instructor to educate and inform, and also answer questions to help them feel better prepared. Then, something happens when "it's time", and that information is somehow trumped with adrenaline, excitement, or even fear. The doula is there to relieve them of remembering what position to get her into for back labor, what the contraction pattern should be when heading to the hospital to avoid getting there too early or too late. The doula reminds the partner to eat and drink as well, to feel free to step out for a restroom break, update family members knowing that the birthing woman isn't alone - because the doula is that one constant support person.

By having a birth doula present, it has been proven that labors are shorter, there are less unnecessary interventions, less chance of a cesarean birth, greater breastfeeding success, and less chance of postpartum depression. Fear is a common emotion that is felt by parents prior to the birth of their child. Most expectant moms are watching television shows on birth and what they are exposed to is fear; i.e. the baby is past due, the baby is too big, we need to induce, the baby's heart rate is dropping – then we cut to commercial. This is not a true reflection of birth! Birth is more often calm, supported, without cameras or drama for television. We, as doulas, build a woman's trust in herself to simply birth her baby. We assure women that interventions have a time and a place, but that she is a part of the team who decides if she is at peace with that intervention.

157

It's my personal hope and mission that by having a birth doula, families will be able to experience less fear and more confidence. Less fear, because we do our best to educate them about their options as well as being on hand encouraging and supporting them in whatever decisions they make. Birth doulas instill more confidence, as we remind and reassure families to stay strong because they are safe in their decision making. Families need to be reminded that they have made well-researched and educated choices and can smoothly transition into parenthood with trust in themselves and confidence.

Rena' Koerner, founder of Integrative Childbirth Services, is certified in the following areas: Dual certification with CAPPA and DONA as a Birth Doula, Postpartum Doula, Lactation Educator, Childbirth Educator, Happiest Baby on the Block Instructor, Reiki Practitioner. For more information, visit: www.integrativechildbirth.net.

Postpartum or Postnatal Doula

A postpartum doula is the extension of a new mother, providing the day-to-day assistance (day or night) she needs so she can get rest. The postpartum doula is a trained professional that offers physical, emotional, and spiritual support to a new mother and the rest of the family. Postpartum doulas also offer breastfeeding support, light household maintenance, family nurturing, and instruction to mom and/or other family members in the care of a newborn.

The postpartum doula's job is to make the transition to parenthood easier for new parents, to help mom during her recovery period, and to ascertain what the family needs help with and provide the instruction. The main objective of the postpartum doula's role is not to take over complete care of the newborn, but to educate and support the family so that they will feel empowered to care for their newborn themselves. Postpartum doulas *do not* offer any medical advice or perform any medical or clinical procedures, but instead can offer parents referrals to appropriate studies and published books. Postpartum doulas should be good with children, patient, non-judgmental, and knowledgeable about newborn care and breastfeeding.

A postpartum doula may provide the following services:
- Physical support
- Household assistance
- Emotional support
- Sibling care
- Spiritual support
- Meal preparation
- Baby care instruction
- Breastfeeding and bottle feeding
- Errand running

POSTPARTUM DOULA WISDOM

Darla Burns, Executive Director of Postpartum Doulas for CAPPA, Childbirth and Postpartum Professional Association, the largest childbirth education organization in the world: *As Americans, we are under the impression that new moms are "Superwomen" and can return to life as it was before baby. We must remember to celebrate this new mother and emulate the other cultures that honor new mothers by caring for them, supporting them, and placing value on the magnificent transformation she is going through. This is the greatest gift we can give to new mothers & newborns.*

I have worked with hundreds of families in the United States, whether it's during birth, teaching childbirth education classes, breastfeeding classes, baby care classes, or as a postpartum doula and what I find interesting is the lack of focus on the mother-baby bond and overall care of the mother after birth. It seems that here in the U.S., after the birth, the focus quickly shifts to the baby. But what about the mother? Is she being supported? Is she being cared for, fed, and comforted? Many families in the US do not have extended family that live nearby and the father is required to return to work soon after the birth. This leaves this new mom to not only take care of her newborn, but also to resume life as she did before the baby. Cooking, cleaning, laundry, and additional household chores are expected to be taken care of by new mothers because of our unrealistic "Superwoman" expectations. We wonder why our postpartum depression rate is so high and why our breastfeeding rates are so low, when it's clear that our new mothers are not being properly cared for. This is where the postpartum doula can be such a vital addition to the new family's well-being. A postpartum doula works with the family after the birth and her main goal is to educate, support, and nurture the new parents so they can care for their newborn with confidence. Postpartum doulas help new mothers with breastfeeding, teach the parents baby care techniques, calming and soothing techniques, do light meal preparation, baby laundry, make sure mom is eating, drinking plenty of fluids and resting. We find when new moms feel loved and are well-supported, they transition to motherhood much more easily, have greater breastfeeding success, heal better, are less likely to develop severe postpartum mood disorders, and have confidence in their role as a mother.

Darla Burns, founder of In Due Time Doula Services, is certified in the following areas: Postpartum Doula, Birth Doula, Lactation Educator, Childbirth Educator, Happiest Baby on the Block Instructor, and Infant Massage Instructor. For more information, visit: www.induetimedoulaservices.com.

In addition to doulas, a burgeoning profession that compliments the services a postpartum doula provides is that of a traditional post-pregnancy practitioner.
If you are interested in finding out more information or hiring doulas, take a look at these websites or search the Internet to find one in your area. Normally, there is a doula organization in every state.

- Childbirth and Postpartum Professionals Association, www.CAPPA.net.
- DONA International, www.DONA.org.

Midwives, the Baby Catchers

It's not just the making of babies, but the making of mothers that midwives see as the miracle of birth.

Barbara Katz Rothman

Midwives, like doulas, believe that childbirth is a natural event and should not be considered a medical procedure but rather a process controlled by a woman. Therefore they believe in facilitating a natural childbirth as much as possible. While there are different types of midwives practicing in various settings, all midwives are trained to provide comprehensive prenatal care and education, guide labor and birth, address complications, and care for newborns.

Geraldine Simkins, President of the Midwives Alliance of North America (MANA) affirms, "The safety of mothers and babies is of utmost importance including the rights of women to make informed choices about where and with whom they give birth."[1]

Midwives are trained healthcare professionals that are fully equipped to help a woman birth her baby in normal, low-risk situations. Midwifery is a healthcare profession in which professionals offer care to childbearing women during pregnancy, labor and birth, as well as during the post-pregnancy period. They also help care for the newborn and assist the mother with breastfeeding. Midwives will refer women to general practitioners or obstetricians when a pregnant woman requires care beyond their area of expertise. Most midwives are women although there are male midwives, but very rarely.

Midwives are trained to handle certain more difficult deliveries, including breech births, twin births and births where the baby is in a posterior position, using noninvasive techniques.[2] According to MANA, The Midwives Model of Care™ is a fundamentally different approach to pregnancy and childbirth. Midwifery care is uniquely nurturing, hands-on care before, during, and after birth. Midwives develop a trusting relationship with their clients which results in confident, supported labor and birth.

Types of Midwives

Midwives go through comprehensive training and examinations for certification. Certification is offered by the American College of Nurse Midwives (ACNM) and the

161

North American Registry of Midwives (NARM). The practice and credentials related to midwifery differ throughout the United States. Below is a description of each of type of midwife as per the Midwives Alliance of North America (MANA) website:

Certified Nurse-Midwife (CNM)

A CNM is trained and licensed in both nursing and midwifery. Nurse-midwives possess at least a bachelor's degree, and many have a master's degree in nursing as well as course work in midwifery, from an accredited institution of higher education and are certified by the American College of Nurse Midwives. CNMs tend to work in hospital settings or free standing birthing clinics.

Certified Professional Midwife (CPM)

A CPM is a knowledgeable, skilled and professional independent midwifery practitioner who has met the standards for certification set by the NARM and is qualified to provide the midwifery model of care. The CPM is the only international credential that requires knowledge about and experience in out-of-hospital settings.

Direct-Entry Midwife (DEM)

A DEM is an independent practitioner educated in the discipline of midwifery through self-study, apprenticeship, a midwifery school, or a - college or university -based program distinct from the discipline of nursing. A DEM is trained to provide the Midwives Model of Care to healthy women and newborns throughout the childbearing cycle primarily in out-of-hospital settings.

Certified Midwife (CM)

A CM is an individual educated in the discipline of midwifery, who possesses evidence of certification according to the requirements of the American College of Nurse-Midwives. Certified Midwife (CM) is also used in certain states as a designation of certification by the state or midwifery organization.

Lay or Direct-entry Midwife

The term "Lay Midwife" has been used to designate an uncertified or unlicensed midwife who was educated through informal routes such as self-study or apprenticeship rather than through a formal program. This term does not necessarily mean a low level of education, just that the midwife either chose not to become certified or licensed, or there was no certification available for her type of education (as was the fact before the Certified Professional Midwife credential was available). Other similar terms to describe uncertified or unlicensed midwives are traditional midwife, traditional birth attendant, granny midwife and independent midwife.

In Europe, midwives and doulas assist in the majority of births. In the U.S., however, midwives and doulas lost their status at the end of the 1800s, when doctors took over the job of childbirth. But in recent decades, women have been embracing more natural ways to give birth simply by believing in what their bodies have been made to do. As a result, women have begun researching and choosing to give birth at birthing centers or at home and employing the services of midwives and doulas.

> *Good beginnings make a positive difference in the world, so it is worth our while to provide the best care for mothers and babies throughout this extraordinarily influential part of life.*
>
> **Ina May Gaskin**[1]

If you are interested in finding out more about midwives or hiring one, please visit the MANA website: www.mana.org.

---

[1] Internationally recognized midwife, birth activist, and recipient of many awards, including the Right Livelihood Award in Dec 2011 (equivalent of the Nobel Peace Prize).

Baby Nurse, Newborn Care Specialist or Night Nanny?

Child birth professionals that mainly focus on newborn care have a variety of titles:
- Baby Nurse
- Newborn Care Specialist
- Night Nurse
- Maternity Nurse
- Night Nanny

The skills and knowledge of these professionals tends to overlap. The designation of Newborn Care Specialist (NCS) or Baby Nurse (BN) is most commonly known and used. Regardless of the title, the function of a BN is virtually the same. These types of professionals are trained and skilled in all aspects of newborn and infant care and parent support. They are normally engaged when parents need assistance at night so they can get much needed rest, lactation support, a sleep specialist or an extra set of hands. The specific needs and concerns of parents will determine whether or not a licensed nurse is needed.

The term BN is often used to describe a NCS, Night Nurse or Night Nanny. A Baby Nurse may is not be a licensed nurse, RN (Registered Nurse) or LPN (Licensed Practical Nurse) but is an extremely caring and knowledgeable person that aids parents with overnight infant care needs. This means that although they may not be trained in certain medical procedures, BN's are able to tend to the basic care of the baby or babies. Their main role is care giving rather than medical provision. On the other hand, a BN who works in a maternity ward may be a registered nurse.

A NCS provides expertise and will help nurture newborns while providing guidance and education for the parents. The primary role is to provide assistance and education after childbirth. This assistance may include scheduling, feeding, sleep training and help with breast feeding. A NCS can work overnight, feeding the baby with a bottle or bringing the baby to the mother to nurse. After the feeding the baby is burped, changed and put back in bed. During the day the NCS will provide similar services and also create a stimulating environment for the baby during waking hours. Specialists document the baby's patterns and keep a log of sleeping feeding and changing times to assist in transitioning the baby to a schedule. NCS normally do not work with children older than six months.

There are NCS that are experienced with preemies, multiples and infants that have special needs such as: being on oxygen, using apnea monitors, have reflux, colic or other medical issues. The best way to determine whether you need a NCS or BN, or even a postpartum doula, is to assess your needs and then find a person that has the skill set that makes you feel confident in your hiring decision. I'd recommend also interviewing postpartum doulas as they provide some of the same newborn care services that overlap with a NCS. Also, it is common that NCSs and BNs are also trained as postpartum doulas.

Traditional Post-pregnancy Practitioner

A traditional post-pregnancy or postpartum practitioner (TPP) is most likely one of the oldest professions on earth, as women have been birthing babies and recovering since the beginning. A TPP is knowledgeable and skilled in traditions of holistic post-pregnancy wellness and recovery encompassing a mother's diet, activity, and personal care after childbirth. Such traditions are based on the Humoral Theory of health (hot vs. cold state). The focus is on rebalancing a mother's internal body temperature as it transitions to a non-pregnant state. A TPP believes that a woman's body begins healing from the day she gives birth and thus must be cared for from that day forward. A woman who has just given birth must be allowed complete rest for a minimum of three weeks; otherwise, there is a risk of the mother having an unbalanced recovery resulting in various post-pregnancy-related conditions.

A TPP is skilled in specific body and uterine massages along with various spa-like treatments and abdominal wrapping, which encourages a post-pregnancy body to heal in a shorter time period. The massages are not deep tissue, but shallow, with the purpose of energizing and invigorating the body to stimulate the body to release water, fat, and flatulence at a faster rate. A mother should feel energized after a massage; if she feels sore the next day, then the massage is being wrongly given. A TPP also provides dietary guidelines and can prepare special meals if she so chooses to offer this service. Quite often, she may also offer the same services of a postpartum doula—for example, newborn care, breastfeeding advice, baby massage, and so on. A TPP may provide the in-home spa services at a client's home, her own home, or elsewhere.

If you are interested in finding out more about traditional post-pregnancy (or postpartum) practitioners, please visit: Post-pregnancy Wellness, www.postpregnancywellness.com.

Hypnosis for Childbirth: What Is It - and Does It Work?

Mention the words "labor and delivery" to an expectant mom in her last trimester, and chances are good that her heart will begin to race and her mind flood with concern -- and in some cases, panic. She knows that the day is coming when a force much bigger than herself will take over and her body will govern itself completely.

For some women, birth is a very fearful event. For "hypnomoms," it is merely a challenge.

What Is Hypnosis, Anyway?

These wise "hypnomoms" use hypnosis to eliminate pain and fear from the birthing experience. In the past, the word "hypnosis" conjured up images of stage hypnotists re-creating Elvis or mesmerizing others into creating embarrassing situations. Now it is common for hypnosis to be used therapeutically in many areas of medicine, dental anesthesia and personal therapy sessions. Even so, many misconceptions remain regarding hypnosis that can dissuade those contemplating this powerful tool.

Here are a few facts about what hypnosis can do:

- All hypnosis is self-hypnosis; the hypnotherapist is only the guide. A person chooses to enter into a hypnotic state, stay in it and come out of it at will.
- It is estimated that approximately 90 to 95 percent of the population can be hypnotized. Willingness, belief and motivation have great influence over hypnotizability.
- During hypnosis you are neither asleep nor unconscious. You will always "come out" when you wish.
- Stronger-minded and stronger-willed people are easier to hypnotize, not the other way around as is usually assumed.
- You cannot be made to divulge information or do anything against your will while in hypnosis.
- Hypnosis is not satanic or oriented toward religion or spirituality at all. It is simply a way to direct your inner mind toward the positive.

167

So What About Hypnosis For Childbirth?

Hypnosis is used with great success in medical and dental procedures by patients who have life-threatening allergies to anesthetics, allowing them to undergo surgeries with no drugs and no pain. We know therefore that the mind can be trained to experience discomfort as only pressure, and that is what is achieved in childbirth hypnosis as well.

During labor, the more relaxation the mother experiences, the more comfort she will have. The depth of relaxation necessary can easily be achieved with hypnosis, as physical relaxation is learned and practiced daily in preparation for birth using guided visualizations followed by positive hypnotic suggestions. When the critical conscious mind is bypassed with hypnosis, the inner mind can literally be reprogrammed to believe that birth will be comfortable, easy and joyous. It's software for your mind!

Managing Fears and Expectations

In other cultures, childbirth is regarded as a natural, normal event in a woman's life. Birthing women are given support from other women, and children are often present to witness the event. In this way, birth is celebrated and honored.

Young girls grow up with the belief system that birth is a positive event, and their expectations of childbirth reflect this attitude. As a result, their births are similar to those of their predecessors: without pain and fear. They have a positive expectation of childbirth.

In our culture, it is very much the opposite. For many generations, we have been told that delivering a baby is many hours of painfully agonizing work, to be faced with fear and trepidation. We have heard stories from well-meaning friends and family that send shivers up our spines -- and so the legacy continues. We experience pain in childbirth in part because we very much expect to!

When learning about how the mind controls the body, an expectant couple is taught to surround themselves with only positive people and messages, to create a positive view of childbirth and the expectation that their birth will be the beautiful, peaceful experience that they want. Fear-clearing sessions are integral to this process, allowing each person to address fears they have, work through possible solutions and then release them.

Fear in labor can create tension, which creates pain, then more fear ... and the cycle continues. Fear and anxiety can also create adrenaline production in the body, causing the labor to become dysfunctional (a common reason for cesarean section surgery). Freedom from fear can make a huge difference in the birthing experience.

Hypnosis for childbirth teaches a woman how to enter into self-hypnosis instantly and create her own natural anesthesia whenever and wherever she needs it. This is important, since any drugs taken by a laboring woman can be dangerous for her and especially her baby. She has total control over her body and is an active participant in her birth process. As labor progresses, she relaxes even more and goes deeper inside herself, trusting in her body's natural ability to give birth with ease and comfort. Her mind is programmed to give her exactly what she needs.

Too Good To Be True?

Can women give birth experiencing a minimum amount of pain…or none at all? They can, but there are many variables during labor and birth that can affect the outcome. Couples need to have a positive but realistic view of hypnosis for childbirth.

Pregnant women and their partners must take responsibility for the choices they make while in labor and how those choices can affect the dynamics and outcome. Many a wonderful birth has been thwarted by not realizing how to make positive, informed choices. These issues are easily addressed and learned in a good consumer-oriented childbirth class or by doing research beforehand. Without a doubt, women using hypnosis are much calmer and more relaxed during labor, which automatically creates more comfort. They also benefit from powerful post-hypnotic suggestions to actually eliminate pain and fear.

How Effective Is This?

Statistics vary by program and method, depending on the length and number of hypnosis sessions, the materials used in each and the skill of the hypnotherapist or teacher as well as the dedication and compliance to the program of each birthing couple. Ideally, childbirth hypnosis instructors have backgrounds in both hypnotherapy and childbirth education and are able to address each woman's personal needs.

With adequate preparation and trust in the natural process of birth, most women can have much more relaxed and comfortable births, with many actually free of pain. It is important to know that the childbirth hypnosis program you choose to use will directly affect your success in having a comfortable birth, so educate yourself before choosing.

Benefits of using hypnosis for childbirth:
- Fewer drugs or no drugs at all means less risk of side effects to mother and baby.
- Shorter labors are likely based on decreased or eliminated resistance of the birthing muscles as a response to pain.
- Mothers are awake and energized, based on total relaxation throughout the birthing process.
- The birthing environment is calm and peaceful.
- Hypnosis provides the ability to turn breech and posterior babies.
- Hypnosis is associated with fewer interventions and complications during labor.
- Babies sleep and nurse better because they have fewer drugs in their systems.

How To Study: Where Do You Start?

Couples who are ready to begin their hypno-journey will benefit by researching all of their options to find a practitioner who allows them to achieve their goals. Seek out a qualified hypnotherapist in your area for office sessions. You will want to make sure to interview them beforehand and ask what type of program they offer for childbirth using hypnosis. Not all hypnotherapists have an effective program in place in their practice. A good childbirth hypnotherapist will offer at least four sessions in the office (six to seven are optimal), the last occurring one week before the estimated due date. You should receive at least one tape or CD to listen to at home by yourself and one or more cues for your birth companion to learn and practice that helps you to relax and go deeper into hypnosis.

Many hypnotherapists have developed their own childbirth hypnosis programs that are very effective. Some use and modify existing ones such as Gerald Kein's Painless Childbirth Program. The attraction to this kind of program is that it allows the hypnotherapist to adapt the program to fit the needs of their own practice, creating their own scripts and tapes from the original program sessions and fully modifying them to the needs of each woman. This helps tremendously with women who have personal issues that need to be resolved, such as VBAC moms, those who have had a past negative birth experience and those who have specific deep-seated fears about childbirth.

To find a hypnotherapist in your area, look in your phone book under "hypnosis" or "hypnotherapy," or contact the International Medical and Dental Hypnotherapy Association for a referral at (248) 549-5594 or (800) 257-5467.

You can seek out hypnosis for childbirth classes in your area. Some are taught at local hospitals and birth centers, and others are taught at an instructor's home. The backgrounds of the instructors can vary widely: hypnotherapist, nurse, doula, childbirth educator. Obviously, the more training and experience they have in the fields they are teaching, the better the class. To find a class, call local hospitals and physicians' offices or do a search on the Internet for "hypnosis, childbirth, education."

Screening Potential Instructors
You may want to ask prospective childbirth hypnosis instructors a few questions.

- Do you have a background in hypnotherapy? A hypnotherapy background is helpful so that they will be able to help you with individual issues.
- Do you have a background in childbirth education? This is also helpful to ensure that no other childbirth classes will be necessary, as they may differ greatly from the philosophy and teachings of the hypnotherapy class.
- How long have you been teaching hypnosis for childbirth classes, and where do you teach the class?
- How many classes do you teach, and how long is each one?
- What materials do you provide with the class? Books, tapes, CDs, scripts and phone help are possibilities.
- How much is the class fee, and is it a group class or private?
- Do you attend births as a hypno-doula, and if so, how many have you attended? If not, have you trained any local doulas for this?
- How many of your former students have been successful using their childbirth hypnosis course? This is something they should know.
- Why did you become a childbirth hypnosis instructor? Hopefully they have a passion for childbirth and a love of natural, unmedicated birthing.

You can also choose a home study course, of which there are many. To find one, search on the Internet for "hypnosis, childbirth, home study." An adequate home study program provides detailed information on hypnosis and how to use it during childbirth as well as hypno-tools for you to achieve your goals, including books, tapes, CDs, handouts and hypnosis scripts. Because you will be studying on your own, it is your responsibility to gain as much knowledge as possible, so choose well.

It is well worth the time to look into hypnosis for childbirth, both for yourself and for your baby. It is important to remember that many drugs given to a woman in labor reach the baby in adult doses in less than five minutes. Using hypnosis techniques can help avoid needing drugs. The deep relaxation has even helped many a nervous dad to cope with their children's birth! The skills you will learn for relaxation and hypnosis will benefit you for the rest of your life.

By Kerry Tuschhoff, HCHI, CH, is a certified hypnotherapist, childbirth educator and Director of Hypnobabies Network in Cypress, California. She is the author of Hypnobabies: Eyes Open Childbirth Hypnosis, The Birth Hypnosis Workbook for Professionals and The Hypno-Doula Training Workbook. For more information, visit: www.hypnobabies.com.

Reprinted with permission by the author.

The Genius of the Placenta

From the beginning of the third month of pregnancy a fetus and a mother maintain completely separate blood systems. This is one of the miracles of the placenta: it both integrates mother and child while also maintaining their integrity as individual and separate systems.

Ibu Robin Lim, CPM, CNN 2011 Hero of the Year
Yayasan Bumi Sehat,(Healthy Mother Earth Foundation)

The study of the placenta, with its benefits and rich nutritional value, is in its infancy stage in most Western countries. It is largely thought of as just another organ that serves no purpose other than to house a growing baby, and should be discarded immediately after birth otherwise it could actually do harm. This is a serious misconception which is being changed as people like Robin Lim (Guerilla Midwife and CNN's Hero of the Year, December 2011), midwives, doulas, child birth educators, independent placenta encapsulators and others like them feel passionate enough to make it their life's work. Many people put pen to paper and written informative books and articles, from a medical perspective, of how a placenta not only protects and grows a baby in utero but how it may continue to play a role after childbirth if allowed. In traditional cultures the value, and genius, of the placenta, medically, nutritionally and spiritually, is well documented and unquestioned, but in the west we have to fight for the right for our placenta.

Your Placenta Is Yours If You Want It

Most women choose to give birth in a hospital setting. However, as more information comes to light that there are additional birthing options available, more and more women are taking control of their birth experience. This is leading to a growing trend of women choosing free standing birthing centers or their own home to have their baby. Contrary to what most people believe it isn't against the law not to have a baby in a location other than a hospital. Actually, it is a woman's right to choose to give birth wherever she feels most comfortable and confident with. Women who give birth outside of a hospital setting have no challenges in keeping their placenta. After all it is a woman's own organ and therefore it belongs to her right? Unfortunately this isn't the case in hospital births.

In most Western countries, it is hospital policy that a woman's placenta is classified as "medical waste" and disposed of as such by incineration or sold to cosmetic companies, normally <u>without</u> a mother's knowledge or consent. This is truly a crime against something that traditional cultures claim is a 'miracle organ' and is referred to

173

as "the tree of life." I don't think any woman would dispose of their placenta if they knew of the continuing benefits it has for their child after being born as well as for themselves for their post-pregnancy recovery.

Placenta, the Miracle Organ

Six days after fertilization, a placenta will have been fully developing and would have completely embedded itself in the uterus. Placental circulation and maternal circulation begin to make exchanges, yet the mother's blood does not enter or mix with the infantile placenta. A normal placenta weights one pound and looks like a purple, blue and red tree of life. During pregnancy and after birth the placenta makes maternal and child survival possible. It provides for the nutritional needs and aids in development. It acts as a barrier guarding mother and child against harmful bacteria and most foreign molecules.

The Umbilical Cord

The umbilical cord is composed of one vein that carries oxygenated, nutrient-rich blood to the fetus, and two arteries that carry deoxygenated, depleted blood from the baby to the mother for her excretory system to dispose of. The cord is strong, but flexible, covered with a jelly like substance and is normally about twenty inches (50 cm) long and less than one inch in diameter (2 cm). The placenta chooses and transports nutrients needed for the formation of the baby's tissues. It ensures a steady supply of enzymes for metabolism, ions of calcium to build bone, iron to produce blood as well as oxygen to the baby. Waste products of carbon dioxide flow back via the mother's endometrial veins. The mother and baby's blood in the placenta come close enough to exchange gases but are never mixed.

A good read for anyone that would like to learn about how the placenta functions during pregnancy and afterwards is the book by Robin Lim, *Placenta the Forgotten Chakra*, Half Angel Press (2010). It succinctly explains the genius of the placenta from a scientific, medical and spiritual standpoint and includes real life stores of the experiences Robin and other parents have had in witnessing the miracle of what the placenta can do if it abilities are understood.

Delayed cord clamping and cutting

Cord clamping has become the accepted norm so much so that delayed clamping is generally considered a new or unproved intervention.

David Hutchon, MD, United Kingdom

During pregnancy, the placenta, or "afterbirth," filters and oxygenates fetal blood. The process of birth pushes about two ounces of blood back up the cord into the afterbirth. It is believed that this blood engorges the placenta and helps it remain adhered to the uterine wall through changes in contour, such as when the bag of water breaks.

Blood is Redistributed, or Transfused, at Birth
The newborn receives approximately 3.5 ounces of blood from the placenta, which occurs within the first four minutes after birth. In addition passing through the blood vessels of the lungs, blood also goes to the intestines and the kidneys, preparing them for digestion and elimination.

As the baby begins to breathe and oxygenate his own blood, the arteries in the umbilical cord which carried blood to the placenta slowly begin to close. Each time the mother has a contraction, blood from the placenta is pumped to the baby through the umbilical vein, which is twice as large as the arteries and has no valves. Thus, the baby's body easily maintains the proper amount of blood; any excess can flow back to the placenta. Physical cord closure occurs 1 – 3 hours after birth. If the cord is going to be clamped early, the baby should be kept within four inches above or below the placenta (on the mother's lap if she is sitting up) to get the greatest physiological transfusion in the short time available. When cord clamping and cutting is delayed until the placenta is delivered, it doesn't matter where the baby is placed--anywhere within cord's length (the mother's arms) is fine.

Even waiting at the bare minimum of ten minutes will be very beneficial if you feel you cannot wait any longer. However, before it is clamped look at and feel the umbilical cord. If it is still pulsing, then the placenta is continuing to transfer healthy t-cells to your baby and clamping should be further delayed. Traditional practices of three hours or more are documented, with many more women choosing to delay severing the cord for even longer periods of twenty-four hours even to the point of letting the cord detach itself spontaneously. These types of births are called a partial Lotus birth and full Lotus birth.

> *A baby whose umbilical cord is severed at the moment of birth does not receive the bonus of blood from the placenta. Instead of perfusing the gut and other organs, survival dictates that available blood is directed to the heart, lungs, and brain. Loss of needed blood results in some pathological symptoms of shock in the newborn. If the cord is cut before the baby has a chance to take a few breaths, the important transition to extra-uterine life may be marred by first breaths that are taken in an overwhelming sense of fear and panic.*
>
> **Mary A. Earhart, Author,**
> **Retired RN, BSN, Licensed Midwife**

Good Changes are Coming

More and more scientific studies of the benefits of delayed cord clamping and cutting of the umbilical are coming to light. The blood in the cord and the placenta belongs to the baby it supported throughout pregnancy. The entire industry of cord blood banking is built around the value of the blood, which contains T-cells, in the umbilical cord at birth. Why not let your child have this precious blood at birth rather than the costly exercise of banking it when it has a limited shelf life and it is uncertain whether or not you will need it in the future? In my opinion allowing a baby to have this precious blood in the very beginning of life would be more beneficial as it is known to prevent anemia in the first three months of life and enriches iron stores and ferritin levels for as long as six months. Remember a baby is born without a developed immune system; getting a full blood supply at birth is a way to prevent future illness.

"Late clamping (or not clamping at all) is the physiological way of treating the cord, and early clamping is an intervention that needs justification. The "transfusion" of blood from the placenta to the infant, if the cord is clamped late, is physiological, and adverse effect so the transfusion are improbable…but in normal birth there should be a valid reason to interfere with the natural procedure." World Health Organization

Lotus Births

A full lotus birth involves leaving the umbilical cord intact to dry out and release naturally, which typically occurs in three to nine days. A partial lotus birth is when the umbilical cord is left intact until the cord stops pulsing, which takes approximately three hours.

Placenta Encapsulation

My abridged definition of Placentophagy is: the consumption of the placenta after childbirth. This normally conjurors up all sorts of disturbing images for most modern mothers as we have all heard the stories of Asian women consuming their placentas in one way or another. A well-known traditional usage for the placenta is for hemorrhaging mothers. In an emergency situation Ibu Robin, pulls off a small piece of the meatiest part of a mother's placenta, covers it in honey and has her consume it. In a matter of minutes the hemorrhaging ceases due to the placenta's high oxytocin content.

Our Western mindset, and tummies, usually can't stomach the thought of eating our own organ, and I can't blame you as I wouldn't be able to consume my placenta that way as well. The savior for women like us is placenta encapsulation. Placenta encapsulation allows us to consume the placenta in a non-offensive way. Think of it as a "placenta pill." We are used to taking medication in capsule form so it wouldn't be anything unusual.

176

Why You Should Take Placenta Pills
The placenta is considered to be a very powerful medicine as it is a life-giving organ and stores the vital essence for the baby. The placenta contains vitamins and minerals, such as vitamin B6, that may help fight depression symptoms. It is also rich in iron and protein, which would be useful to women recovering from childbirth.

Your Encapsulator and the Process
The process should be carried out by an experienced individual with good health, mentally and emotionally, as well as possessing good credentials. Your placenta is sacred and should be handled with care during this preparation. The process begins with the placenta being collected anytime after birth, normally within 48 hours after birth if you choose to do a partial Lotus Birth. You can also encapsulate after a full Lotus Birth, but the strength of the placenta's efficacy may be diminished. However it can still be beneficial. Your placenta should be refrigerated if preparation is not possible within 24 hours and it could be put in the freezer for up to two weeks. However, it may be less effective at this point. The placenta is placed in a food dehydrator, which preserves it. Then is it ground into powder form and placed in empty capsules to be taken as a daily supplement after childbirth. This allows the mother to benefit from it for weeks instead of just the first few days postpartum. The capsules can also be frozen, extending their use from weeks and months to years. Since the capsules also help with fatigue and milk production, they can be taken any time a mother feels worn down or needs to increase her milk supply.

Specific benefits of placenta pills are that they may help to:
• Increase general energy.
• Facilitate a quicker return to health after birth.
• Increase production of breast milk.
• Decrease likelihood of baby blues and post natal depression.
• Decrease likelihood of iron deficiency.
• Decrease likelihood of insomnia or sleep disorders.

Considering that the placenta is a completely natural substance, created by a woman's own body, encapsulation of the placenta is definitely worth considering as part of a holistic postpartum recovery for every expectant woman. If you are having a hospital birth, you need to make your intention known well in advance to all the professionals and people involved in your birth experience. If hospitals are informed well in advance that you would like to take your placenta for health or religious purposes, then there shouldn't be any problem.

Placenta Tincture

A tincture is an alcoholic extract or solution. A placenta tincture is an added bonus as it can be used long after placenta capsules are gone. Tincturing a small piece of the placenta in high-grade alcohol such as vodka, brandy or ethanol increases the shelf-life of the placenta so the mother can enjoy its benefits for an extended time. The tincture can be used at any time the mother experiences trauma, transition, emotional distress, and even later in life during menopause, It can even be turned into a homeopathic remedy. A suggested dosage is ten to forty drops in water, two to three times a day. If kept in a cool, dry place, a placenta tincture should last indefinitely.

It is recommended to allow the placenta to steep for at least six weeks before use. The tincture is very shelf-stable if kept in a cool dark place such as a cupboard, and will last for many, many years. If you are interested in having enough placenta tincture to last the lifetime of mother and child, you can continue to add eighty or one hundred proof high grade alcohol to the bottle as the tincture is used, never allowing it to get below half full, or even better, three-fourths full.

TRADITIONAL CEREMONIAL HANDLING OF A PLACENTA

In Indonesia, Malaysia, and Thailand as well as other cultures, the placenta is considered to be a baby's first protector, guardian angel or twin soul. (I love this belief! The idea of a baby and its placenta having an intimate relationship, like a security blanket wrapped around the baby is comforting.) A baby's placenta is handled with gentleness and treated with respect. What normally takes place is the blood is washed off with some sort of traditional wash. For example, tamarind paste is used in Malaysia. It is packed in salt, wrapped in a cloth and placed in a clay jar. Sometimes parents place items with the placenta as wishes for talents the parents wish their child to have. For example Ibu Robin Lim placed a guitar pick with her son's placenta and he has cultivated a love and skill for music as he grew up. A ceremony is performed, or prayer said, and the earthen jar is normally buried near the house, and a tree or a plant is planted on top of it. If a family moves house the placenta jar is dug up and taken with the family and reburied in the new location.

The placenta in Vietnamese and Chinese cultures is viewed as a life-giving force and it is dried and added to specific placenta recipes in order to increase the mother's energy and vitality. In Korean culture, the placenta is often burned. The ashes are kept to make a liquid which is believed to help the child recover from any illness. X

It is customary of the Navajo Indians of North America to bury a child's placenta within the sacred four corners of the tribe's reservation as a binder to ancestral land and people. Objects are buried with it to signify the profession they hope the child will pursue, for example a pen to signify a writer. X

In Hawaii, the placenta is washed and then buried following a religious ritual with a tree planted on top of it. It is believed this binds the child to his or her homeland. The "iewe" (placenta) of the newborn child is sacred and must be handled in a sacred manner in order to provide for the physical health of the child. X

I love such traditions surrounding the placenta as I never saw mine nor got to handle or treat it with respect. However, I did get to see my first placenta at Ibu Robin's Bumi Sehat birthing clinic. A young woman gave me permission to see her newborn baby, born just twenty-four hours before, still attached to his placenta. The placenta had been was salted and spiced wrapped in a cloth and placed in a basket next to him with the umbilical cord covered with a light cloth. I'll never forget it as it was a magical experience for me. Mommy and baby so peaceful and the placenta lovingly attached next to the baby. It didn't get in the way or was cumbersome as you may think. An umbilical cord spontaneously unattaches itself in five to nine days depending on the care.

After reading the story below in Ibu Robin Lim's book, *Placenta the Forgotten Chakra*, I had to include this piece. This book is a must read for every woman.

A Conversation Between the Placenta and Child
By Joel Garnier

Placenta: "Hey, I'm the placenta, OK?"

Baby: "OK."

Placenta: "Oops, mom's water just broke, don't panic."

Baby: "OK."

Placenta: "Soon we are going out through there, ok, and you are going to have to learn to breathe air right away."

Baby: "OK?"

Placenta: "Just sort of be as slippery and calm as you can, and I'll be right behind you."

Baby: "I'm ready."

Placenta: "That's the spirit!" "Good pun!" "Nice work, you've got your head out. I've heard that's a trip, now relax one of your shoulders and you should glide right out."

Baby: "OK, I'm out. There are people here. Now what?"

Placenta: "You gotta blow your nose and clear your throat and start breathing air. I'll be out soon."

Baby: "Someone just rested me in the crook of mom's arm. I'm breathing. I think it's safe to come out. Hey that thing you said about breasts, you were right. Awesome!"

Placenta: "OK I'm out too, and these are good people. I'm over here in a bowl of flowers, still connected to you by our umbilical cord. I suggest you and mom catch up on some zeds and I'll be here when you wake up."

Baby: "Cool."

Placenta: "OK, its morning, so wake up sleepy head."

Baby: "Yeah, really fresh, good smells."

Placenta: "Perfect, that is a really good sign."

Baby: "Now what?"

Placenta: "Ah, this is the part where we wait and see what they decide to do, you know, the parents. Don't take this the wrong way, but there's going to be some baby talk and a whole bunch of babbling and laughing at you and I won't understand." You might see some things, wait, I can't believe I forgot, did you open your eyes yet?"

Baby: "Yeah, I told you I saw the breasts."

Placenta: "Right, right, sorry. Say have you, you know, suckled?"

Baby: "Yep, and let me tell you sister, this is the best!"

Placenta: "OK, I'm a little jealous but I have all I need for the time being."

Baby: "You know, I noticed the babbling and laughing and crying. What are they going on about?"

Placenta: "Who knows? It's always different."

Baby: "Yeah, I know. I noticed that too. At least we get to stay connected for a little while longer."

Placenta: "Yeah. Go to sleep. When you wake up I won't be here anymore. I can tell by what we've seen so far that you and mom are going to be fine, and I'll be fine too. And if you listen carefully, you see that I have not really left you, OK?"

Baby: "OK, goodnight, I love you."

Placenta: "I love you too. Sweet dreams."

Views are changing regarding the purpose of a woman's placenta during pregnancy and afterwards. It is not only an organ that grows in a woman's body to house a growing baby, it is much more than that; and only now this is being realized by modern science. The placenta is Mother Nature's "going away" gift to mothers and babies after pregnancy to ensure they get that *little extra* to ensure they have what both their bodies need. For the mother, to gain back her strength after pregnancy and childbirth; and for the baby, the cord blood that it needs to start this life healthy and strong.

The Miracle of Kangaroo Care

This snuggling of an infant inside the pouch of their parent's shirt, much like a kangaroo's pouch, led to the creation of the term "Kangaroo Care."

Kangaroo care has been studied in depth since 1983 and was first officially implemented it in Bogota, Colombia, due to the high infant mortality rate of 70%. It was an inexpensive and very beneficial to babies, and so effective the mortality rate fell to 30%.

Newborn Expectations
A newborn at birth is wide awake for the first sixty to ninety minutes and has certain sensation that he is to be met. For example, he hears mommy's familiar voice and heartbeat, and her smell and breast milk are familiar as well. With these expectations met, a newborn then feels safe, which results in his body calming down. A baby's heart rate, breathing and oxygen saturation, blood pressure, and temperature all stabilize much faster when in contact with mommy than when separated. A baby will have had all his basic needs of warmth, food, and protection satisfied.

Kangaroo Care Position
A diaper-clad baby is placed on a parent's bare chest, tummy to tummy, in between the breasts. A skull cap can be placed on the baby's head if it's too cool, and then the baby's body is covered with a blanket or piece of clothing. The baby's head is turned so that the ear is placed above the parent's heart. The mommy or daddy's body heat keeps the baby feeling safe and warm as he listens to their heartbeat. Any medical procedures are conducted around this skin-to-skin contact without separating them. There is a major movement in Western countries to make kangaroo care the standard method of care for all newborn babies, both premature and full-term, as there are many benefits for both baby and parents.

Benefits for the Baby:
- Stabilization of the baby's heart rate.
- Improved (more regular) breathing pattern.
- Improved oxygen saturation levels (an indicator of how well oxygen is being
- delivered to all the newborn's organs and tissues).
- Gain in sleep time.
- More rapid weight gain.
- Less crying.
- More successful breastfeeding episodes.
- Earlier hospital discharge.

Benefits for the Parents:
- Improved bonding, feelings of closeness with their baby.
- Increased breast milk supply.
- Increased confidence in ability to care for their baby.
- Increased confidence that their babies are well cared for.
- Increased sense of control.

Skin-to-skin contact should ideally be for twenty-four hours, with the mommy and daddy taking turns throughout the day so that your baby is never separated from its parents; this way stress for the baby is minimized.

Increases Supply of Breast Milk

In kangaroo care, a baby instinctively makes movements toward its mommy's breast and will start to suckle on his own. With a proper latch, production of breast milk will be stimulated early. A mother's breasts have the innate capability to automatically warm if her baby's body is cool and will cool if her baby's body is too warm. Kangaroo care is even more important to stabilize premature babies, or preemies.

The True Miracle of Kangaroo Care

The power and effectiveness of kangaroo care, there was highlighted in a newspaper article about a woman in Australia who gave birth to a premature baby. After twenty minutes of trying to get the baby to breathe, the doctor finally pronounced him dead. The parents overcome, with grief said that if their baby was on his way out of this world, they wanted him to know who his parents were and how much they loved him before he died. So the mother, in kangaroo care style, cuddled her baby for two hours. However, after only five minutes, her baby started displaying short, startled movements, which became more pronounced, and eventually their beautiful baby boy opened his eyes to say hello!

Specialized Garments

There are comfortable and breathable maternity garments designed by women specifically for kangaroo care. These women through their own experiences are passionate advocates for kangaroo care. It is easier than you think, and it is up to you to do it for as long as you'd like.

Baby Planners, Much More Than Just Baby Showers

A professionally certified baby planner is a trained maternity consultant with experience and knowledge in all aspects of maternity, far beyond just helping a woman select baby products, prepare for a baby shower, or planning for the single event of the birth. If you examine the depth of knowledge and services in the market place, hiring a baby planner isn't really such a luxury service as is largely thought to be, and will mostly save expecting parents money, time and undue stress. This is because a baby planner must be on top of the latest, greatest and most convenient technology, products, gadgets and so on this lets parents off the hook from having to figure out which products are good, which are not so good, which have been taken off the market, recalled or have been sold out and on back order. This is where undue stress is relieved.

Baby planners tailor their services to suit a client's specific needs, lifestyle and preferences, as well as help them determine the types of resources, services and products that will be most useful and essential for them as they prepare for parenthood and beyond. A planner is able to introduce options regarding birthing, feeding, sleeping, health, fitness, nutrition, eco-friendly living, safety, post-partum support, budgeting, and baby gear, to name a few. Planners can also provide options regarding pre-conception, pregnancy, postnatal. Other parenting topics may also be recommended if requested by a client. Additional services a baby planner may provide is organizing special events such as a baby shower, baby moon or maternity retreat or even a photo shoot or design of the birth announcement.

By determining the types of resources, services and products that best suits their requirements, parents are paired with the most suitable and reputable services and products in the market place. After engaging the services of a baby planner, parents feel informed and empowered to make the best decisions for their growing family.

Disclaimer

The information contained in this book is not meant to be a substitute for persons seeking the advice of a qualified healthcare provider. It is not intended to diagnose, treat, cure, or prevent any disease or illness. Always consult your healthcare provider about the use of any product or herbs, especially during pregnancy, when nursing a baby or with children. The information is not in any way offered as prescription, diagnosis, or treatment for any disease, illness, infirmity, or physical condition. Any form of self-treatment or alternative health program necessarily must involve an individual's acceptance of some risk, and no one should assume otherwise. Persons needing medical care should obtain it from a physician. Consult your doctor before making any health decision.

Postpartum Support International (PSI)

Postpartum Support International (PSI) is dedicated to helping women suffering from perinatal mood and anxiety disorders, including postpartum depression, the most common complication of childbirth. PSI has members and volunteer coordinators in every US state and in over 37 countries around the world. This organization links professionals with education and training specific to Perinatal Mood Disorders and recovery. PSI strives to educate family, friends and healthcare providers so that moms and moms-to-be can get the support they need and are able to have a solid recovery. This is done by bringing together families who are at risk of crisis related to Perinatal Mood and Anxiety Disorders (PMADs), trained volunteers, and the professionals who research and treat this type of condition. Awareness that this illness is the number one complication of childbirth is essential.

The PSI project is to increase consumer and provider awareness and knowledge of education, advocacy, and social support related to mental health issues related to childbearing.

It is important that: Moms are not alone. Moms are not to blame, and with help, they will be well.

For more information, visit: www.postpartum.net

Ibu Robin Lim 2011-2012
CNN HERO OF THE YEAR
Certified Professional Midwife, Birth Activist

Every baby's first breath on Earth could be one of peace and love. Every mother should be healthy and strong. Every birth could be safe and loving. But our world is not yet there.
Ibu Robin Lim

Ibu (Mother) Robin Lim, Grandmother and Certified Professional Midwife (CPM) with the North American Registry of Midwives and Ikatan Bidan Indonesia, is a founder and executive director for Yayasan Bumi Sehat, an international non-for-profit organization located in Indonesia. Ibu Robin is also an accomplished author and has been celebrated for her service and charitable works with marginalized people in need.

Awards:
2005: Women of Peace Award by the Women's Peace Power Foundation
2005: Asian American Volunteer person of the Year award, shared with her daughter Deja Bhernhardt.
2006: Alexander Langer International Peace Award.
2008: Woman of the Month Award by the United Nations Entity for Gender Equality & the Empowerment of Women (UNIFEM).
2011: CNN 2011 Hero of the Year

Books by Robin Lim
- After the Baby's Birth, A Complete Guide for Postpartum Women
- Eating for Two...Recipes for Pregnant and Breastfeeding Women
- Obat Asli...The Traditional Healing Herbs of Bali
- The Geometry of Splitting Souls
- Indonesia, Globe Trotters Series
- Butterfly People

Books in Bahasa Indonesia
- ASI Eksklusif Dong
- Ibu Alami

Film Documentary
- Guerrilla Midwife by Deja Bernhardt, script by Robin Lim.
  An award winning documentary about Robin's work, Bumi Sehat and the importance of gentle bird for a peaceful planet.

Bumi Sehat Foundation International
(a not-for-profit organization)

Background: Robin Lim's foundation, Yayasan Bumi Sehat (Healthy Mother Earth Foundation) was founded in Bali in 1995, expanded its services to Ache immediately after the 2004 tsunami and, in 2010, was an early responder to the earthquake in Haiti. Bumi Sehat is an advocate for marginalized, displaced, low-income people of all faiths and cultures, and from its humble beginnings as an Indonesian not-for-profit organization, has grown to have international impact from its charitable works.

Vision: We believe that access to quality healthcare is a human right. We believe that each individual is an essential societal component of peace and that, by caring for the smallest citizens: the babies at birth, we are building Peace, one Mother, on Child, one Family at a time.

Our service is built on three simple Principals:
- Respect for Nature,
- Respect for Culture and
- Respect for the wise implementation of the Science of Medicine

Our focus is on culturally appropriate, sustainable family healthcare, gentle maternal services and infant survival with an emphasis on breastfeeding (the best start and nutritional sustainability for all babies.) We believe that each individual is a miracle of hope and a promise of peace.

Activities: In the villages of Nyuh Kuning, Bali, and Gampong Cot, West Aceh in Indonesia, we operate maternal, infant, and family healthcare clinics. Our patients come from all parts of Bali and Aceh including displaced people from many Indonesian islands. We provide early responder care in the event of natural catastrophes. Bumi Sehat also manages, coordinates and operates a Youth Center in Bali, where a variety of programs are provided for the elderly; projects supporting education and capacity building are offered, as well as projects focusing on environmental protection.

Please help Ibu Robin and the Bumi Sehat team create Peace on Earth, one Precious Baby at a time.

Donations of cash or immediate supplies on Robin's Wish List can be made through: www.bumisehatbali.org.

Thank you so much for your support!

An important documentary in the making...

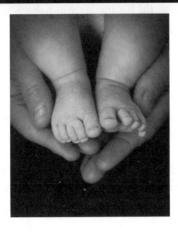

AFTER BIRTH PROJECT

Bringing awareness and compassion to the *after birth* needs of the developing family.

The After Birth Project will expose the startling and largely unknown facts and conditions existing in our culture for families after the birth of a child. It will reveal why having a baby in our country can be one of the most isolating and sometimes even dangerous experiences. 1 out of every 8 women experience significant depression, anxiety, intrusive repetitive thoughts, panic, or post-traumatic stress disorder after childbirth. Left untreated, some cases have had fatal consequences for moms and babies.

Filmmakers Elizabeth Reynolds and Joanna Whitlow are traveling the country to connect with families and experts creating a grass-roots formula for an ideal support network.

They [have] documented the up-to-date findings presented at the 2010 Postpartum Support International (PSI) Annual Conference held in conjunction with The International Marcé Society in Pittsburgh, Pennsylvania. The principal aim of the Marcé Society is to promote, facilitate and communicate about research into all aspects of the mental health of women, their infants and partners around the time of childbirth.

The After Birth Project will detail the post-birth experience in America in contrast to other cultures. Other nations demonstrate more positive postpartum experiences through diverse and nurturing options. We will present examples of these and also American local communities and organizations that have established a positive model. Please join Elizabeth and Joanna's journey in their quest to create a more aware, compassionate and healthy world for moms and babies.

FILMMAKERS:

Elizabeth Reynolds ~ *Director/Producer/Writer*
Elizabeth has co-produced and made contributions in direction, editing and writing on one-minute, three-minute and 30-minute television shows and numerous testimonials and interviews. Projects include productions for Ricki Lake, Jack Canfield and Alison Armstrong. She is a coordinator for PSI (Postpartum Support International) and founder/president of Elizabeth Reynolds Lux Aromatics, essential oil blends for well-being. The mother of two daughters, age 25 and 18, Elizabeth lives in Ventura, California.

Joanna Whitlow ~ *Director/Writer*
A professional in the pregnancy, birth and postpartum field since 2002, Joanna is an IBCLC, Certified Birth and Postpartum Doula, CAPPA faculty member and childbirth educator. Joanna founded the non-profit organizations About Families, Inc., and is currently the Executive Director. Joanna is also the local coordinator of Postpartum Support International (PSI) in California. Her own company For Moms and Babies offers resources, education and support for pregnancy, birth and parenting. For more information, visit, www.formomsandbabies.com. Joanna lives in Indio, California with her husband and four sons.

For more information or to make a donation to support the production and distribution of this important documentary, please visit www.afterbirthproject.com.

192

Notes

Preface
1. The Government of Malaysia, Ministry of Health Malaysia, Traditional & Complementary Medicine Division, *Traditional and Complementary Medicine Practice Guidelines on Malay Postnatal Care*, First Edition June 2009.

Chapter 1 – The Postpartum Epidemic in America
1. Center for Disease Control & Prevention, *National Vital Statistics System, Birth data*, last modified on August 11, 2011, http://www.cdc.gov/nchs/births.htm.
2. Post-pregnancy Support International, accessed on January 15, 2009, http://post-pregnancy.net.
   Wikipedia, the free Encyclopedia, Post-pregnancy Depression, last modified on October 13, 2011, http://en.wikipedia.org/wiki/Post-pregnancy_depression.
3. Post-pregnancy Support International, accessed on January 15, 2009, http://post-pregnancy.net.
4. Katherine Stone, "How many women really get PPD?," *Post-pregnancy Progress Blog*, http://post-pregnancyprogress.org/2011/02/how-many-women-really-get-post-pregnancy-depression/
5. American Diabetes Association, Diabetes Statistics, accessed on August 11, 2011. http://www.diabetes.org/diabetes-basics/diabetes-statistics/.
6. Stroke Center, Stroke Statistics, US Statistics, accessed on August 14, 2011, http://www.strokecenter.org/patients/about-stroke/stroke-statistics/
7. Breast Cancer, US Breast Cancer Statistics, last modified on October 19, 2011, http://www.breastcancer.org/symptoms/understand_bc/statistics.jsp
8. US Census Bureau, *The 2012 Statistical Abstract*, http://www.census.gov/compendia/statab/cats/population.html
9. Center for Disease Control & Prevention, *National Vital Statistics System, Birth data*, last modified on August 11, 2011, http://www.cdc.gov/nchs/births.htm
10. Ibid.
11. Negative Population Growth, NPG 2011 Population Fact Sheet, March 2011, http://www.npg.org/edmaterials/2011%20Student%20Fact%20Sheet.pdf
12. Ibid.
13. Finnigan, Annie, Everyone but U.S: The State of Maternity Leave, Working Mother web, accessed October 20, 2011, http://www.workingmother.com/best-companies/everyone-us-state-maternity-leave
14. United States Department of Labor, *Wage and Hour Division: Family and Medical Leave Act*, accessed October 20, 2011, http://www.dol.gov/whd/fmla/
15. Human Rights Watch, US Lack of Paid Leave Harms Workers, Children, February 23, 2011, http://www.hrw.org/news/2011/02/23/us-lack-paid-leave-harms-workers-children
16. The Associated Press, "U.S. stands apart from other nations on maternity leave," *USA*

Today, August 26, 2005. http://www.usatoday.com/news/health/2005-07-26-maternity-leave_x.htm.

17. National Institute of Mental Health, "Women and Depression: Discovering Hope," accessed December 3, 2008, http://www.nimh.nih.gov/health/publications/women-and-depression-discovering-hope/complete-index.shtml.

18. Wikipedia, the free Encyclopedia, Post-pregnancy Depression, last modified on October 13, 2011, http://en.wikipedia.org/wiki/Post-pregnancy_depression.

19. Ibid.

20. Susan Hatters Friedman, M.D., "Post-pregnancy Mood Disorders: Genetic Progress and Treatment Paradigms," *The American Journal of Psychiatry*, 166:1201-1204, November 2009, http://ajp.psychiatryonline.org/cgi/content/full/166/11/1201.

21. Merritt, Tracie, Kuppin, Sara, and Wolper, Michelle, B.A., "Post-pregnancy Depression Causes and Correlates," *The International Electronic Journal of Health Education*, 2001; 4:57-63, http://www.iejhe.org.

22. Stein, Rob and St. George, Donna, "Unwed Mothers Increases Sharply in U.S., Report Shows," *The Washington Post*, May 14, 2009, http://www.washingtonpost.com/wp-dyn/content/article/2009/05/13/AR2009051301628.html.

23. Washington, Jesse, Blacks struggle with 72 percent unwed mothers rate, MSNBC website, November 7, 2010, http://www.msnbc.msn.com/id/39993685/ns/health-womens_health/t/blacks-struggle-percent-unwed-mothers-rate/#.Tp_tu5uBqU8.

24. National Organization of Mothers of Twins Club, Inc. Multiple Birth Statistics, accessed January 14, 2009,
http://www.nomotc.org/index.php?Itemid=55&id=66&option=com_content&task=view.

25. Ibid.

26. US Census Bureau, *The 2012 Statistical Abstract*, http://www.census.gov/compendia/statab/cats/population.html

27. Heyes, J.D., "Antidepressants increase risk of breast cancer," *Natural News*, July 23, 2011, http://www.naturalnews.com/033099_antidepressants_breast_cancer.html

28. Ibid.

29. Barthlow, Michael PharmD, "Top 200 Prescription Drugs of 2009," *Pharmacy Times*, May 11, 2010, http://www.pharmacytimes.com/publications/issue/2010/May2010/RxFocusTopDrugs-0510

30. Ibid.

31. Selander, Jodi , 'Placenta: Happy Pills for Post-pregnancy Recovery,' Placenta Benefits, accessed on October 14, 2010, http://placentabenefits.info/FunFitLife_article.asp, originally printed in Fun & Fit Life Magazine, March 2010.

32. Lim, Robin, After the Baby's Birth: A Complete Guide for Post-pregnancy Women, (Bali, Indonesia: Celestial Arts) 1991, p. 9-10.

33. Ibid.

34.

35. Lim, Robin, After the Baby's Birth: A Complete Guide for Post-pregnancy Women, (Bali,

Indonesia: Celestial Arts) 1991, p.9-10.

36. Ibid.
37. Obata, Mary L., M.A., MFT, "Clinical Social Work Society, Guidelines for Treating Post-pregnancy Mood Disorders," Clinical Social Work Society, 2004, accessed September 26, 2011, http://clinicalsocialworksociety.org/docs/continuing_education/Guidelines.pdf.
38. Ibid.
39. Ibid.
40. Ibid.
41. Pregnancy or Postpartum OCD, Postpartum Support International, accessed on November 21, 2011, http://www.postpartum.net/Get-the-Facts/Postpartum-OCD.aspx.
42. Saju, Joy, MD, MS, Postpartum Depression; Overview of Postpartum Mood disorders, Medscape Reference, last revised, October 5, 2011, http://emedicine.medscape.com/article/271662-overview.

Chapter 2 – What Do American Women Do to Recover from Pregnancy?

1. Wagner, Marsden, Born in the USA: How a Broken Maternity System, must be fixed to put Women and Children First, University of California Press, 2006.
2. Wikipedia, The Free Encyclopedia, Feminist movement, last revised on October 13, 2011, http://en.wikipedia.org/wiki/Feminist_movement
3. Ibid., identified source Messer-Daviddow, Ellen, Disciplining feminism: from social activism to academic discourse (Duke University Press 2002)
4. Ibid., identified source: Butler, Judith, 'Feminism in Any Other Name', *differences* vol. 6, numbers 2-3, pp. 44-45.

Chapter 3 – Taking Care of Mom = Taking Care of Baby

1. Kim-Godwin, Yeoun Soo, Phd, MPH, RN, "Post-pregnancy Beliefs and Practices Among Non-Western Cultures," *The American Journal of Maternal/Child Nursing*, Volume 28 Number 2, pp 74-78, March/April 2003.
2. Malaysian Government, Hasan, Zahara, Beauty is Beyond Skin Deep: Traditional Treatments for Women, Malaysian Agricultural Research and Development Institute, MARDI, Malaysia, 2007.
3. Ibid., p. 67.
4. Ibid, p. Preface.
5. Doula and Labor Support, Women and Children Services, Unity Hospital, accessed October 25, 2011, http://www.allina.com/ahs/unity.nsf/page/Unity_doula_home

Chapter 4 – The Womb is a Woman's Life Force

1. PR Newswire website, Anthem Blue Cross and Blue Shield Offers Newborn and Parenting Resources to Ease New Mothers' Transition Back to Work After Maternity Leave, Eight weeks of free resources and one-on-one coaching available to new moms. http://www.

prnewswire.com/news-releases/anthem-blue-cross-and-blue-shield-offers-newborn-and-parenting-resources-to-ease-new-mothers-transition-back-to-work-after-maternity-leave-70193917.html

2. Changes After Delivery, I am pregnant, The site for pregnancies and babies, accessed on January 4, 2010, http://www.i-am-pregnant.com/encyclopedia/Birth/Changes-after-delivery

3. Manderson Lenore, "Roasting, Smoking and Dieting in Response to Birth: Malay Confinement in Cross-Cultural Perspective," *Social Science & Medicine. Part B: Medical Anthropology*, Volume 15B, pp 509-520, 1981. http://www.sciencedirect.com/science/article/pii/0160798781900259

4. Bogumil, Connie, Humoral Theory Food and Culture, Humoral Theory In Cultural Food Beliefs, Oregon State University, June 10, 2002, http://food.oregonstate.edu/ref/culture/humoral.html.

5. Mollison, Hazel, "Can a pregnant woman's temperature rise and fall?" Livestrong, September 2, 2011, http://www.livestrong.com/article/531586-can-a-pregnant-womans-temperature-rise-fall/.

6. Klainin, Piyanee, Gordon, Arthur David, "Post-pregnancy depression in Asian cultures: A literature review," *International Journal of Nursing Studies*, 46 pp1355–1373, February 29, 2009. http://www.journalofnursingstudies.com/article/S0020-7489(09)00070-4/abstract.

7. Lee, Minh Thi; Pasandarntorn, Wanawipha; Rauyajin, Oratai, "Traditional Practices among Vietnamese Mothers in Anthi District, Hung Yen Province," Hanoi School of Public Health, Mahidal University, Thailand, accessed December 10, 2011, http://www.sh.mahidol.ac.th/hssip/theses/2002/3.pdf.

General Reading

1. Asian confinement; Malay pantang: An overview, Baby Center, accessed September 24, 2010,

2. http://www.babycenter.com.my/pregnancy/asian-postnatal-practices/malay-confinement/.

3. Kim-Goodwin Yeoun Soo, PhD, MPH, RN, MNC, "Post-pregnancy Beliefs and Practices Among Non-Western Cultures," *The American Journal of Maternal/Child Nursing*, March/April 2003, volume 28 Number 2, pps 74-78, http://www.nursingcenter.com/prodev/ce_article.asp?tid=408218.

Chapter 5 – Why You Need A Mommy Plan

1. How long is Pregnancy?, Baby2See, accessed August 22, 2011, http://www.baby2see.com/pregnancylength.html.

2. Salgueiro, Nancy, Dr., Your Birth Coach, e-mail communication, October 7, 2011, http://yourbirthcoach.com/.

3. Weeks? Months? Trimesters? Lunar months? Days?, Baby2See, accessed August 22, 2011, http://www.baby2see.com/pregnancylength.html.

4. Mom and Baby at 40 Weeks Pregnant, Women's Health Care Topics, accessed august 24, 2011, http://www.womenshealthcaretopics.com/pregnancy_week_40.htm
5. Vedder, Julie, Oxford Companion to the Body, Pregnancy, July 2011, http://www.answers.com/topic/pregnancy.
6. Holley, Casey L., "4 Ways to Cope With Negative Feelings During Pregnancy," Live Strong, November 18, 2009, http://www.livestrong.com/article/10994-cope-with-negative-feelings-during/#ixzz1aTE7pJsh\
7. Druxman, Lisa, "Your Post-Baby Body: Part I," e Not Alone, You are Not Alone, 2007, http://www.enotalone.com/health/17166.html
8. Ibid.
9. "Lesson 6: Changes of the Postpartal Patient," Obstetric and Newborn Care – II, Medical Education Division, The Brookside Associates, 2007, Accessed October 14, 2010, http://www.brooksidepress.org/Products/Obstetric_and_Newborn_Care_II/lesson_6_Section_1.htm
10. Bennett, Dr. Shoshana, Clinical Psychologist, http://www.drshosh.com/.
11. Kim-Goodwin, Yeoun Soo, PhD, MPH, RN, MCN, "Post-pregnancy Beliefs and Practices Among Non-Western Cultures," The American Journal of Maternal/Child Nursing, Volume 28, Number 2, March/April 2003, pp. 74-78. http://www.answers.com/topic/pregnancy

Chapter 6 – Post-pregnancy Precautions: Diet DONTS

1. Editor-in-chief: Gerard Bodeker, Health and Beauty from the Rainforest, Malaysian Traditions of Ramuan, Didier Millet Pte Ltd, Malaysia, 2009. p 14.
2. Lamxay, Vichith and de Boer, Hugo, "Plants used during pregnancy, childbirth and postpartum healthcare in Lao PDR: A comparative study of the Brou, Saek and Kry ethnic groups," Journal of Ethnobiology, September 8, 2009, http://www.ethnobiomed.com/content/5/1/25.
3. Relaxin, Wikipedia, the free Encyclopedia, last modified Oct 4, 2011, http://en.wikipedia.org/wiki/Relaxin.
4. Reviewed by Hirsch, Larissa MD, Recovering From Delivery, Kids Health From Nemours, June 2008, http://kidshealth.org/parent/pregnancy_center/childbirth/recovering_delivery.html.
5. Ibid.
6. Ibid.
7. Ibid.
8. Ibid.
9. Ibid.
10. Ibid.
11. Skin Changes During Pregnancy, Baby Centre, January 2008, http://www.babycentre.co.uk/pregnancy/antenatalhealth/skinchanges/.
12. Melasma Cures, The Earth Clinic, last revised October 22, 2011, http://earthclinic.com/CURES/melasma.html.

13. Gagne, Steve, "The Energetics of Cooling Foods?," Macrobiotics Guide, May/ June 2008, http://macrobiotics.co.uk/articles/coolingfoods.htm.

14. Chemicals in Household Products, Breast Cancer Fund, accessed October 15, 2011, http://www.breastcancerfund.org/clear-science/chemicals-linked-to-breast-cancer/household-products/.

15. Fife, Bruce, ND, "Coconut Oil and Medium-Chain Triglycerides," Coconut Research Center, 2003. http://www.coconutresearchcenter.org/article10612.htm.

16. Ibid.

17. Nightshades – Substitutes, Food for Awakening, accessed on September 4, 2011, http://www.foodforawakening.com/nightshade-substitutes/.

18. Bolen, Barbara Bradley PhD, "Top Six Gassy Foods: Foods that Contribute to Intestinal Gas, Bloating and Flatulence," About.com Guide, last revised August 3, 2011, http://ibs.about.com/od/ibsfood/a/GassyFoods.htm.

19. Aflatoxins, Wikipedia, the free Encyclopedia, last modified Oct 22, 2011, http://en.wikipedia.org/wiki/Aflatoxin.

20. All about nightshades: explore the hidden hazards of your favorite food with macrobiotic nutritionist Lino Stanchich, CBS Interactive Business Network Resource Library, *New Life Journal*, April – May 2003, http://findarticles.com/p/articles/mi_m0KWZ/is_5_4/ai_111734421/

21. "The Toxins in our food'" Arthritis Insight, accessed September 14, 2011, http://arthritisinsight.com/archives/test8808.htm.

22. Holley, Will Chris, Nightshade Plants in a Nutshell, Archure, accessed on August 17, 2011, http://www.archure.net/salus/nightshade.html.

23. Ibid.

24. Nall, Rachael, "Citric Acid in Fruits," Livestrong, June 15, 2011, http://www.livestrong.com/article/471927-citric-acid-in-fruits/.

25. Bolen, Barbara Bradley PhD, "Top Six Gassy Foods: Foods that Contribute to Intestinal Gas, Bloating and Flatulence," About.com Guide, last revised August 3, 2011, http://ibs.about.com/od/ibsfood/a/GassyFoods.htm.

26. Sherpa, Coupon, "Top 15 chemical additives in your food", Phys Org, January 19, 2010, http://www.physorg.com/news183110037.html

27. The Glycemic Index, http://www.glycemicindex.com/.

28. Sherpa, Coupon, "Top 15 chemical additives in your food", Phys Org, January 19, 2010, http://www.physorg.com/news183110037.html.

29. Short-term effects of alcohol, Wikipedia, the free Encyclopedia, last modified Oct 4, 2011, http://en.wikipedia.org/wiki/Short-term_effects_of_alcohol.

Chapter 7 – Post-pregnancy Precautions: Diet DO'S

1. Editor-in-chief: Gerard Bodeker, Health and Beauty from the Rainforest, Malaysian Traditions of Ramuan, Didier Millet Pte Ltd, Malaysia, 2009. p 18.

2. Viewers Comments, "Your Post baby Belly; Why It's Changed and How to Tone It," Baby Center, September 24, 2011, http://www.babycenter.com/0_your-post-baby-belly-

why-its-changed-and-how-to-tone-it_1152349.bc.

3. Ibid.

4. Schneider, Andrew, "Tests Show Most Store Honey Isn't Honey, Ultra-filtering Removes Pollen, Hides Honey Origins," Food Safety News, accessed November 7, 2011, http://www.foodsafetynews.com/2011/11/tests-show-most-store-honey-isnt-honey/.

5. Gagne, Steve, "The Energetics of Cooling Foods?," Macrobiotics Guide, May/ June 2008, http://macrobiotics.co.uk/articles/coolingfoods.htm.

6. Andrew, Saul, "The Produce Without The Poison: How to Avoid Pesticides," Doctor Yourself, 2003, http://www.doctoryourself.com/pesticides.html.

7. Omega rich foods and Pregnancy, Pregnancy Info, accessed October 19, 2011, http://www.pregnancy-info.net/omega3.html.

8. Fogoros, Richard N., M.D., "Eating Fish – Healthy, or Toxic? FDA releases guidelines for avoiding mercury in fish," About.com Guide, revised March 22, 2004, http://heartdisease.about.com/cs/riskfactors/a/fishmercury.htm.

9. Sherpa, Coupon, "Top 15 chemical additives in your food", Phys Org, January 19, 2010, http://www.physorg.com/news183110037.html.

10. Jacquot, Jeremy Elton, Boiling Water for Better Drinking, Done Right, Tree Hugger, July 17, 2007, http://www.treehugger.com/files/2007/07/boiling_water.php.

11. Laurence, Ruth A., M.D., "Herbs and Breastfeeding," Breastfeeding, accessed May 14, 2011, http://www.breastfeeding.com/reading_room/herbs.html.

12. Reinagel, Monica M.S., L.D./N, "Is MSG Safe? Part 2," Nutrition Diva, http://nutritiondiva.quickanddirtytips.com/is-MSG-bad-for-you.aspx, last revised on October 19, 2011.

13. Nuts and Seeds, Veg Health Guide, accessed October 1, 2011, http://www.veghealthguide.com/nuts-seeds/.

14. Ibid.

15. Drinking Milk while Breastfeeding, Urban Mommies: Your On-line Parent Magazine, June 1, 2007, http://www.urbanmommies.com/babies/drinking-milk-while-breastfeeding/.

16. Egg Yolk, Wikipedia, the free Encyclopedia, last revised October 22, 2011, http://en.wikipedia.org/wiki/Egg_yolk.

17. Rothwell, Sherry RHN, CD, "Pregnancy Brain may be First Sign of EFA Deficiency during Childbirth Years," Natural News, March 18, 2010, http://www.naturalnews.com/028391_pregnancy_nutrition.html

18. The Developing Brain, Developing Childhood, accessed September 30, 2011, http://www.developingchildhood.com.au/the_developing_brain.

19. Black, Alexis, "Brain health dramatically improved by intake of omega-3 fatty acids and fish oils," Natural News, January 2, 2006, http://www.naturalnews.com/016353.html

20. Rothwell, Sherry RHN, CD, "Pregnancy Brain may be First Sign of EFA Deficiency during Childbirth Years," Natural News, March 18, 2010, http://www.naturalnews.com/028391_pregnancy_nutrition.html.

21. Barakhah, Anisah, Ensiklopedia Perbidanan Melayu, Utusan Publications & Distributors Sdn Bhd, 2007.

22. Ibid.
23. Lim Robin, Eating for Two: Recipes for Pregnant and Breastfeeding Women, Celestial Arts, 2003, p52.
24. Interview: Zaini Amnah binti Adnan, Traditional Post-pregnancy Practitioner, interviewed by Valerie Lynn, many discussions and e-mail exchanges from October 2009.
25. Hasan, Zahara, Beauty is Beyond Skin Deep, Traditional Treatments for Women, Malaysian Agricultural Research and Development Institute, (MARDI), p. 17-18.

Chapter 8 – Post-pregnancy Precautions: Activities

1. Newborn Immune System, Wellness, accessed October 20, 2011, http://www.wellness.com/reference/allergies/newborn-immune-system/
2. Hasan, Zahara, Beauty is beyond skin deep, Traditional Treatments for Women, Malaysian Agricultural Research and Development Institute (MARDI), 2007, pg. 63.
3. Reflexology, Wikipedia, the free Encyclopedia, last revised October 14, 2011, http://en.wikipedia.org/wiki/Reflexology

Chapter 9 - Post-pregnancy Precautions: Personal Care

1. Hasan, Zahara, Beauty is beyond skin deep, Traditional Treatments for Women, Malaysian Agricultural Research and Development Institute (MARDI), 2007, pg. 63.
2. Reflexology, Wikipedia, the free Encyclopedia, last revised October 14, 2011, http://en.wikipedia.org/wiki/Reflexology.
3. Mokhtar, Nor Ashikin, OBGYN, "A Belly Good Wrap," The Star Newspaper, July 4, 2010, http://thestar.com.my/health/story.asp?file=/2010/7/4/health/6596850&sec=health.

General reading

1. Kanagaratnam, Tina M., Coconut Belly Rubs: Traditional Midwifery Care in Malaysia & Indonesia, Childbirth Solutions, accessed December 1, 2011, http://childbirthsolutions.com/articles/coconut-belly-rubs-traditional-midwifery-care-inmalaysia-indonesia/

Chapter 10 – Herbs to Avoid While Breastfeeding

1. Herbal safety for nursing moms, Kelly Mom, last revised August 1, 2011, http://kellymom.com/momblog/bf/can-i-breastfeed/herbs/herbal_safety/
2. Jacobson, Hilary, DH.HU.SI, "Latogenic Foods and Herbs, Mobi Motherhood, accessed on October 27, 2010, http://www.mobimotherhood.org/MM/article-diet.aspx
3. Ibid.

Chapter 11 – Turmeric, the Healing Spice

1. Turmeric Root, Natural Wellbeing, accessed October 25, 2011, http://www.naturalwellbeing.com/learning-center/Turmeric_Root
2. Ehrlich, Steven D., N.M.D., Turmeric, University of Maryland Medical Center, last

reviewed on May 5, 2011, http://www.umm.edu/altmed/articles/turmeric-000277.htm

3. Gallant, Lisa C.A.S., "Turmeric, The Golden Goddess," California College of Ayurveda, accessed September 16, 2011, http://www.ayurvedacollege.com/articles/students/turmeric

4. Turmeric-Curcumin, The most powerful compound in botanical medicine; The world's most important herbal extract, Turmeric-Curcumin, accessed on October 25, 2011, http://www.turmeric-curcumin.com/.

5. Health Benefits of Turmeric, Natural Health Cure, last revision June 22, 2010, http://www.naturalhealthcure.org/food/health-benefits-turmeric.html.

6. Gallant, Lisa C.A.S., "Turmeric, The Golden Goddess," California College of Ayurveda, accessed September 16, 2011, http://www.ayurvedacollege.com/articles/students/turmeric.

7. Ibid.

General reading

1. Dr. Ramli b. Abdul Ghani, former Head of Traditional and Complimentary Medicine Department, Ministry of Health of Malaya, interviewed by Valerie Lynn, August 11, 2011.

2. Zaharah Hasan, Author, interviewed by Valerie Lynn, September 17, 2011.

3. Zaini Amnah binti Adnan, Traditional Post-pregnancy Practitioner, interviewed by Valerie Lynn, many discussions and e-mail exchanges from October 2009.

Chapter 12 – The Daddy Plan

1. Perinatal and Postpartum Depression a Top Priority, American Congress of Obstetricians and Gynecologists, May 17, 2010, http://www.acog.org/About_ACOG/News_Room/News_Releases/2010/Perinatal_and_Postpartum Depression_a_Top_Priority.aspx.

2. What is Post-pregnancy Depression (PPD)?, MedEd, Last Updated: 10/17/2011 http://www.mededppd.org/default2.asp.

3. Stone, Katherine, "How Many Women Get Post-pregnancy Depression? The Statistics on PPD," Post-pregnancy Progression, October 8, 2010, http://post-pregnancyprogress.com/?s=erectile+dysfunction.

4. Stone, Katherine, "Post-pregnancy Depression by the Numbers," Post-pregnancy Progress blog, last revision, January 11, 2008, http://post-pregnancyprogress.com/?s=erectile+dysfunction.

5. Ibid.

6. Viewer Comments: Post-pregnancy Depression – Symptoms, MedEd, accessed on September 14, 2011, http://www.emedicinehealth.com/post-pregnancy_depression/discussion_em-725.htm.

7. Potash, James M.D., "US House Acts on Post-pregnancy Depression," ABC News, October 19, 2007, http://abcnews.go.com/Health/Depression/story?id=3747576&page=1.

8. Discussions, Post-pregnancy Wellness, May 2010, https://www.facebook.com/Post-pregnancyWellness.

9. Viewer Comments: Post-pregnancy Depression – Symptoms, MedEd, accessed on September 14, 2011, http://www.emedicinehealth.com/post-pregnancy_depression/discussion_em-725.htm.

10. Faces of Post-pregnancy Depression, State of New Jersey, Department of Health and Senior Services, accessed September 15, 2011,

11. http://www.nj.gov/health/fhs/post-regnancydepression/facesofpmd/danafaces.shtml.

12. Frequently Asked Questions, Post-pregnancy Support International, accessed on October 17, 2011, http://www.post-pregnancy.net/Get-the-Facts/Frequently-Asked-Questions-about-the-Facts.aspx.

13. Dealing with Rejection, Post-pregnancy Dads, February 13, 2009, http://www.post-pregnancydads.org/.

14. Ibid.

15. Doula, Wikipedia, the free Encyclopedia, last revised October 25, 2011, http://en.wikipedia.org/wiki/Doula.

16. Bartell, Dr. Susan S., "Fighting Post-pregnancy Blues: It's Harder with Two than One," Having another baby, October 30, 2010, http://www.havinganotherbaby.com/articles/ppd.html.

17. Mistakes, Post-pregnancy Dads, accessed on November 1, 2011, http://post-pregnancydads.wordpress.com/z-mistakes/.

18. Recovery, Post-pregnancy Dads, accessed November 1, 2011, http://post-pregnancydads.wordpress.com/recovery-steps/.

19. Helping Men Beat the Baby Blues and Overcome Depression, Post-pregnancy Men, accessed on October 27, 2011, http://www.post-pregnancymen.com/.

20. Ibid.

21. Ibid.

General Reading

Johannes, CB; Arauio, AB; Feldman, HA; Derby, CA; Kleinman, KP; McKinlay, JB, "Incidence of erectile dysfunction in men 40 to 69 years old: longitudinal results from the Massachusetts male aging study." New England Research Institute, Journal of Urology, Feb 2000, pp460-463. http://www.ncbi.nlm.nih.gov/pubmed/10647654.

Mommy's Notes
What's the Difference between Midwives and Doulas?
General reading

Edwards, Molly, "What's the difference between a midwife and a doula?" TLC website, accessed December 12, 2011, http://tlc.howstuffworks.com/family/difference-between-a-midwife-and-doula.htm

Doulas Do A Lot

1. Doulas: Don't Give Birth Without One, Birthing from Within Westchester, April 7, 2011,

http://birthingfromwithinwestchester.com/tag/cesarean-birth/.

2. What is a doula?, Your Doula, accessed on November 1, 2011, http://yorubadoula. wordpress.com/what-is-a-doula/.

3. Wonderfully Made Bellies and Babies, Whats a DoolaDo?, accessed November 1, 2011, http://wonderfullymadebelliesandbabies.blogspot.com/2007/05/whatsa-doola-doo. html.

4. Klaus, Kennell, and Klaus, Mothering the Mother, New York, Addison-Wesley Publishing Company, 1993.

5. Ibid.

6. Born Doula Services, accessed on November 2, 2011, http://www.borndoulaservices. com/.

Midwives, the Baby Catchers

1. Simkins, Geraldine, MANA website, MANA's President Responds to Recent Controversies in the Media September 24, 2011, http://mana.org/pdfs/ MANAResponsetoMediaControversy9-24-2011.pdf.

2. North American Registry of Midwives, accessed December 12, 2011, http://narm.org/.

General reading

1. Midwives Alliance of North America (MANA), accessed on December 12, 2011, http:// mana.org/.

2. Midwives, American pregnancy, last revised March 2011, http://www.americanpregnancy.org/labornbirth/midwives.html.

3. Midwifery, Wikipedia, the free Encyclopedia, last revised on October 28, 2011, http:// en.wikipedia.org/wiki/Midwifery.

The Genius of the Placenta

Sources & General Reading

1. Lim, Robin, CPM, Placenta the Forgotten Chakra, (Bali, Indonesia, Half Angel Publishing), 2010.

2. Selander, Jodi, "Placenta for Healing," Placenta Benefits, accessed on November 15, 2011, http://placentabenefits.info/medicinal.asp.

3. Earhart, Mary, "When to Cut the Umbilical Cord: Advantages of Delayed Cord Clamping," Pregnancy and Childbirth, Suite 101, accessed on November 17, 2011, http://mary-earhart.suite101.com/when-to-cut-the-umbilical-cord-a170448#ixzz1f3vGYrlU.

4. Earhart, Mary, "Cord Clamping Should be Delayed," Pregnancy and Childbirth Suite 101, accessed on November 17, 2011, http://www.suite101.com/news/cutting-the-cord-afterbirth---experts-now-recommend-waiting-a307849#ixzz1f4C7TqX8.

5. Wingeier, Kristina, & Shapiro, Jamie, Placenta Tincture, Placenta Apothecary, last revised November 1, 2009, http://placentalove.blogspot.com/2009/11/placenta-encapsulation. html.

6. Pereira, Sara, Mommy Feel Good, last revised July 8, 2010, http://mommyfeelgood.wordpress.com/2010/07/08/now-offering-placenta-tinctures/.

7. Chang, Momo, "Motherhood Rooted, Asian and Pacific Islander moms in the United Staetes embrace ancient post-birth traditions, Hyphen Magazine, accessed on January 6, 2021,

8. http://www.hyphenmagazine.com/magazine/issue-23-bittersweet/motherhood-rooted

9. Glanville, Carina, Then Culture of Parenting – A Postnatal Journey of the World, Natural Parenting, accessed January 7, 2012,

10. http://www.naturalparenting.com.au/flex/the-culture-of-parenting-a-postnatal-journey-of-the-worl/341/1.

11. Independent Placenta Encapsulation Network, http://www.placentanetwork.com/remedies/Tincture.asp.

12. Placenta Traditions, Birth to Earth, accessed January 7, 2012,

13. http://www.birthtoearth.com/FAQs/Placenta+Traditions.html

Kangaroo Care

1. "Why Kangaroo Mother Care Works," Kangaroo Mother Care, accessed on November 21, 2011;
http://www.kangaroomothercare.com/why-kmc-works.aspx.

2. Larimer, Krisanne, "Kangaroo Care Benefits," Premature Baby, Premature Child, 1999, accessed
on November 21, 2011, http://www.prematurity.org/baby/kangaroo.html.

3. Wikipedia the Free Encyclopedia, Kangaroo Care, last revised on October 23, 2011,
http://en.wikipedia.org/wiki/Kangaroo_care.

4. Richardson, Holly, "Kangaroo Care," Midwifery Today, accessed on November 21, 2011,
http://midwiferytoday.com/articles/kangaroocare.asp.

5. Inbar, Michael, "Mom's hug revives baby that was pronounced dead," MSNBC Parenting Today,
http://today.msnbc.msn.com.

INDEX

About the Author

Valerie Lynn (McDonough) is a mother, wife, daughter, sister and a friend to many. She moved away from the United States in 1994 and has lived in Japan, England, Australia, Indonesia and most recently Malaysia, where she has settled down in the capital, Kuala Lumpur, since 2000. She is married to Scott McDonough, an Australian, and they have one son named Jordan, who is five years old at this time. She now divides her time between the United States, Malaysia, and Australia.

Valerie became interested in traditional post-pregnancy beliefs and practices after witnessing the remarkable recovery of friends who received customary post-pregnancy services from traditional post-pregnancy practitioners in Malaysia. She was attracted to the Malay after-birth traditions and practices because of their holistic approach to ensuring the new mommy's recovery. In 2010, she had the honor of being the very first foreigner to complete the Traditional Malay Postnatal Massage course at Universiti Teknologi Malaysia (UTM) in Kuala Lumpur, Malaysia.

Valerie is a graduate of Rutgers University, New Jersey, USA (1992) and postgraduate of the University of London, School of Oriental and African Studies (2000). Valerie founded the Post-Pregnancy Wellness Company in order to provide women with the knowledge, information and tools needed to develop a holistic plan for recovery after childbirth. Valerie is the Asia-Pacific Volunteer Coordinator for Postpartum Support International and is on the Advisory Board of the documentary-in-the-making, the After Birth Project. In early 2012 collaborated with one of Malaysia's top culinary universities, Berjaya University College of Hospitality, Kuala Lumpur, to develop post-pregnancy recipes based on the guidelines contained in this book. These recipes are the basis for the future book called The Mommy Plan cookbook.

She dreams that wonderful, all-natural post-pregnancy recovery products and traditions will become part of Western cultures so more women will have a balanced recovery from childbirth. Her mission and vision is to create supportive post-pregnancy cultures in countries that do not have them in an effort to seriously reduce the rate of postpartum-related mood disorders.

Valerie can be reached at valerie@postpregnancywellness, valerie@mypostpartumwellness, or info@themommyplan.com.

Websites: www.postpregnancywellness, www.postpartumwellness or www.themommyplan.com